Discover

Cyprus

and North Cyprus

In this book, 'Cyprus' refers to the island as a whole before the Turkish intervention of 1974, and thereafter to the area controlled by the government of the Republic of Cyprus, south of the Green Line. 'North Cyprus' refers to the area which has now declared itself independent under the name of the Turkish Republic of North Cyprus.

Price conversions quoted in this book are at the rate of
C£1 = £1.30 = $2.10.

Cover: New and old in the harbour at Paphos.

Discover

Cyprus

and North Cyprus

Terry Palmer

HERITAGE
HOUSE

DISCOVER CYPRUS and North Cyprus
First published January 1991
ISBN 1.85215.022X
Typesetting extrapolated in 8.5 on 9.5 Rockwell on
Linotronic 300 by Anglia Photoset, St Botolph St,
Colchester, from in-house computer setting.
Printed by Colorcraft Ltd, Hong Kong.
Distributed in the UK and major outlets overseas by Roger
Lascelles, 47 York Rd, Brentford, TW8 0QP.
Published by Heritage House (Publishers) Ltd, King's Rd,
Clacton-on-Sea, CO15 1BG.

© **Terry Palmer, 1990.**

Acknowledgements: The staff of the Cyprus Tourism Organisation,
Nicosia and London; the staff of the TRNC tourist office, Nicosia and
London; John Aristides, restauranteur, Kakopetria; Nicos Papadopoulos,
Pano Panayia; Harry Papantoniou, Skarinou; Eleni Christoforidou, curator
National Struggle Museum, Nicosia; Yilmaz Samlı, Girne Belediye; and
friends on both sides of the Green Line who have told me of their
experiences in 1974 and consequently wish to be unidentified.

Bibliography: *Rendezvous in Cyprus,* Barbara Toy, Murray, 1970; *Romantic Cyprus,* Kevork Keshishian, Nicosia.

Also by Terry Palmer: *The Ghost At My Shoulder* (Corgi),
The Ghost Who Loved Me (Heritage House), *The Cairo
Alternative* (Heritage House).

Titles in the 'Discover' series, in print or in preparation, include:

Discover The Channel Islands Discover Czechoslovakia
Discover Cyprus
Discover Florida
Discover The Grand Canyon State   Discover Gibraltar
Discover Iceland
Discover Morocco
Discover Tunisia
Discover The Dominican Republic
Discover The Gambia
Discover Malta
Discover the Seychelles
Discover Turkey

CONTENTS

DISCOVER CYPRUS
REPUBLIC of CYPRUS

TURKISH REPUBLIC of NORTH CYPRUS

INDEX OF MAPS

CYPRUS

248-9

246-7

244-5

Terry Palmer on the uphill side of the newlyweds' rock in Kakopetria
— might it slide down again?

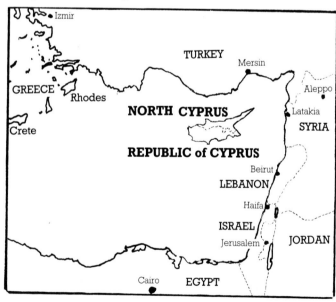

1: WHY CYPRUS?

The friendly isle

CYPRUS IS ALMOST AS OLD AS HISTORY. Neolithic Man was here 9,000 years ago, leaving traces still visible today. Five thousand years later, Bronze Age Man found and worked copper and zinc on the island; civilization arrived in 1,450BC when the Mycenaeans came from Greece, followed by Alexander the Great in 325BC.

Later ruled by Phoenicians, Assyrians, Egyptians, Persians, Romans, Byzantines, English — a Queen of England was crowned here — the Knights Templar, the French, the Venetians and the Ottomans, Cyprus came back into the British Empire in 1878 and stayed there until independence in 1960.

Where? Cyprus is an Asiatic island that clearly considers itself to be European. With an area of 3,572 square miles (9,251 sq km) — 1,295 sq miles (3,354 sq km) of it in the Turkish Republic of North Cyprus — and a total population of around 680,000, of whom 165,000 are in the Turkish north, Cyprus is small. It is slightly smaller than the English counties of Norfolk and Suffolk, and marginally bigger than the states of Delaware and Rhode Island put together.

The island's northernmost and easternmost point is in the near-inaccessible Khlides Islands, off the tip of the Kırpaşa (Karpass) Peninsula, at 35° 41' N, 34° 37' E. The southernmost headland is Cape Gata — Cape of the Cat — at 34° 32' N, on the Akrotiri RAF base and so out of bounds to Cypriots and tourists alike; and the westernmost point is the inaccessible flank of the Akames Peninsula at 32° 14' E.

Mt Olympus. Cyprus's highest point is also inaccessible to the average traveller. A Royal Air Force radar installation sits on the 6,401ft (1,950m) summit of Mt Olympus (Khionistra in Greek) in the Troodos Mountains, controlling movements of aircraft on the Akrotiri base. But skiers, hikers — and the average motorist — can reach the 6,200ft contour with no problems, provided cameras are not pointed at the radar base.

In the Turkish-controlled part of the island the highest point is Kyparissovouno (the Turks don't seem to have a name for it), at 3,150ft (1,024m) near the western end of the Kyrenia Mountains, the Girne Dağlar in Turkish.

Despite being divided since 1974, the people of this beautiful and rugged island, be they to the north or the south of the Green Line, are probably the friendliest in the Mediterranean. If you are among the

1,400,000 visitors a year who go to the Republic of Cyprus — 550,000 of them from Britain — or if you join the small but growing number of tourists to North Cyprus, you will be assured of a welcome almost without parallel.

ΚΑΚΟΠΕΤΡΙΑ
Kakopetria 24km
ΤΡΟΟΔΟΣ
Troodos 43km
ΜΟΝΗ ΚΥΚΚΟΥ
Moni Kykkou 60km
B 9

ΑΣΤΡΟΜΕΡΙΤΗΣ 1km
Astromeritis

ΠΕΡΙΣΤΕΡΩΝΑ 4km
Peristerona
ΛΕΥΚΩΣΙΑ 34km
Nicosia
B 9

But sometimes the road signs are all in Greek.

2: WHICH CYPRUS?

The divided island

ACCORDING TO INTERNATIONAL LAW there is only one Cyprus, the republic that gained its independence from Britain in 1960. This Cyprus is divided into the administrative districts of Famagusta, Paphos, Kyrenia, Larnaca, Limassol and Nicosia, with a House of Representatives in Nicosia city, the capital. Between the Turkish invasion — or liberation, according to your point of view — which began on 20 July 1974, and the cease-fire on 16 August, Republican Cyprus lost all the district of Kyrenia, most of Famagusta, and pieces of Nicosia and Larnaka districts, as well as almost half the ancient walled city of Nicosia. The Turks captured only 37% of the country but, according to Republican Cypriot statistics, that area held 83% of the dockyards, 65% of the tourist hotel beds and 56% of mine and quarry production, and produced 48% of the crops and 41% of the livestock. In all, the Greek-ruled part of Cyprus lost 70% of its national income — and saw the Turks come within 700 feet (200m) of the seat of government.

Shattered economies. The Cypriot economy was shattered, with unemployment soon reaching 39% in the Greek-held south, and probably more in the Turk-held north.

Between 180,000 and 200,000 Greek Cypriots fled south; Morphou, now Güzelyurt, was 95% Greek, Kyrenia (Girne) was 75%, and Famagusta (Gazimağusa) was 60%. But between 35,000 and 45,000 Turkish Cypriots fled north, including 30% of the population of Paphos, 12% of Limassol and 5% of Larnaca, as well as the entire population of around 60 villages. The figures are disproportionate because the population was split 77% Greek, 18% Turkish and 5% others, including British and Maronites, the latter a sect of Christians originating in Syria.

Only a tiny percentage of Turkish Cypriots remained in the south, though the Cypriot Republican government has a policy of assuring all Turkish Cypriots that, as Cypriots first and Turks second, they are welcome. Since 1974 only a very few have gone back from the north. Several hundred Greek Cypriots in the Karpasian Peninsula stayed on in 1974 and are still there today, their food supplied by UNFICYP and the Green Line open to them for occasional escorted visits to the south.

Abandoned hotels. At the end of the conflict the Turks had most of the water and the Greeks had all the power station; scores of roads were cut, thousands of peasant houses were in ruins, a narrow strip of forbidden territory ran through the centre of Old Nicosia, and almost all the tourist hotels in Famagusta as well as the island's best beach were left in no-man's-land. Surprisingly, this is the situation today, with the Turkish north totally dependent on the Greek south for its electricity, and weeds growing in the abandoned streets of the two largest cities.

The Republic of Cyprus maintains its claim to be the legitimate government of the entire island, a claim supported by every country in the world except Turkey. To most Greek Cypriots, Kyrenia and Famagusta are still part of the motherland and only temporarily out of reach. Road signs, including those on the new Highway south from Nicosia, give directions to Famagusta and Kyrenia, although the Turks now call these places Gazimağusa and Girne and totally ban all Greek Cypriots wanting to come north and visit those cities. The Cyprus Telecommunications Authority, based in the south, lists names and numbers in the Turkish north as they were on the morning of 20 July 1974, not knowing if the lines exist − some of the subscribers were among the Greek Cypriots who fled south − and not being able to check as there is neither postal nor telephone connection across the Green Line which now divides the island.

Turkish Cypriots have similar problems if they want to visit the south and perhaps see their former homes from a safe distance. They need either a job in Republican Cyprus, in which case they go south and lose the right to come back to the north; or a job on the Dhekelia base, which allows them to use the Four-Mile Crossing as they please (and once on the British base they are theoretically free to travel anywhere in the south though liable to awkward questions if stopped by the police); or a valid reason such as urgent medical attention not available in the north.

To sum it up: each side grants its people free exit to the other side, but neither accepts routine entry of the other side's people.

Crossing points. There are several places where the Green Line may be crossed, the most notable being the **Ledra Palace Crossing** in Nicosia, the only one which tourists and expatriate Britons living in the north may use; it's also used by diplomats and UNFICYP personnel. The **Four Mile Crossing** links the British Sovereign Base of Dhekelia with Gazimağusa (Famagusta) and is used by UNFICYP, by British troops and their families wishing to visit the north − provided they have the right documents − and by Turkish Cypriots who have jobs on the British base. Tourists and others are not allowed through. Other crossings are for UNFICYP personnel only.

Diplomatic tangle. Every country in the world with the single exception of Turkey acknowledges that the Republic of Cyprus is the legitimate government of the entire island of Cyprus, and none except Turkey has diplomatic, postal or telephone links, trade agreements, or direct air connections with the unrecognised government in the north.

It's hard work planting banana trees: this is near Polis.

Despite this non-existent status, North Cyprus has a growing number of friends in influential places, particularly in the Arab World; Britain is its biggest export customer, and there is a British Consular Section in Lefkoşa, the Turkish part of Nicosia.

Turkish support. The Turkish Republic of North Cyprus could not survive without Turkish military and economic support; Turkey has around 35,000 troops in the north and has brought in 65,000 settlers from Asia Minor: in international talks on the Cypriot problem (to which North Cyprus itself is excluded) Turkey claims that these immigrants were needed to replace the fleeing Greeks in key jobs, but Greece (and the Republic of Cyprus, which *is* granted a voice in international talks) claim that these newcomers owe allegiance to Turkey and not to Cyprus.

Turkish Republic of North Cyprus. In February 1975 the north of the island was named the Turkish Federal State of Cyprus, but on 15 November 1983 it declared itself an independent country with the new name of the Turkish Republic of North Cyprus, sometimes also called *Northern* Cyprus, but Kuzey Kıbrıs Türk Cumhurieti in Turkish. It now has its own flag and government, and it has banned the Cypriot pound in favour of the much-devalued Turkish lira.

Although the Turkish Republic of North Cyprus does not exist in international law and diplomacy, it is nonetheless there. It has recovered much slower than Republican Cyprus to the south and still suffers from some of the political and economic ills of Turkey itself.

11

Shunned by Greece which campaigns bitterly against it in the European Community (North Cyprus has no right of reply), ignored by international aid foundations who send all available funds to the Republic of Cyprus, the TRNC has entered the international package-holiday market. It has a rudimentary tourist office and is building hotels; it opened the civil airport at Ercan in 1986 on the former RAF base of Tymbou, replacing the Geçitkale airfield; and it has a good promotional slogan as well: *a corner of Earth touched by Heaven.*

Quandary. The existence of two *de facto* but not *de jure* countries on one small island puts the writer of guide books in a quandary. As the TRNC is now in the tourist market I feel it has a place in this book, but I am avoiding passing any personal opinion on the political issue. The Greeks call the 1974 incident an invasion; to the Turkish Cypriots it was a liberation, officially known as the Peace Operation, but I shall call it an intervention.

Author's compromise. As a compromise, throughout this book I use the word 'Cyprus' or the term Greek Cyprus to refer to the internationally-accepted Republic of Cyprus, even though its effective rule is now confined to the south of the Green Line and, in a historical context only, to the entire island; the term 'North Cyprus' and the abbreviation TRNC refer to the Turkish Republic of North Cyprus.

Turkish names replace Greek. As North Cyprus has adopted the longstanding Turkish version of almost all town and village names in its part of the island, and uses these names on the TRNC's map and on all road signs, it is pointless using the Latinised Greek name in those chapters featuring the north, yet as Greek Cyprus and all map publishers outside the TRNC use only the Greek names, I have retained them for reference.

What's on offer: Cyprus. Cyprus is thoroughly reintegrated into the tourist market, promoting the image of a beautiful island that was the birthplace of Aphrodite, the Greek goddess of love known as Venus to the Romans. She rose from the sea on a wonderfully scenic stretch of coastline near Paphos, and took her name from the Greek word for sea-foam, *aphros.*

But Cyprus has much more than legend to offer. It has many beaches, though most are tiny and only a few have large stretches of golden sands. The countryside ranges from flat, south of Nicosia, to the splendid rugged beauty of the Troodos, with Mt Olympus snow—capped from December into April; in spring the green meadows are ablaze with wild flowers that would have been killed off by herbicides years ago in northern Europe.

There is history, starting with the Neolithic ruins of Khirokitia and including the large sprawl of ancient Paphos, the Kolossi Castle in Limassol, and the Venetian walls of Old Nicosia. And, particularly in the Troodos, there are the monasteries, many decorated with gilded icons and some which offer hospitality to overnight travellers. South Nicosia and Limassol are among the best shopping centres in the eastern Mediterranean for their size, rivalling Tel Aviv.

And there is the cuisine, mainly Greek but with strong influence from Turkey, Britain and, to a lesser extent, Lebanon. The knights of the Order of St John of Jerusalem began Cyprus's wine-exporting business in the 13th cent, and the country's wines, fortified wines and brandies are now sold around the world from the United States to Australia.

What's on offer: North Cyprus. North Cyprus is new to the tourist industry and has yet to present itself to the market with the professionalism that is necessary for mass appeal. The inevitable touchdown at a Turkish airport makes the flight a little more tedious, and there are many small problems yet to be solved, such as transport from Ercan Airport for the independent traveller.

But once you have arrived in North Cyprus you find yourself amid friendly people, many of whom speak good English and (as with Greek Cypriots) carry British passports and have family or friends in Britain.

Ancient history begins with the ruins of Soli and Salamis, while the medieval castles of St Hilarion, Buffavento and Kantara stand on the craggy ridge of the Kyrenia Mountains offering splendid views across the central plain to the Troodos and, on exceptionally clear days in winter, to the snow-capped Taurus range of southern Turkey. Girne (Kyrenia) harbour must be among the most picturesque in the world.

Most beaches in the north are as tiny as those in the south, but there are good sands in parts of Gazimağusa (Famagusta) Bay, while on the southern shore of the tip of the Kırpaşa Panhandle is what I consider to be the most attractive beach on the island, almost empty of human activity because of its remoteness — a good thing, perhaps, as turtles come ashore to lay their eggs in these sands. North Nicosia and Famagusta are the best shopping centres but are a long way behind those south of the border.

Cuisine is less adventurous, mainly Turkish but with a strong British flavour. Local and imported wines are plentiful and cheap, and Scotch whisky, bottled in North Cyprus, sells at around £2 ($3.20) for 70cl. Nightlife of distinction is confined to a few of the main tourist hotels.

It's only money: the stable Cypriot pound and the devalued Turkish lira.

John Aristides looks out over Kakopetria, the village he helped save.

3: BEFORE YOU GO

Paperwork and planning

CYPRUS IS SO POPULAR that you will probably need to book your flight months in advance if you plan a high-season holiday. North of the Green Line, tourism is still in the embryo stage and you can usually fly off at short notice, but the schools' summer holidays give a massive boost to the airlines as much of the Turkish Cypriot community of north London wants to go home for a few weeks. In low-season the flights are sometimes less than half-booked, with travellers going to and from Turkey helping to swell the payload.

PASSPORTS and VISAS
CYPRUS
All visitors to Cyprus require passports, excluding only those citizens of The Lebanon who are forced to leave their country at short notice. Visas are *not required* for citizens of the European Community, Austria, Iceland, Malta, Scandinavia, Finland, Yugoslavia, a growing number of east European countries, the entire North and South American continents, Australia, New Zealand, and Japan; the visa desk you see at Larnaca airport is for Syrians. Nationalities not covered in this list must get visas before reaching Cyprus.

No entry. Turkish citizens are not allowed entry, nor is *anybody whose passport shows he or she has visited North Cyprus. You may not make your first entry through the Ledra Palace crossing in the Green Line (see below).*

NORTH CYPRUS
All visitors to North Cyprus, including Turks, require passports. Greek citizens must apply for visas, which are granted only in exceptional cases; visas are *not required* for citizens of anywhere else in western Europe, North America or Australasia.

No entry. As the immigration authorities are aware of the Greek and Cypriot ban mentioned above, they will put your passport stamp on a loose paper insert — but only at your request. A TRNC passport is recognised only by Turkey, thus excluding many North Cypriots from the opportunity to travel.

INDEPENDENT or PACKAGE?
CYPRUS

The great majority of visitors come on a package holiday, but those of independent spirit and many of those on return visits, choose to make their own arrangements. Many tourist hotels sell their entire accommodation to tour operators, leaving nothing for the casual visitor: if you want a fortnight based, for example, in the five-star Grecian Bay Hotel in Ayia Napa, you will obviously book a package deal.

There is ample scope for independent travellers but they must be prepared to accept whatever accommodation is available, particularly during high summer. Ayia Napa is likely to be booked solid in July and August, but in the smaller coastal resorts such as Polis in Paphos district, you'll find accommodation specially prepared for the casual caller. The CTO states that accommodation is not available in private homes but in the small villages far from the tourist track you'll have little trouble, other than linguistic, in renting a room or even an empty house, but remember that nobody has any right to ask for rent for an abandoned Turkish property. You won't have many of the comforts of home, but you'll have a much better understanding of the Cypriot way of life.

If you plan to see the country by car, make your rental agreement as soon as you have your flight booked as there's heavy demand for hire cars. But even in high summer you should be able to find a small auto-rental firm in the backstreets of Larnaca or Limassol that has a vehicle for immediate use.

Cyprus has several official camping sites, but there is no problem in bringing your own lightweight tent and camping in the countryside, provided you avoid military areas, get permission if you're on private land — and take your rubbish away. And don't forget the monasteries: most of those in the Troodos have rooms for travellers, although a few will not allow women over the threshold on any pretext.

NORTH CYPRUS

Lack of organisation and the political stalemate make North Cyprus a more difficult destination for the independent traveller. The North Cyprus tourist map mentions just 25 hotels, for the most part giving just the name, star rating, phone and telex number; it also lists 18 hotel-apartments, otherwise known as apart-hotels or self-catering establishments. The tourist office in London lists others, but the information is often inaccurate and confusing. As the unclassified hotels — *pansiyon* in Turkish in the singular form — are inspected and licensed by the *belediye,* the town hall, the tourist office ignores them. This book doesn't.

Similarly, some of the airlines are not interested in arranging car hire for flight-only passengers, and the international agencies do not operate in this unrecognised country. As many flights land at Ercan after the airport's car hire offices have closed for the day, the independent traveller must make his own arrangements in advance; this book lists most rental companies with their phone numbers.

Despite this seeming indifference, North Cyprus is desperate for tourism.

The package traveller, as always, has everything arranged, but may find problems such as last-minute hotel changes because of overbooking during Ramadan.

HEALTH and INSURANCE

Cyprus is remarkably healthy, and the Cyprus Tourist Organisation stresses that even the common infectious diseases are rare. There is no need for any injection or vaccination, malaria was eradicated years ago, and there are few insects to bother you.

MONEY MATTERS
CYPRUS

The Cyprus pound is a steady currency, ranging in value from 0.75 to 0.88 to the pound sterling (0.40 to 0.50 to the US dollar) in the past ten years, and with a comfortably low inflation rate. It is one of the few currencies whose unit value is greater than the pound sterling.

The Cyprus pound, C£, is divided into 100 cents, with notes for 50c, C£1, C£5 and C£20; coins have values of 1, 2, 5, 10 and 20 cents. The currency is not traded internationally, but your bank should be able to buy it provided it is given sufficient notice.

Banks. Cyprus has no shortage of banks, and all but the smallest village has a branch of at least one bank, even though business there may be restricted to one morning a week. **Banking hours are 0830-1200, Monday-Saturday,** but in tourist areas several banks operate an **afternoon tourist service,** 1500-1730 Mon-Fri.

Credit cards. Credit and charge cards are widely accepted for hotel bills, better-class restaurants, shops selling luxury goods, travel agencies and car rental agencies, but you cannot buy petrol with a credit card.

You can buy cash with a credit or charge card thus:

▦ – Popular Bank.

▬ – Barclays; Bank of Cyprus; Cyprus Popular Bank; Hellenic Bank.

▣, **Carte Blanche** – Bank of Cyprus.

◣, **Euro Card** – Bank of Cyprus; National Bank of Greece.

Many branches of these banks have cash dispensers for the relevant credit card, but you will need to know your Personal Identity Number.

Personal cheques. People with current accounts in British banks can draw cash with personal cheques at any branch of Barclays Bank; if you bank at Barclays you can draw up to £100 sterling a day, but the limit is £50 for accounts at other British banks. There is a small commission on each transaction.

How to take money. You have a wide choice. Dollar bills, sterling, or any other major currency; travellers cheques in those currencies; Eurocheques, British cheques — or buy your money as you need it on your credit card. Bear in mind the risk of losing your wallet, handbag or money belt, though you are highly unlikely to have it stolen.

NORTH CYPRUS

The Turkish lira, TL, which superceded the Cyprus pound in November 1983, suffers from permanent inflation. As an example, a pound sterling bought 260TL in April 1982, 300TL in 1983, 460TL in 1984, 630 in 1985, 1,000TL in 1986, 1,300TL in 1987, 2,300TL in 1988, 3,400TL in 1989 and 4,300TL in 1990. The value erodes so steadily that it's worth buying your money as you need it, remembering that banks receive the day's rate around 0900 and most are closed at noon — but licensed money exchanges stay open much later. The airport bank sticks to banking hours and is therefore almost useless; bring any TL you may need for immediate expenses.

Some shops, the airport taxis, and most tourist hotels accept payment in any major foreign currency, a few also accepting the Cyprus pound.

As the Turkish lira — it's never called just 'lira' — is so unstable I have converted all prices into pounds sterling and US dollars. When spending, your main problem is counting the zeros on your banknotes.

Salamis's theatre was lost for centuries under drifting sand.

Personal cheques. People with current accounts in British banks can draw cash at most North Cypriot banks, provided the cheque is supported by a guarantee card; you may have to help the cashier fill in his forms and there is a small commission. Without a guarantee card the process involves setting up a local account and waiting a month.

How to take money. For convenience, take your money in currency or in travellers' cheques, *not* Eurocheques. You risk losing your cash, but you'll not have it stolen.

Credit cards. Credit and charge cards are *not* acceptable for drawing cash at banks or money exchanges, nor are they accepted at some of the tourist hotels and restaurants. Many tourist shops deal in Visa and Mastercard (Access), but Amex and Diners Club are less popular. You cannot buy petrol with a plastic card.

Banks and banking hours. Banks which change money for tourists are: KT Koop Merkez Bankası, Türk Bankası Ltd, Kıbrıs Kredi Bankası Ltd, TC İş Bankası, TC Ziraat Bankası, As-Bank Ltd, Birinci Döviz Alım-Satım, Ertuğrul Akbel & Sons Ltd. Britain's Barclays Bank is not in the country.

Türk Bankası is open longer than most other banks: see 'business hours' in Chap 4 for full times. There is no tourist afternoon service.

Money exchanges. Money exchange offices in the major towns buy currency and travellers cheques (not personal cheques) at a marginally higher rate than the banks, and don't make any deduction for their services. They are open in the afternoons, usually until 1800.

DRESS SENSE
CYPRUS

Dress as casually as you like in the tourist areas, but be prepared to put on more clothing in the towns and countryside. Men won't be welcome in monasteries in shorts or tee shirts, nor will women in short skirts or plunging necklines, but there is no need to wear a hat. Tourists overwhelm the monastery in Ayia Napa and almost anything seems to be accepted, despite notices asking for modesty in dress.

Evening. Formal dress, particularly for men, is expected only in the most expensive hotels and restaurants. For your own comfort, take a light jumper for evening wear unless you're travelling at the height of summer.

On the beach. Topless bathing for women presents no problems at all, even on the town beach at Larnaca. In Ayia Napa and the beaches in the Paphos area, bikini bottoms are sometimes so small that they are invisible from the rear, but the ultimate — total nudity — has yet to be reached.

In the mountains. Snow lingers in the Troodos Mountains into April, so come prepared for cold nights at any time of the year, and for bitter frosts in winter.

NORTH CYPRUS

The same general rules apply, but less strictly. Men and women are welcome in any mosque in any normal street clothing; there is no need for women to cover their head or forearms, but bermuda shorts and mini-skirts would be a little offensive. There is no need to take your shoes off if you avoid treading on the mosque's carpets.

Topless bathing is accepted, but doesn't feel right on the tiny beaches of the north; keep it for Club Acapulco at Girne or the municipal beach at Gazimağusa.

DISABLED

Cyprus is only just beginning to cater for the large potential market for disabled visitors. The CTO's annual hotels guide includes services for the disabled among the selling points of every approved hotel, but of the 25 of all categories in Nicosia, only three — the Hilton, the New Ledra and the Kennedy — qualify for inclusion. The 25 hotels in Ayia Napa, a town which lives entirely on the tourist trade, have 10 listed which accept disabled guests. In North Cyprus I know of only the Salamis Bay Hotel with special ramps for wheelchairs.

Tourist coaches can carry wheelchair-bound travellers, but I am not aware of any coach that is specially adapted. Service taxis and hire cars present the same problems that they do anywhere else.

Much of scenic Cyprus is hilly, making wheelchairs difficult to push, though the towns of Nicosia, Larnaca, Limassol and Gazimağusa are flat enough; there's a moderate hill in Ayia Napa and a steeper one in Girne — but forget Paphos.

Sightseeing from a wheelchair is also a daunting task due to the proliferation of steps, kerbs and gradients, yet several people manage it in Greek Cyprus; I have yet to see a wheelchair of any kind on the Turkish side.

Who can deny Paphos harbour's beauty?

WHAT TO TAKE

For a conventional holiday there is nothing special that you need to take, as Cyprus, north or south of the dividing line, can supply it. If your interests run to specialist sports you will, of course, take your gear, though the amateur will find windsurfing, scuba diving, water skiing and other wet sports catered for, though less so in the north. Don't bring your golf clubs: the only course is a six-holer at Güzelyurt (Morphou) on which serious play is almost impossible.

Clothing. Evenings can be cool except during high summer, so a light jumper is useful. For walking in the Troodos Mountains you will need full hiking gear, including waterproofs, at any time of year except high summer, and in winter you should be prepared for sub-alpine conditions.

Self-catering. Greek and Turkish coffee and tea have flavours that are different from those of western Europe and the USA; you might consider taking an adequate supply. If you plan to rent a room or apartment off the tourist circuit, try to take an old-style British round-pin power plug; in the absence of this, take a screwdriver so you can change your own plugs. Non-British residents should take an adaptor to fit British-style square-pin sockets.

Films. Films of all standard sizes, speeds and brands are available everywhere.

Power cuts. North Cyprus suffers from irregular and localised power failures at any time, particularly in early evening in winter. Unless you're staying in a large hotel with its own generator, take a torch or candle, and keep it nearby as soon as dusk falls.

Bath plugs. A few of the middle-range tourist hotels in North Cyprus and virtually all the pensions, and some of the cheaper places in Greek Cyprus, fail to provide plugs for baths and basins. Britons could consider taking spares, size 1½ (37mm) and 1¾ (44mm).

TOURIST OFFICES
CYPRUS

The Cyprus Tourism Organisation is active not only in promoting tourism, but also in maintaining standards. Its officers inspect all accommodation listed in its comprehensive *Hotels Guide,* updated each year and available free from any of its offices; anything on offer that is not in this guide is unofficial and the CTO cannot help settle any grievances.

The CTO is financed by several 'tourist pavilions' operating restaurants at locations such as Curium, and by a 3% tax on all restaurant meals: it also controls the minimum size of each serving. You're benefiting from the CTO's vigilance, and paying for the service, so you may as well use the CTO to the full.

Welcome to Cyprus. The CTO even has its own radio programme, *Welcome to Cyprus,* on the Cyprus Broadcasting Corporation's channel two, on 498m, 603KHz, from June through September. The half-hour programme gives the latest information on what to see and do, and also has a touch of world news. Hours are: 0800 in German, 0830 in English, 0900 in French, 0930 in Swedish and 1000 in Arabic, Mon-Sat.

CTO offices in Cyprus:
Ayia Napa: 17 Archbishop Makarios Ave, ✆821796.
Larnaca: Democratias Sq, ✆654322.
Limassol: 15 Spyros Araouzos St, ✆362756.
Nicosia: Laiki Yitonia, ✆444264; head office for postal inquiries, 18 Theodotou St, (PO Box 4535), ✆443374, telex 2165, fax 366744. (On second floor of small office block facing small square).
Paphos: 3, Gladstone St, ✆232841.
Platres (Troodos): village centre, closed in winter, ✆321316.

CTO offices abroad:
United Kingdom: CTO, 213 Regent St, London W1R 8DA, ✆071.734.9822.
Belgium: Dienst voor Toerisme van Cyprus, 83 Weststraat, 1040 Brussel, ✆02.230.5984.
Germany: Fremdenverkehrszentrale Zypern, Kaiserstrasse 13, D-600 Frankfurt am Main, ✆284708.
Netherlands: Dienst voor Toerisme van Cyprus, Prinsengracht 600, 1017 KS Amsterdam, ✆244358.
Sweden: Cypriotiska Statens Turistbyra, Vasagatan 11S, 111 20 Stockholm, ✆115578.
Switzerland: Fremdenverkehrszentrale Zypern, Gottfried Keller Str 7, CH8001 Zürich, ✆262.3303.
U.S.A: CTO, 13 E 40th St, New York, NY 10016, ✆(212).213.9100.

The CTO also has offices in Austria, Bahrain, Belgium, France, Greece, Italy and Japan.

NORTH CYPRUS

Turkish Republic of North Cyprus tourist offices:

In North Cyprus:
Kyrenia, the harbour; **Famagusta,** Fevzj0akmak Cad; **Nicosia,** Kyrenia Gate (opening 1991), Mehmet Akif Cad: see maps for locations.

TRNC offices abroad:
United Kingdom: 28 Cockspur St, London, SW1Y 5BN, ✆071.839.4577.
Austria: Starchantgasse 13, B1, 1160 Wien, ✆911.2744.
Belgium: 284-286 Avenue Louise, BTE 10-1050, Brussel, ✆648.4756.
Canada: 300, John St, Suite 330, Thornhill, Ontario L3T 5W4, ✆731.4000.
Germany: Willinger Str 88, 5303 Barnheim-Widding.
U.S.A: 821 United Nationa Plaza, 6th Floor, New York, NY 10017, ✆687.2350; and 1667 K Street, Suite 690, Washington, DC 20006, ✆887.6198.

In addition, there are offices in Italy and Japan, a consulate in

Istanbul and the country's only embassy in Ankara.

In North Cyprus, offices are on the harbour front at Girne, on Fevziçakmak Cad in Gazimağusa, and at Kyrenia Gate Lefkoşa (opening 1991), with the head office on Mehmet Akif Cad, Lefkoşa.

TOUR OPERATORS
CYPRUS
British: Airtours, Rossendale; Amathus Holidays, London; Aspro Travel, Cardiff; Azure Holidays, London; Bonaventure, London; Boswell & Johnson, Gloucester; Cadogan Travel, Southampton; Club Eurotravel, Margate; Cyplon Travel, London; Cyprair Tours, London; Cypriana Holidays, London; Cyprosun Travel, Birmingham; Delta Travel, Manchester; Falcon Holidays, London; Global Holidays, Bromley; Golden Sun Holidays, London; Greece & Cyprus Travel Centre, Sutton Coldfield; Horizon Holidays, Birmingham; Intasun Holidays, Bromley; Jasmin Tours, Gerrards Cross; Krislan Travel, London; Lancaster Holidays, Bromley; Libra Travel Holidays, London; Martin Rooks Holidays, London; Nicholas Travel, London; Olympic Holidays, London; Pan-World, London; Priceright Holidays, London; Redwing Holidays, Crawley; Saga Holidays, Folkestone; Samanda Travel, Ilford; Select Holidays, Hertford; Sol Holidays, Bradford; Soler Touriste, Chessington; Southfields Travel, London; Sunfare Holidays, Glasgow; Sunseekers, Huddersfield; Sunspot Tours, London; Sunvil Travel, London; Thomas Cook, Peterborough; Thomson Holidays, London; Tjaereborg, London; Travellers Abroad, London.

United States: Amphitron Holidays, Washington; Arista Tours, New York; Cyprus Airways, New York; Cyprus Trade & Tours, New York; Cyprus Tours, New York; Fly Away Vacations, Peabody, Mass; Galilee Tours, New York; Travel Air, Rockville, MD; Virgin Atlantic, New York.

A mighty Makarios outside his Archbishopric.

Canadian: World Adventure Tours, Winnipeg; Eliva Tours, Quebec; Aphrodite Holidays, Vancouver; Cyprair Tours, Toronto.

Dutch: Allsun, Rotterdam; Arke Reizen, Enschede; Belair, Rotterdam; Evenements Reizen, Amsterdam; Gulliver Flytours, Leiden; Holland International, Rijswijk; Interkerkelijke Reisorganisatie, Dreibergen; Jan Hofstrareizen, Drachten; More International Travel, Hilversum; N.B.B.S, Leiden; PC Reizen, Amsterdam; Raptim Nederland, Den Haag; Vliej Educatieve Reizen, Degstgeest; Amicitia, Zwijndrecht; Amro Facet Reizen, Amsterdam; Concorde Reizen, Baarn; D-Tours, Amsterdam; Gil Travel, Rosmalen; Gyrath Trips, Amsterdam; Ilios Travel, Zaandam; Hotelplan, Rijswijk; JD Travel, Strijen; Lidia Hofman Reizen, Amsterdam; Mobiplan, Ambacht; Neckerman, Amsterdam; Near East Tours, Amsterdam; Passpartout, Rotterdam; Stichting 55+, Baarn; Sunsnacks, Breda; Teener Twen Tours, Den Helder; Transvakantiereizen, Amersfoort; Travel Air, Bussum; Yugotours, Amsterdam.

Danish: Fritidsrejser, København; Spies Rejser, København; Tjaereborg, Tjaereborg.

Finnish: Aurinkomatkat Suntours, Helsingfors; Lomamatkat, Helsingfors; Tjaereborg, Helsingfors; Hasse, Helsingfors; Spies Matkat, Helsingfors; Startour, Helsingfors; Karair, Helsingfors.

Norwegian: Saga Tours, Oslo; Gullivers Reiser, Mjöndalen; Startour, Oslo; Tjaereborg, Oslo; Vingreiser, Oslo.

Swedish: Atlas Resor, Göteborg; Fritidsresor, Stockholm; Royal Tours, Stockholm; Spies Resor, Stockholm; Vingresor, Stockholm; Always Tours, Göteborg.

German: there are 57 German tour operators who travel to Cyprus.

NORTH CYPRUS

British tour operators: CTA Holidays, London; Celebrity Holidays, London; Cricketer, Crowborough; Fatosh, London; Happy Days, London; Metak, London; Mosaic, London; New Image Holidays, Huntingdon; Pilot Travel, Thirsk; Prime Travel, Bradford; Regent Holidays, Shanklin; Steep West, London; Sunquest, London; Tele-Service, London; Topaz Travel, London; Turquoise Holidays, London.

EMBASSIES and HIGH COMMISIONS
CYPRUS

All these diplomatic offices are in Nicosia unless otherwise mentioned.

British High Commission: Alexander Pallis St, ✆473137.

Australian High Commission: 2nd floor, 4, Annis Komninis St, ✆473001.

Canadian Consulate: Julia House, 3 T. Dervis St, ✆451630.

Danish Consulate General: 39 Artemis Ave, LARNACA, ✆652427.

Finnish Consulate General: 9 A'bish Makarios Ave, ✆444277.

German Embassy: 10 Nikitaras St, ✆444362-4

Irish Consulate: Flat 301, C. Armenias Ave & Calypso St, ✆499544.

Netherlands Consulate General: Athens & O'Connor St, LIMASSOL, ✆366230.

Norwegian Consulate General: 4, Meletiou Metaxaki St, ✆472024.

Swedish Consul General: 2nd floor, Princess Zena de Tyras Palace, 442483.

Swiss Embassy: Commercial Union Tower, A'bish Makarios Ave, ✆446261.

United States Embassy: Dositheos & Therissos St, ✆465151.

NORTH CYPRUS

As North Cyprus is not recognised internationally, it has diplomatic relations only with Turkey . . . yet there is a British Consular Section in Lefkoşa. Before the Turkish intervention of 1974 the British High Commissioner to Cyprus had his residence on Shakespeare Ave, Nicosia, with his office (above address). The Green Line now separates the buildings, so the High Commissioner's new residence is in south Nicosia.

British Consul? But the former residence, on the renamed Mehmet Akif Cadessi, now holds the British Council and the British High Commission Consular Section, the latter open Mon-Fri 0730-1300. The High Commissioner or one of his staff comes to a small office behind Girne (Kyrenia) post office every Saturday from 1000-1200. So how can Britain have a consulate in a country whose existence it doesn't acknowledge? The answer I received was that the consulate does not recognise the TRNC but is there to help the interests of the many British expatriates who live in North Cyprus.

Larnaca Castle's inner court seen from the minaret of the neighbour-ing mosque.

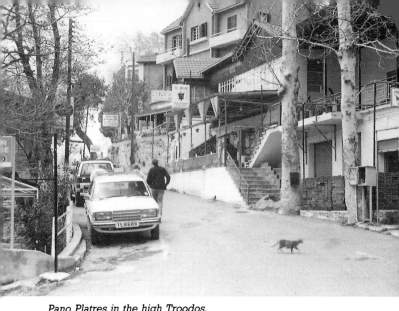

Pano Platres in the high Troodos.

Kyrenia's shipwreck Museum holds this relic from the 4th cent BC.

4: CYPRIOT FACTFILE

Facts and figures

AFFILIATIONS
CYPRUS
Cyprus is a member of the United Nations, the Commonwealth, the Council of Europe and the Non-Aligned Movement, and applied in 1990 to join the European Economic Community.

NORTH CYPRUS
As North Cyprus doesn't legally exist, it cannot be a member of anything. Turkey, the country which brought North Cyprus into existence, is a member of NATO, the United Nations, and is an associate member of the European Economic Community. Its application for full membership was refused in February 1990. Turkish Cypriots resent Greek Cyprus's EEC application being for the entire island, without consultation with the north.

ARMED FORCES
CYPRUS
Cyprus has a National Guard of around 13,000 troops, most of whom are conscripted for nine months and serve in the infantry, the mechanised infantry, or the light artillery brigades. Air defence falls on one Maritime Islander light aircraft and two AB47 light helicopters. Rumours circulating in North Cyprus claim the south is rearming with foreign help.

The British Sovereign Bases of Episkopi, Akrotiri and Dhekelia were never ceded to Cyprus on independence and remain under British control: see Chapter 17. British troops did not join in the defence of Greek Cyprus in 1974 even though the Turkish Army occupied territory up to the Dhekelia base boundary.

NORTH CYPRUS
North Cyprus's military strength is not published, but the Ministry of the Interior of Cyprus claims there are 35,000 Turkish and Turkish-Cypriot troops in North Cyprus. Among their weapons are T34 tanks. The Turkish military presence is obvious but not overpowering; the soldiers, few of whom speak any English, are friendly towards tourists and don't mind being photographed in the street – but not on their bases.

All North Cypriot males must serve two years in the army, but eligible young men who return home after working abroad may buy their release from service for £4,000 ($6,400), or 18 months of it for £2,000.

BUSINESS HOURS
CYPRUS
Banks: 0830-1200, Mon-Sat. In tourist areas most banks also operate the 'afternoon tourist service' from 1500 to 1730. This service is purely for changing currency and travellers cheques.

Post Offices: 1 Oct-31 May, 0730-1330, Mon-Sat; in summer (1 June-30 Sept) post offices close at 1330.

Telephones: Cyprus Telecommunications Authority offices, the easiest places to make a phone call home, are open 24 hours in Nicosia, Limassol and Larnaca, but from 0700-1915 daily in Paphos.

Government offices: Summer, 0730-1330, Mon-Sat; winter, Mon-Fri, 0730-1400, Sat, 0730-1300.

Museums: Jun-Aug, Mon-Sat 0730-1330; Sep-May, Mon-Sat, 0730-1400, with any variations being mentioned in the text.

Petrol (gas) stations: 0600-1800 Mon-Fri; 0600-1600 Sat. Of the 200 gas stations in Cyprus, around 20 are open on Sundays, 0700-1600, in rotation: the *Cyprus Weekly* lists them in advance.

Shops: 30 Apr-1 Oct, 0800-1300, 1430-1730 Mon-Sat; 1 May-30 Sept, 0800-1300, 1600-1900, *but note that they are closed on Wednesday and Saturday afternoons throughout the year.* There are numerous exceptions: small, family-run businesses selling basic commodities are often open all day and every day, even in the remote hill villages, but they may close during church services if they would otherwise offend their customers.

Shops in the tourist areas are usually open in the evenings and on Sundays.

NORTH CYPRUS
Banks: Türk Bankası's hours are **summer:★** Mon, 0830-1330, 1530-1800; Tu-Fri, 0830-1400; Sat, 0830-1330: **winter:** Mon & Fri 0830-1300, 1400-1700; Tu, Wed, Thur, Sat, 0830-1400. Most other banks close at 1200 in summer, and there are other small variations on times. There is no tourist afternoon service.

Money exchanges are open 0800-1300, 1430-1800 Mon-Fri and 0800-1300 Sat, and give better rates.

Post Offices: summer:★ Mon, 0730-1400, 1530-1800; Tu-Fri, 0730-1400 only; Sat 0830-1230: **winter:** Mon-Fri 0800-1300, 1400-1700; Sat 0830-1230.In the absence of an English sign, look for 'postahane.'

Telephones: 0730-2030 every day. In the absence of English, look for the sign 'Telekomünikasyon.'

Government offices: including the 'Belediye'(town hall) in general: Mon, 0730-1400, 1530-1800; Tu-Fri 0730-1400.

Museums: times vary.

CLIMATE

TEMPERATURES

Maximum and minimum, in COASTAL AREAS:

in degrees Fahrenheit:

JAN	FEB	MAR	APR	MAY	JUN	JUL	AUG	SEP	OCT	NOV	DEC
62/46	62/46	65/49	72/52	79/59	85/67	89/70	91/71	87/67	81/61	73/56	65/49

in degrees Celsius:

JAN	FEB	MAR	APR	MAY	JUN	JUL	AUG	SEP	OCT	NOV	DEC
16/8	17/8	18/9	22/11	26/15	30/19	32/21	33/22	30/19	27/16	23/13	18/8

Maximum and minimum, in UPLAND AREAS (but not in the high Troodos Mountains):

in degrees Fahrenheit:

JAN	FEB	MAR	APR	MAY	JUN	JUL	AUG	SEP	OCT	NOV	DEC
47/36	48/34	54/39	62/45	70/52	79/60	83/64	84/65	77/59	69/53	60/46	51/39

in degrees Celsius:

JAN	FEB	MAR	APR	MAY	JUN	JUL	AUG	SEP	OCT	NOV	DEC
8/2	9/2	12/4	16/7	21/11	26/15	28/18	29/18	25/15	20/11	15/8	8/4

AVERAGE RAINFALL in millimeters and inches:

	JAN	FEB	MAR	APR	MAY	JUN	JUL	AUG	SEP	OCT	NOV	DEC
NICOSIA	68/2.7	40/1.6	38/1.6	19/0.8	21/0.8	10/0.4	~	3/0.1	10/0.4	30/1.2	30/1.2	80/3.2
KYRENIA	109/4.4	69/2.8	64/2.6	23/0.9	11/0.8	2/0.1	~	~	5/0.2	46/1.8	71/2.8	143/5.7
PAPHOS	100/4.0	59/2.4	43/1.7	17/0.7	7/0.3	~	~	~	3/0.1	30/1.2	54/2.2	111/4.4
Mt OLYMPUS	275/10	200/7.9	160/6.3	55/2.2	49/1.9	19/0.8	~	4/0.1	16/0.6	54/2.1	85/3.3	275/10.8

SEA TEMPERATURES in degrees F and C:

JAN	FEB	MAR	APR	MAY	JUN	JUL	AUG	SEP	OCT	NOV	DEC
60/16	59/16	61/17	64/18	68/20	73/23	77/25	79/26	79/26	75/24	70/21	65/18

(~ = trace) Source: Cyprus Tourism Organisation.

Petrol (gas) stations: from early morning to late evening, every day, including Sunday. Petrol stations open at 0600 in the small towns such as Yenierenköy (Yialousa) and close at 2000, to cater for people travelling to work in the cities; urban stations open at 0800. All times are subject to local variation and unwound alarm clocks.

Shops: in general, summer, Mon-Fri 0730-1330, 1600-1800; Sat, morning only; winter, Mon-Sat 0800-1730, but there are many exceptions with small family shops staying open all day and every day, including Sunday.

Tourist offices: summer:★ Mon, 0730-1400, 1530-1800; Tu-Fri, 0730-1400 only: **winter:** Mon-Fri, 0800-1300, 1400-1700. These hours are to suit the staff, not the tourist.

★ **Summer** begins on the first Monday in May and winter on the first Monday in October.

COST OF LIVING
CYPRUS

The cost of living in Cyprus is noticeably less than in western Europe, and lower than in the USA, but the Cypriots don't benefit as their earnings are proportionately lower.

As more than 30% of British package-holiday visitors choose self-catering accommodation, I have tried to give a balanced idea of costs in this Cypriot shopping-basket, priced in C£, sterling, and US dollars.

bread, kg loaf	25c-30c	**31p-39p**	51¢-61¢
butter, 8oz (227gm)		25c **32p**	51¢
local cheese, kg	from C£2	**2.56**	$4.05
milk, fresh, litre		24c **30p**	50¢
−, condensed, can		32c **41p**	65¢
eggs, 12		40c **51p**	82¢
corned beef, 340gm	63c-90c	**80p-£1.15**	$1.28-$1.84
luncheon meat, 340gm	42c-52c	**54p-67p**	85¢-$1.05
meat, pork, kg	from C£1.20	**1.54**	$2.43
−, beef, kg	from C£2	**2.55**	$4.05
−, chicken, kg	from 90c	**1.15**	$1.84
coffee, Maxwell House, 50gm	92c	**1.17**	$1.86
−, Nescafe, 50gm	82c	**1.05**	$1.66
fruit, kg, in season:			
−, oranges	20c-50c	**25p-65p**	41¢-51¢
−, grapefruit	15c-30c	**19p-39p**	31¢-61¢
−, melons	15c-25c	**19p-32p**	31¢-51¢
−, apples	60c-90c	**78p-£1.15**	$1.22-$1.84
−, grapes	25c-50c	**32p-65p**	51¢-$1.02
−, bananas	25c-75c	**32p-96p**	31¢-$1.52
fruit juice, litre	35c-50c	**45p-65p**	72¢-$1.02
Keo beer, 75cl		32c **41p**	65¢
local table wines, 73cl	83c-C£1.10	**£1.06-£1.40**	$1.68-$2.24
Keo brandy, 70cl	90c-C£1	**£1.15-£1.28**	$1.84-$2.05

Keo rum, 70cl .... C£1.20 **£1.54** $2.43
Cinzano bianco, 75cl .... C£2.99 **£3.85** $6.08
Whisky, 75cl .... from C£9.25 **£11.85** $18.75
cigarettes, pkt 20 .... from 56c **72p** $1.14
theatre ticket .... from C£2 **£2.56** $4.05
cinema seat .... from C£1.25 **£1.60** $2.59
night club .... from C£3 **£3.85** $6.08
Kodacolour Gold film, 35mm 36 exp .... C£2.90 **£3.72** $6
petrol: *see Chapter 7*
Salaries, monthly, gross
teacher, ... C£400-C£500
bus driver (scheduled service) .... C£300
bus driver (tourist coach) .... C£450
building trade (the range) .... C£250-C£600

NORTH CYPRUS

This shopping list is priced only in sterling and US dollars:

bread, standard size .... **12p** 20¢
tomatoes, kg .... **8p** 12¢
lettuce .... **6p-12p** 10¢-20¢
potatoes, kg .... **35p** 56¢
home-made soft cheese, kg .... **50p** 80¢
Halloumi cheese, kg **£2.55** $4.10
Holland brand ham, tin, 1lb **£2.10** $3.35
corned beef, 340gm .... **65p-£1.50** $2.40
Earl Grey tea, 100gm **80p** $1.32
Nescafé standard, 200gm **£3.50** $5.60
– Gold Blend, 7oz (200gm) **£5.25** $8.40
Ceylon tea (coarse), 1kg **£3** $4.80
Metro Çakulet (Mars bar) .... **13p** 21¢
Cadbury's Dairy Milk, 200gm (7oz) **£1.60** $2.55
Camping Gaz, 95cc cylinder .... **60p** 96¢
6 candles **£1** $1.60
Scotch whisky, bottled in TRNC, 70cl .... **£2-£3** $3.20-$4.80
(Johnny Walker, litre, in Ercan duty-free shop, ... **£6.50** $10.80)
Harvey's Bristol Cream, litre **£4.50** $7.20
Country Satin Cream, litre **£7.50** $12
Smirnoff vodka, 75cl **£6.15** $9.85
Yeni Rakı, 75cl **£1.40** $2.25
Aphrodite wine, 75cl **90p** $1.45
cheapest table wine, 75cl .... from **35p** 56¢
Efes (Ephesus) Pilsen lager, Turkish, 50cl **70p** $1.12
Silk Cut cigarettes, 20 .... **45p** 72¢
(Marlborough, 200, in Ercan duty-free shop, ... **£6.50** $10.80)
spa water from Turkey, 150cl .... **30p** 48¢
petrol: *see Chapter 7*
minimum legal salary per month **£75** $120
unskilled labourer, per month **£100** $160

Fruit costs around the same in North Cyprus as in the south. Clothing is much cheaper throughout the island than in western Europe, but specific examples are meaningless.

1 litre = 1.76 Imp pints, 2.1 US pints; 1 ounce (oz) = 28.35gm

DRUGS

The drug trade is not an obvious hazard in Cyprus, but the word on the street is that drugs are smuggled in from Syria aboard small boats, almost always for onward transit. The Cypriot authorities are aware of the problem and intercept suspicious small craft. Northern Cyprus appears to be free of the drugs menace.

ECONOMY and INDUSTRY

Mining. Copper has been mined in Cyprus since the Bronze Age, and was certainly being smelted in 3,000BC from a number of small and shallow mines: the Cyprus Museum in south Nicosia has details of the sites. **Copper** was so important in the island's early history that the name Cyprus derives from the Latin *cuprum,* meaning 'copper' – or did the metal take its name from the island? The debate continues.

In 1911 an American mining engineer, C. G. Gunther, found a reference in a New York library to those early mines. The Cyprus Mines Corporation, based in Los Angeles, USA, was soon producing copper from seams at Phoucassa – 'Smoke Hill' – near Skouriotissa, followed by more workings at Lefka, with the metal being railroaded down to Morfou Bay.

Then came the 1974 intervention, leaving Smoke Hill in the buffer zone and Lefka and Morphou, renamed Lefke and Güzelyurt, in the Turkish-held area: a few months later the company surrendered its lease.

The Hellenic Mining Company still extracts copper pyrites from near the ancient city of Tamassos, a deposit that was first exploited 4,000 years ago.

Pano Amiandos in the Troodos Mountains is overwhelmed by its open-cast **asbestos** mine, which produces around 22,000 tons of finished asbestos in its ten-month season, work ceasing when snow is too deep. The Greek writer Homer mentioned asbestos, believing it to be fibre from a plant. The ancient Greeks called the material 'unquenchable' – *asbeston* in the accusative case – but Cypriots knew it as *amianthus,* which has given the village its name. *Pano* just means 'upper' with *Kato* being 'lower.'

The limestone mountains are the source for around 850,000 tons of **cement** each year, much of it produced at, and shipped from, the Vassiliko processing plant at Zyyi (Zygi, or Zyghi) on the south coast. Come at the wrong time of day and you'll see a stream of dust and vapour going far out to sea.

Umber, the brown clay used in paints and dyes, is found near

Limassol, and Larnaca's salt lake by the airport can yield 5,000 tons of sea-salt each summer.

The chromium mine just north of Mt Olympus closed around 1974, the zinc mine between Kampia and Kapedes suspended work in 1977, and the copper mine south of Polis ran out of ore in 1979 after 97 years of production.

There is no significant mining in North Cyprus, but limestone is quarried from the Kyrenia Mountains.

Products of the land. Cyprus has been famed for its wines for centuries, but see Chapter 13 for more on the subject. Other products of the land include the full range of citrus crops, and around Easter you can see fruit and blossom on the trees at the same time. There are plenty of carob (locust bean) and olive trees, and the small fields of the small farms grow the full range of soft fruits and vegetables.

The island's breadbasket, the central plain between Nicosia and Gazimağusa, is in North Cyprus, giving the Turkish Cypriots a distinct advantage in the production of grain. This is a featureless part of the island, green only in winter and early spring, and after the May cereal harvest goats graze the stubble.

The Republic of Cyprus exports around 170,000 tons of new potatoes, 150,000 tons of grapes, 130,000 tons of citrus fruits and 110,000 tons of milk a year. Cypriots claim that the Sponda variety of potato, dervied from Scottish stock, is the island's best.

Leather and lace. The island of Cyprus has thriving leather and lacemaking industries, with around 7,000,000 pairs of shoes produced each year in the republic and 140,000 in the north: you'll find prices for all leather goods can be half what you'd expect to pay in Europe.

Lacemaking is still a traditional cottage industry on both sides of the Green Line, but tourists arrive by the coachload to see the women at work in Pano Lefkara in southern Cyprus.

Despite being a country that doesn't exist officially, North Cyprus manages to sell $36,000,000 of exports, mainly agricultural, each year to Britain, its biggest customer.

EDUCATION

Education is compulsory from 5½ years to 15; in the Republic of Cyprus this takes in primary school and the *gymnasium* or lower secondary school, after which comes the optional *lyceum* to the age of 18. In North Cyprus the Mariif College in Lefkoşa holds the British '11–plus' exam in preparation for colleges in USA and the UK. English is a compulsory subject in all schools, with nine hours a week devoted to it in the north.

There is not a university on the island, but the University College in Gazimağusa has engineering, business and computer courses.

Many British expatriates educate their children at the British Sovereign Base of Dhekelia.

ELECTRICITY

The island's supply is 240v 50 cycles, AC, a legacy of British rule. Power sockets in newer buildings take 13-amp square-pin plugs, but in older buildings in remoter areas the 15-amp round-pin socket is still to be found.

During the 1974 intervention the Turks destroyed the gas-fired power station at Ayios Amvrosios, now Esentepe, and North Cyprus is now waiting for its generator at Güzelyurt to come on stream; in the meantime it buys all its power from the south and must tolerate irregular blackouts.

FESTIVALS
CYPRUS

Festivals emerge from major events in the religious or cultural calendar, or from historic landmarks. Cyprus's calendar of festivities is therefore closely tied to its public holidays, but sporting and tourist-related promotions are crowding into an already busy schedule; for the latest information ask for the CTO's diary of events.

These hotels in Famagusta have been empty since July 1974.

New Year's Day is dedicated to **Ayios Vasilis,** Saint Basil, when people exchange presents and cut the Ayios Vasilis cake, baked the previous day. Epiphany, 6 January, marks the end of 12 days in which evil spirits have been at large, and people placate them by throwing food, usually pancakes, onto their roofs where the demons lurk. On the same day the **Ceremony of the Baptism** sees religious processions going down to the sea at Ayia Napa, Paphos, Paralimni, Larnaca and Limassol, with a priest baptising the Cross then throwing it into the sea; a diver brings it back later.

At the beginning of Greek Orthodox Lent, **Green Monday** is marked by carnivals around the country before the 50 meatless days leading to Easter. Around the same time, Paphos holds its kite competition.

The Greek Orthodox Church agrees with the Catholic and Protestant churches that **Easter** is the first Sunday after the first full moon after 21 March (the equinox), yet Greek Easter sometimes comes a week later than the others. It is, however, the main religious feast of the year, with special cakes for the Thursday of Holy Week (the week ending on Easter Sunday). Church sepulchres (tombs, symbolic in this sense) are decorated with flowers on Good Friday, and carried in procession around the community that evening; in Kathikas, Paphos, the priest carries the Holy Cross through the village during the afternoon. Easter Sunday begins with midnight mass, with celebrations lasting into Tuesday, particularly in Ayia Napa and Paralimni, Polis and Paphos.

On the Saturday before Holy Week (eight days before Easter), **Larnaca** remembers its patron saint, Lazarus, first Bishop of the town, with a procession around town led by priests carrying Lazarus's icon.

Cypriots mark **Greek National Day** with street parades, dances, and athletic events, while **Ayia Napa** starts its summer-long festivals of music and folk-dancing in Monastery Square – but these are aimed purely at the tourist market.

The ancient Greek feast of Dionysos, the god of the theatre, has been revived as **Anthestiria,** now the festival of flowers – *anthos* means 'blossom.' Go to Engomi (Nicosia), Paphos, Paralimni, Larnaca or Limassol to see the floral processions. Around the same time, Nicosia holds its **May Fair** near Famagusta Gate.

The two-day **Limassol Folklore Festival** in late May starts in Kolossi Castle then moves to the town gardens; Paphos is also holding its own two-day **May Festival** around the same time.

Kataklysmos, the Festival of the Flood, is an ancient celebration unique to Cyprus. Held at Pentecost – the Whitsun weekend from Saturday through Monday – it marks the Biblical Flood as well as the ancient Greek legend of Deukalion; in the first, Noah and his family were saved, while in the second Deukalion and *his* wife were the chosen people.

Kataklysmos is celebrated only on the coast: at Ayia Napa, at nearby Fig Tree Bay, and at Larnaca, Limassol, Paphos and Polis, with water sports, folk dances and singing — and throwing water at each other on the Monday. Tourism has added a touch of colour to the modern festival.

More that 50 communities hold their own small **village festivals** in August, September and October, celebrating their own particular claims to local fame and featuring folk dancing in local costume. Ask the CTO for details of the timetable in your area and at your time.

The **Limassol Wine Festival,** spanning 12 days from late August into September, is a public relations exercise for the industry, but offers plenty of free food and wine for everybody; ₵363103 (Limassol Municipality) for more information.

Christmas is less important in Cyprus than in western Europe, but by tradition has 40 days for preparation, ending on Christmas Eve (24 December) with the baking of special bread and carol singing by the children. Christmas Day is for Mass, and for feasting, followed by 12 days of piety, a standstill period marking the shift of Christmas when Christianity changed from the Julian to the Gregorian calendar, introduced from 1582. If mere mortals can move Christmas, no wonder the demons come out to play!

NORTH CYPRUS

Festivals play a far smaller role in the community life of North Cyprus, and they're more likely to be spontaneous affairs celebrating the end of the harvest in a particular village. Güzelyurt has its orange festival, Yeşilırmak in the far west celebrates the end of its strawberry season, and Bostançı, south of Güzelyurt, has its water melon festival.

The dates are fixed locally and at short notice by the *mukhtar,* the village head man, and if you come upon such a festival you can be certain it is the genuine thing, with no hint whatever at playing for an audience of tourists.

FLAG

The flag of the Republic of Cyprus, agreed at independence, is an orange-coloured silhouette of the island mounted on a white background, with two olive branches beneath — as shown on the rear cover of this book.

Since the Turkish intervention of 1974, Cypriots in the south have emphasised their Greek origins and affiliations with such vigour that the flag of Greece is now much more common that the Cypriot banner.

The Turkish flag, a white crescent moon holding a small white star, on a red background, has replaced them both in the north of the island and, since November 1983 and North Cyprus's declaration of independence, has been joined by the flag of the Turkish Republic of North Cyprus, a colour reversal of the Turkish flag but with red horizontal stripes top and bottom. Go to either side of the Paphos Gate or the Ledra Street blockades in Nicosia and you can see all four flags at the same time.

GAS

The small 190-gm canisters of butane gas suitable for camping stoves, are available in most service stations in south Cyprus, as well as in a variety of shops from hardware stores to the village supermarket. Prices range from 30c to 55c (40p-71p).

Turkish Cypriots have used the big bottles as cooking fuel for years, but the small canisters have been available since 1989 at around 58p. You'll need to ask at ironmongers or service stations — but I bought one in a video rental shop.

These gas canisters, whether unopened or in use on a stove, are forbidden aboard airliners.

GOVERNMENT and CONSTITUTION
CYPRUS

The 1960 Constitution of the newly-independent Republic of Cyprus recognised the Turkish-Cypriot minority, with 35 seats in the House of Representatives guaranteed to Greek Cypriots and 15 to Turkish Cypriots. Public service appointments, including jobs in the 2,000-strong police force, were divided in the ratio of 70:30, and the National Guard's 2,000 men were recruited in the ratio of 60:40.

Recently the Government has increased the membership of the House of Representatives from 50 to 80. The number of Greek members has risen from 35 to 56, and the Turkish from 15 to 24; despite the events of 1974 the Government still recognises Turkish Cypriots as citizens of the Republic of Cyprus and helps those who want to come south, but such movements are so rare they make headline news in the Cypriot press.

The 1985 elections gave the Democratic Rally 33.5% of the vote, with 19 seats; the Democratic Party 27.6%, 16 seats; AKEL, the Communists, 27.4%, 15 seats; and EDEK, the Socialists, 11%, 6 seats. The Turkish seats were not contested and are left vacant.

In the Presidential Election of 14 February 1988, Spyros Kyprianou was defeated in the first round along with Klerides, allowing Yeoryios Vassiliou to become president with 51.6% of the vote.

NORTH CYPRUS

North Cyprus declared itself independent on 15 November 1983, and in the election of 8 December 1985, the National Unity Party won 24 seats, the left-wing Republican Turkish Party won 12, the centre-left Communal Liberation Party 10, and the right-wing New Birth Party 4. Rauf Denktaş remained president.

In presidential elections on 22 April 1990, Denktaş was returned with 66.7% of the vote. Two weeks later, on 6 May, the National Unity Party (Ulusal Birlik Partisi) won 34 seats against the 16 gained by the Democratic Struggle Party, a coalition of the other three parties, who favoured some sort of compromise with the Greek Cypriots.

See Chapter 10 for a fuller account of Cyprus's present status as a divided island.

HOLY DAY and REST DAY

Cyprus has always held Sunday as the day of rest. Turkey adopted Sunday in the early days of Kemal Atatürk's rule when he westernised the country and dropped Arabic script in favour of the Latin alphabet. North Cyprus, therefore, has Sunday as the day of rest although Friday is the Islamic holy day.

MAPS

The best map of Cyprus available in Europe is in the Bartholomew Clyde Leisure series, at a scale of 1:300,000. It has generous street plans of Nicosia, Paphos, Larnaca, Limassol and Ayia Napa, plus the Paralimni Coast and Limassol Beach at 1:34,000 and, on the reverse, the Troodos Mountains in colour contours for walkers at 1:71,500. UK price is £3.50.

Freytag & Berndt's map and cultural guide at 1:250,000 has town plans plus historic sites, and names in the Greek alphabet as well as Latin, for £5.50. The Greek information is useful for visitors who venture into the mountains.

Geo Project's map is also at 1:250,000, with plans of Larnaca, Limassol, Nicosia and Paphos, for £5.95. Hildebrand's road map at 1:350,000 has no town plans and sells at £3.50. The official Survey of Cyprus at 1:250,000 is the best for contours but has no town plans. It sells at £4.95 — but for £16.95 you can have a set of four maps at 1:100,000 also from the Survey of Cyprus and covering the entire island. Information on North Cyprus is likely to be out of date.

Incomplete information. None of these maps gives any extra information on North Cyprus and none marks the buffer zone, the former no-man's-land surrendered by the Greeks but not captured by the Turks. This is amazing, as it's an area of south Cyprus that tourists are urged not to enter without authority. Even more amazing is the fact that every map I have seen, including official ones north and south of the Green Line, fail to show that southern Famagusta is out of bounds to *everybody* except UNFICYP troops.

The Cyprus Tourism Organisation issues on request a free road map of the island; it is slightly out of date on details north of the Green Line, names few places of interest, but marks almost every village and hamlet in Latin characters. The information on the Highway from Nicosia to Larnaka and Limassol, and the Larnaca-Limassol link road, is out of date.

The Turkish Republic of North Cyprus tourist office issues a free road map with all towns and villages renamed in Turkish — the only map which does this — but with no detail at all south of the Green Line; if you're driving in North Cyprus this map is essential for recognising the Turkish names and getting the latest information on the road to Ercan Airport. The map, in English and Turkish, gives good street plans of Girne, Lefkoşa and Gazimağusa.

Available in Cyprus. The Cyprus Touring Map, at C£1.50 and a scale of 1:250,000, is well-priced but a bit crude and lacks the Green Line, though it has good town plans; it's published by Apostolos Papadopoulos of Nicosia. On the same scale, the Cyprus, Cypern, ΚΥΠΡΟΣ map by the Efstathiadis Group, Athens, shows contours, the Green Line, and street plans. The TRNC map is on sale in North Cyprus.

The maps in this book are mainly based on the Bartholomew Clyde map and the two free tourist maps, with buffer zone information from UNFICYP, and Famagusta closed-zone boundaries from personal survey.

NEWSPAPERS
CYPRUS

The English-language *Cyprus Mail* is published daily, price 25c, with a circulation of less than 4,000. *The Cyprus Weekly,* priced at 30c, is published on Friday and has a circulation of around 12,000. In the circulation war, both papers give schedules for CBC television and radio, CBC's two radio channels, the BBC World Service, and BFBS radio; the *Weekly* understandably gives the coming week's programmes, while the *Mail* gives just that day's programmes.

There are 11 Greek-language newspapers published in Cyprus.

Foreign newspapers. Foreign newspapers, from Britain, France, Germany, Italy, Scandinavia and the Arab world, are on sale in the tourist areas, at prices from 65c. British Sunday papers are available late on Sunday, for C£1.65. No US papers are available.

NORTH CYPRUS

The English-language *Cyprus Times,* a bright tabloid covering local and international news, began weekly publication in autumn 1989 and sells for 11p (18¢). Among the nine Turkish-language papers are *Kıbrıs* and *Kıbrıs Postası.*

A limited range of European newspapers is available, but no US papers get this far.

PHOTOGRAPHY
CYPRUS

Photography is permitted anywhere in Cyprus except where local signs prohibit it. Sadly, there are many restrictions, including all the military bases be they Cypriot, British or United Nations. With two exceptions you may not use cameras within the Buffer Zone, or take pictures of the Green Line: the exceptions are the blockade at the top of Ledra St, Nicosia, and the Ledra Palace crossing point on Drakos Ave, Nicosia — but the UN is not happy with cameras at the crossing.

If you are seen to be taking photos or video, you will be arrested, very gently. Your video tape will be screened, and your film confiscated by the civilian police, for processing. If you have not filmed anything of military significance — which can be interpreted as a barbed wire fence — your film and tape will be returned; anything controversial will be destroyed.

Sovereign Bases. The ban on photography in the British bases is interpreted loosely as the Temple of Apollo, the old city of Curium and the Convent of St Nikolaos of the Cats are all on sovereign base territory, with no local ban on the camera.

In effect, take whatever pictures you like on the British bases, provided you avoid anything of military significance and don't mind the risk of being detained for an hour or two if you're seen photographing.

No cameras. The mountaintop Monastery of Stavrovouni recently banned photography and has a notice on its gate. The Cypriot National Guard camp at the base of the mountain has 'no photography' signs. The inference is therefore that photography is permitted on the mountain slopes, but when I was arrested I learned that the entire mountain is in a no-photo zone. The RAF radar base on Mt Olympus is similarly off limits to cameramen, though there is no notice: I was cautioned here. Keep your cameras out of sight along the B9 road from Akaki to the Troodos foothills, and never try filming a Greek Orthodox priest unless you have his permission.

NORTH CYPRUS

Signs in Turkish, English, French and German show where photography is banned, usually around Turkish Army bases; the approach road to St Hilarion Castle goes through a banned zone as it

Photography is not allowed in the hilltop Monastery of Stavrovouni, but I was arrested for filming on the open mountain.

overlooks an army base.

There are no other restrictions: you may photograph Turkish troops off base, the interiors of mosques, and Ercan Airport, but there is always the need for common courtesy when pointing a camera at the local people.

POLICE

The Cypriot police force is modelled on the British example, with uniforms in north and south still almost identical, though the North Cypriot police wear light khaki summer clothes. Several officers from the Greek force go to the Police College at Hendon, London, for part of their training.

The police, **ΑΣΤΥΝΟΜΙΑ** in Greek and *polis* in Turkish, are friendly, unarmed, and in my experience ready to help any tourist at any time, and probably have a half-hour conversation as well. Beware the Greek word **ΠΟΛΙΣ** 'polis,' which means 'town,' as in 'metropolis.'

Both forces have traffic police, but I have found road checks only in North Cyprus.

Crime. The island of Cyprus has an amazingly low crime rate. There is virtually no chance of meeting a bag-snatcher, a car thief, a confidence trickster or a rapist. Women walk the streets alone after dark in perfect safety, and motorists leave expensive cars unlocked and with the keys in the ignition, especially in North Cyprus. The crime rate is so low that you can almost *feel* the sense of freedom that it brings − and there is not the remotest indication that tourists might be harassed.

POST OFFICE
CYPRUS

The Post Office is another legacy from British rule, but its business hours are far from British; see Chapter 4.

There are post offices in the towns and larger villages, with postal agencies catering for medium-sized villages.

Postage rates include a one-cent surcharge for the 1974 refugee fund, shown by a special 1c stamp.

The Post Office conducts all normal mail business, but does not have a monopoly on the sale of stamps. It has no connection with the Cyprus Telecommunications Authority.

NORTH CYPRUS

The *Postahane* is a mix of British and Turkish, with complex business hours; see Chapter 4.

To combat North Cyprus's lack of international recognition, all outgoing foreign mail is sent on the car ferry from Gazimağusa to Mersin, Turkey, from where it is treated normally.

Incoming mail: special address. Incoming foreign mail must not mention the Turkish Republic of North Cyprus on the envelope; after the Cypriot postal town must come 'Mersin 10, Turkey,' a special code which directs the mail to this Turkish port and ultimately on the ferry to Gazimağusa.

The Post Office in the north doesn't have a monopoly on the sale of stamps — despite the recognition problems, the TRNC issues its own postage stamps — and it has no connection with the Telekomünika-syon Dairesi, the telephone department.

POWER STATIONS

Cyprus's electrification began in earnest in 1952 with the opening of an 84 mega-watt power station at Dhekelia. In 1966 the 180MW station at Moni, east of Limassol, joined the grid, followed by Dhekelia B in 1983.

The Turkish forces never captured either of the two main stations generating in 1974, so south Cyprus continued supplying electricity to the occupied north, which it still does today; see 'electricity.'

And as a matter of interest, south Nicosia's sewerage system handles much of the effluent produced in the northern part of the city.

PUBLIC HOLIDAYS
CYPRUS

Before the Turkish intervention, Cyprus recognised Moslem as well as Christian feast days as public holidays, but since 1974 the list has been reduced.

★January	1	New Year's Day
	6	Epiphany
#February—March		Green Monday
★March	25	Greek Independence Day
April	1	Greek Cypriot National Day
#March—April		Easter
★May	1	Labour Day
#June		Kataklysmos
August	15	Dormition of the Virgin Mary
★October	1	Cyprus Independence Day
	28	Greek National Day
December	25,26	Christmas

★If these dates fall on a Sunday, the following day is the public holiday.

#These dates are variable. Green Monday is always 50 days before Easter Sunday (8 weeks before Easter Monday). The Greek Orthodox Easter consists of Good Friday, Saturday, Easter Sunday and Easter Monday: Easter Sunday falls on 7 April in 1991, 26 April 1992, 18 April 1993, 1 May 1994, 23 April 1995.

Kataklysmos, the Festival of the Flood (see 'Festivals'), a public holiday for the private sector only, comes 50 days after Easter (7 weeks after Easter Monday)

This 'astronaut' flew in 600BC. See him at the Pierides Museum in Larnaca.

NORTH CYPRUS

January	1	New Year's Day
#April		Ramazan Bayram
	23	National Sovereignty and Childrens' Day
May	1	Labour Day
	19	Youth & Sports Day
#June		Kurban Bayram
July	20	Peace Operation Day
August	1	National Resistance Day
	30	Turkish National Victory Day
#September		Birth of the Prophet Mahomet
October	29	Turkish Republican Day
November	15	Declaration Day

#These dates are in the Islamic calendar and move back 11 days each year, 12 on a leap year. Ramazan Bayram is a three-day celebration marking the start of Ramadan; Kurban Bayram is a four-day sacrifice of animals to Allah, with the meat being given to the poor; it's not widely practised.

Ramazan Bayram begins on 15 April 1991, 4 April 1992, 24 March 1993, 13 March 1994, 2 March 1995. Kurban Bayram begins on 23 June 1991, 12 June 1992, 1 June 1993, 21 May 1994, 10 May 1995. Mahomet's birthday is on 30 September 1991, 19 September 1992, 8 September 1993, 28 August 1994, 17 August 1995.

Childrens' Day was begun in Turkey in 1920 to mark Kemal Atatürk's introduction of democracy, and Turkey has recently suggested to the United Nations that it become a worldwide holiday. July 20 marks the beginning of the Turkish intervention in 1974 and August 30 the end of the operation. August 1 marks the founding of the Turkish Resistance Organisation, and in 1983 November 15 saw the founding of the TRNC.

PUBLIC TOILETS (RESTROOMS)

There are probably more public conveniences per square mile in the Republic of Cyprus than anywhere else in the Mediterranean, and they are usually well-equipped and clean. You will find them in large bus stations, near markets, at airports, at CTO pavilions, at some archaeological sites, and at useful points in the towns. And they are free.

In the south, most are labelled in Greek and English, but if there is no suitable picture of a man or a woman, look for ANΔPON for the gents', and ΓYNAIKΩN for the ladies'.

In North Cyprus, unattended public toilets are noticeably less common and tend to be dirty. Lavatories with an attendant — and a fee of around 5p (8¢) — are smart. In Girne, borrow the lavatory in the Dome Hotel, inside the main door on the left; in Gazimağusa try the attended toilet hiding in the shopping precinct north-west of the Monument of Victory. The relevant Turkish word is *tuvalet*.

RADIO and TELEVISION

Television. The Cyprus Broadcasting Corporation, known as CBC or CyBC, made its first radio broadcast on 4 October 1953 and its first television transmission on 1 October 1957. It is still a small concern, its growth limited by its small audience, and it is now funded by a small levy on almost every electricity bill issued in Cyprus, supplemented by a small income from advertising.

The single channel begins daily transmissions in colour between 1600 and 1700 hrs, with closedown between 2330 and 0100. Most programmes are bought from the BBC but contributions can come from anywhere in the world; local news is in Greek, English and Turkish.

Depending on local topography, Cypriots can also tune into Middle East Television and Türkiye Radyo ve Televizyon, both of which offer programmes in English. Turkish television frequently broadcasts original English-language soundtracks of imported films simultaneously on radio, 95.6MHz or 92.5MHz. But TRT is notorious for altering its schedules at very short notice.

Radio. CyBC's radio programmes on Channel II (498m, 603KHz, or 94.9MHz FM) are on air daily from 0600 to 2400, with news in English at 1000, 1400 and 2000; several other programmes have come from the BBC's domestic output, but there are also transmissions in Greek,

Turkish, Armenian and Arabic. CyBC's classical music programmes have a wide audience in the Near East. Don't forget the CTO's *Welcome to Cyprus* programme: see 'Tourist offices' in Chapter 3 for more details.

There is excellent reception around the clock (except 1030-1200 Mon-Fri) on the **BBC's World Service** on 127MHz broadcast from Bush House in London but transmitted from the British East Mediterranean Relay Station at Zyyi, midway between Limassol and Larnaca; the forest of radio masts identifies the spot from miles away.

The BBC's recommended frequencies for English-language programmes are:

	0300	0400	0500	0600	0700	0800	0900	1000	1100	1200	1300	~	2300	2400
1323KHz														
720KHz														
639KHz														

The British forces in the Sovereign Base Areas have their own radio programmes broadcast by the **British Forces Broadcasting Service,** BFBS (Channel I: VHF, 99.6, 92.1 and 89.7MHz; MW, 1089 and 1503KHz. Channel II: VHF, 95.3, 89.9 and 91.9MHz), with the entire output in English and transmissions 24 hours a day.

The Cypriot press, including the two English-language newspapers, publishes the full schedules for CyBC, BBC World Service, BFBS, and METV (Middle East Television).

NORTH CYPRUS

The north has its own *Bayrak Radyo ve Televizyon* whose single television channel broadcasts Monday to Friday 1800 (or a few minutes later) to 2030, with news in English at 2010. From BRT's shutdown the station relays Turkish television (see above).

Broadcasting, of course, knows no boundaries. Many North Cypriots tune into Turkish television all day long – and some watch CyBC's programmes.

SMOKING

Cyprus grows tobacco, but the increasing recognition of the rights of non-smokers has spread to the south of the island. Smoking is banned in service taxis and many public buildings, and discouraged in others, including shops. No such restrictions exist in the north.

SPORTS
CYPRUS
Spectator sports.   There are stadiums in Nicosia, Limassol and Larnaca for major spectator sports, which include several international football matches and athletics events; details are available through

the Cyprus Football Federation at 1, Stasinou St, Engomi 152 (P.O.Box 5071) Nicosia, (℅02.445341) and the Cyprus Tennis Federation at 20, Ionos St, P.O. Box 3931, Nicosia, (℅(02).366822 or 450875). The federation has 13 member clubs who have a year-round season incuding matches abroad.

The Amateur Athletic Association of Cyprus holds a marathon in Nicosia in winter (summer is too hot for running); ℅(02).444176 for details.

The Rothmans Cyprus Rally, held at the end of September, attracts drivers and spectators from many countries. Call the Cyprus Automobile Association, ℅02.313233 for details.

In addition, there are international contests in athletics, basketball, bridge and shooting, with details available at the CTO.

Participator sports: Skiing is the only participator sport that requires planning and preparation, though the season lasts only from early January to sometime in April. The Cyprus Ski Federation at 21 Diagoras & P. Katelari St, 1st Floor Office 102, P.O. Box 2185, Nicosia, ℅(02).365340, owns and operates four ski lifts which normally operate 0900-1600, serving 13 runs suitable for beginners, intermediate and advanced skiers; and there's a ski shop for the hire of equipment for alpine and cross-country sport. Temporary membership for visitors costs C£15.

Tennis is, of course, available at several of the main tourist hotels.

The Troodos Mountains are also a suitable location for **cycling,** provided you bring all your equipment, from a multi-gear mountain cycle to clothing suitable for low temperatures and rain. Cyclists need not confine themselves to the mountains, but should allow for the high midday temperatures from May to September at any altitude.

Cyprus has a wide range of **watersports** available, with Ayia Napa and Fig Tree Bay being the best place to come. Choose from hiring a canoe at C£1.50 an hour, to parascending at C£20 for half an hour, with mid-priced options including water skiing, hiring a speedboat, and jet-skiing.

A narrower range of watersports is available at Paphos, Polis, and the tourist strips at Limassol and Larnaca.

NORTH CYPRUS

Spectator sports.   Football is the dominant sport, with almost every village having a team. The local council, the *Belediye*, and major tourist hotels provide tennis courts.

Tae kwan do is so popular that the world championships have been held in the country.

Participator sports. On an island, the easiest sports for visitors involve water. Windsurfers can be rented at Salamis Bay, Club Acapulco, and Mare Monte hotels; sailing is available at Deniz Kızı and jetskiing at Salamis Bay. There's horse-riding for you at Karaoğlanoğlu (Ayios Yeoryios) west of Girne, with the island's only golf course waiting at Güzelyurt (Morphou) — six holes that defy serious sport.

TELEPHONES
CYPRUS

In theory, it's easy to use the Cypriot telephone service. In practise it's not so easy, as many call boxes accept phonecards only (you can buy these at post offices and many shops), others are for '199' (emergency) calls only — and of the remainder, a few don't work.

Having found your call box, the procedure *is* simple: lift the receiver, put several 20c coins in the slot, and dial, feeding in more coins during the call; the system will take 2c, 5c and 10c coins as well, but these are useless for long-distance. Unusued coins will be returned when you replace the receiver.

Or you can use the phone in your hotel room, after you dial for an outside line — the code is usually 8 — but remember that calls from hotels always cost more.

Optionally, you can call from the Cyprus Telecommunications office in Nicosia, Limassol or Larnaca (all are open 24 hours), in Paphos (open 0700-1915), or in Prodhromos in the high Troodos (open 0930-1300, 1600-1800 Mon-Fri), where you dial your number, including the international code, and pay at the counter afterwards.

Collect calls (reverse-charge calls) are *not* available from call boxes: use a private phone and dial 198 for the operator.

Cheap rate. There is no time of day or night when calls are cheaper.

New district codes. In March 1990 the old area codes were replaced with new district codes, based on the administrative districts, and all numbers became six-digit, adding a prefix where necessary.

These are the new district codes and prefixes: **Nicosia,** code 02, no prefix; **Famagusta,** code 03, prefix 8; **Larnaca,** code 04, prefix 6; **Limassol,** code 05, prefix 3; **Paphos,** code 06, prefix 2.

Line engaged. It is not possible to phone North Cyprus from Cyprus; use of the Famagusta district code is restricted to the Ayia Napa area.

NORTH CYPRUS

Turkish call boxes and the Turkish telephone system have replaced the old British telephone network in North Cyprus. There is no possibility of calling the Greek sector directly; in an emergency UNFICYP acts as a messenger.

Area codes. The north still uses the area codes that the south has dropped, so Gazimağusa has 036, Girne 081, Lefkoşa 020 and Güzelyurt 071, but in summer 1990 the Telekomünikasyon department began experimentally dropping the area codes, starting with calls from the capital.

Calling home. Calling home is not easy, as all connections go through Turkey and you may have to wait up to an hour to make a call from a cubicle in the Telekomünikasyon office. If you try this method, dial the international access code 00, followed by your number, and pay for your call at the desk.

Optionally, you may try your luck in a call box. First buy around £5 ($10) worth of *normal jeton* or *büyük jeton* (I use the word in the singular as the Turkish plural, -ler or -lar, confuses the issue; you'll get normal or big 'tokens' which replace the devaluing Turkish lira). Slide some jetons in the payment slots, then dial 9. Wait for a change of tone, dial 9 again, then your number. You may get through, or you may lose your jetons.

Calling TRNC from abroad. As all international calls are routed via Turkey, when phoning North Cyprus from abroad ignore the 357 code for Cyprus; use instead the special Turkish code, 905, and delete the zero in the area code. Thus, for Kyrenia (Girne) (081).12345, dial: [your international access code] + 905 + 81.12345.

International codes. These codes apply from anywhere in Cyprus, and follow the **international access code:**

Australia	61	Austria	43
Belgium	32	Canada	1
Denmark	45	Finland	358
Germany	49	Ireland	353
Netherlands	31	Norway	47
South Africa	27	Sweden	46
Switzerland	41	United Kingdom	44
United States of America	(A.B.Devletleri in Turkish)		1

The Laiki Yitonia shows Nicosia's Old City at its smartest. . .

TIME

Cyprus is on GMT+2. Clocks are put forward one hour for summer time (daylight saving time) on the last weekend in March and back one hour on the last weekend in September, matching the EEC countries and many others, but not the UK nor the USA.

Sunset. The sun sets around 1645 in midwinter and around 2000 in summer, allowing for the clocks being altered.

TIPPING

Hotels and restaurants island-wide add a 10% service charge, which includes the tip, leaving private taxi-drivers as almost the only people who expect a gratuity — in this case up to 10%.

WATER

With the exception of Famagusta city, tap water is perfectly safe to drink everywhere in Cyprus, and has no noticeable chlorine, but beware signs saying 'not potable.' Boreholes supplying most of Famagusta have become contaminated with sea water and the result is unpalatable. In the south of the city by the Palm Beach Hotel, soft water is piped over from Republican Cyprus — but pressure is low and there is usually none at all on Sundays. Bottled mineral water is readily available everywhere.

. . . but the Old City has some terrible scars near the Green Line in Lefkoşa.

WEIGHTS and MEASURES

Republican Cyprus has adopted the metric system throughout, but a few old people in the remote villages cling to systems that predate the British arrival in 1878. In North Cyprus distances are measured in miles, petrol and other liquids in litres, but those old systems are still widely used for weighing greengrocery and measuring land.

A *donum* is 1,600 sq yards (1,338sq m, 0.336 acre) and a *pic* or *arsin* is two feet (60.94cm). There are 4.5 *okes*, (pronounced 'oak' in the singluar) to an Imperial gallon, or 5.4 to a US gallon, making one oke worth 0.562 of a pint. But an oke is also 1.278lb (2.826kg).

Trucks and vans in North Cyprus still have their payload marked on the side in hundredweights (1cwt = 50.8kg).

Clothing sizes. Conversion formulae from Cypriot sizes:

Women's clothes: for UK sizes, deduct 28. For USA sizes, deduct 30. Continental sizes are the same.

Men's clothes: use this sliding scale:

UK & USA	34 35 36 37 38 39 40 41 42
Eur & Cyp	42 44 46 48 50 52 54 56 58

Women's shoes: for a rough guide for UK sizes, deduct 33. For USA sizes, deduct 31. Cypriot sizes are slightly different from Continental.

Men's shoes: for UK and USA sizes, deduct 34. Continental sizes are the same.

Men's shirt collars: use this sliding scale:

UK & USA	14 15 16 17 18
Eur & Cyp	37 38 41 43 45.

WHAT YOU WON'T LIKE ABOUT CYPRUS

Too many Cypriot men think that the spring and autumn migrations of birds gives them the right to shoot whatever passes overhead. Many of the 45,000 members of the Greek Cypriot Hunters' Association have joined organised dove shoots each spring, or gone to a remote hilltop and shot whatever flies past, at a time when 250 species of bird use Cyprus on their migration from Africa to Europe; many hilltops are still littered with empty cartridge cases as testimony.

In recent years the conservationists have been increasing their pressure, backed by Friends of the Earth and similar organisations threatening to urge tourists to boycott Cyprus until the spring hunt is banned. The issue is widely debated in the press and broadcast media, with the likelihood that the government will follow the Greek example and ban the spring shoot.

Although there is less hunting in North Cyprus, it leaves considerable room for improvement.

5: LANGUAGE and RELIGION

Greek and Turkish; Orthodox and Moslem

GREEK, ENGLISH AND TURKISH are the official languages of the Republic of Cyprus, though since 1974 Turkish has vanished from normal use. At the last all-island census held, on 11 December 1960, 80% of the population was Greek and 18% Turkish, with the remainder Armenian: the figures exclude British troops and dependents in the sovereign bases.

Before the Turkish intervention of 1974, Turkish Cypriots and Greek Cypriots were scattered at random across the island, though each village tended to polarise as either one or another, a notable exception being Zyyi on the south coast which had 84 Turks and 86 Greeks at the 1960 census. Today, the entire nation is polarised, with very few Turks in the south and only a few hundred Greeks in the north, almost all of them in the Kirpaşa Peninsula.

This arch in the Castle of Forty Columns appears on many postcards.

CYPRUS

It is not essential to understand a single letter of Greek in order to appreciate a holiday in Cyprus, but the more you intend to travel off the beaten track and mix with the locals the more you will appreciate a basic knowledge of the Greek alphabet, even if you confine it to the capital letters.

Why? Because in the remote areas many signposts are only in Greek, and many rural buses going from village to village have their destinations scrawled in Greek on pieces of card. And they all use capital letters.

Greek is the language of the cradle, and while Cypriot children are obliged to study English and French in secondary school, few adults away from the tourist circuit know more than a dozen words in English.

In view of the wide selection of Greek phrase books available, it's beyond the scope of this book to say much on the matter of vocabulary, but here is the Greek alphabet to help you sort out some of those signposts deep in the Troodos Mountains:

Greek letters			Greek	Latin (Eng)	
printed/written			name	equiv.	
cap	cap	small			
A	**A**	α	alpha	A	as in 'hard'
B	β	β	beta	B	as in 'big'
Γ	Γ	γ	gamma	G or Y	(see below)
Δ	Δ	δ	delta	D	as in 'did'
E	E	ε	epsilon	E	as in 'let'
Z	Z	ζ	zita	Z	as in 'buzz'
H	H	η	ita	EE	as in 'meet'
Θ	Θ	θ	thita	TH	as in 'thick'
I	I	ι	iota	EE	as in 'meet'
K	K	κ	kappa	K	as in 'kiss'
Λ	Λ	λ	lamda	L	as in 'look'
M	M	μ	mu	M	as in 'man'
N	N	ν	ni	N	as in 'man'
Ξ	Z	ξ	ksi	X, KS	as in 'fix locks'
O	O	o	omicron	O	as in 'pot'
Π	Π	π	pi	P	as in 'pot'
P	P	ϱ	roh	R	as in 'run'
Σ	Σ	σ	sigma	S	as in 'kiss'
T	T	τ	taf	T	as in 'top'
Y	Y	υ	ipsilon	EE	as in 'meet'
Φ	Φ	φ	fi	F	as in 'fig'
X	X	χ	hi	F(see below)	
Ψ	Ψ	ψ	psi	PS	as in 'caps'
Ω	Ω	ω	omega	O	as in 'pot'

Note: in the following paragraphs, capital letters in quotes, as "G," are Latin letters. Those capitals not in quotes are Greek letters which look (and, in these examples, sound) exactly the same as Latin.

The Greek alphabet. Γ is the problem letter. Before A, O, Ω, it is a hard "G," as in the Spanish *general*, or Arabic *hamsin* ('five'), similar to the German "CH" as in *machen*.

Before E, I, Y, it is pronounced as "Y" in *yes*, making the word ΑΓΙΑ, 'saint,' sound 'aya' as in *Ayia Napa*. So try ΑΓΙΟΣ ΓΕΟΡΓΙΟΣ, 'Saint George,' transliterated as *Ayios Yeoryios*.

Ξ, handwritten as ⤜, is easy when you see it in ΕΞΟΔΟΞ, *exodos*, 'exit,' or ΤΑΞΙ, for 'taxi.' In Greece it is often shown as ⤜.

X is similar to Γ, but a little more like the "CH" in the Scottish *loch* when coming before A, O, Ω. It has the different sound of a faint "H" when coming before E, I, H, Y – but there are exceptions to this rule.

Note that H, I and Y all sound similar, and O is nearly identical with Ω.

Place-names worth recognising:

ΠΛΑΤΡΕΣ	Platres
ΛΕΥΚΩΣΙΑ	Nicosia (Levkosia)
ΛΕΜΕΣΟΣ	Limassol (Lemesos)
ΠΑΘΟΣ	Paphos
ΛΑΡΝΑΚΑ	Larnaca
ΑΓΙΑ ΝΑΠΑ	Ayia Napa
ΤΡΟΟΔΟΣ	Troodos
ΠΕΔΟΥΛΑΣ	Pedhoulas

You'll find these spoken words useful:

Good morning!	*Kaliméra!*
Goodbye!	*Hérete!*
Please	*Parakaló*
Yes	*Ne (short, not 'neee')*
Good evening!	*Kalispéra!*
Pardon!	*Pardón!*
Thank you	*Ef haristó!*
No	*Oh-hi*

A few printed words worth learning:

ΑΠΑΓΟΡΕΥΕΤΑΙΗ ΕΙΣΟΔΟΣ	no entry
ΜΟΝΟΔΡΟΜΟ	one-way street
ΙΔΙΟΤΙΚΟ	private
ΚΛΕΙΣΤΟΝ	closed
ΚΕΝΤΡΟ ΠΟΛΙΣ	town centre
ΔΙΑΤΗΡΕΙΤΕ ΤΟ ΔΑΣΟΣ ΚΑΘΑΡΟ	
keep the forest clean (a common sign)	

NORTH CYPRUS

Turkish is the only official language of the Turkish Republic of North Cyprus. With the departure of almost all the Greeks and the adoption of the Turkish version of all the village names — which involved replacing all the road signs — Greek no longer has a role in the affairs of the north. Even English, the international language, has lost its joint-official status; be thankful that Kemal Atatürk decided to replace Arabic script with the Latin alphabet, which makes Turkish much easier than Greek to read.

The Turks originated in Mongolia but picked up much Arabic vocabulary when they accepted Islam, and since the defeat of the Ottoman Empire the language has been absorbing a steady stream of European words — but it's still a difficult tongue for Europeans.

The alphabet. Turkish letters are pronounced as in English, except: **c** is pronounced as 'j' and **ç** is pronounced as 'ch.' While **g** is always hard as in 'go,' **ğ** is the most difficult letter in the alphabet. It is like a softer version of the 'ch' in the Scottish 'Och!' or the same letters in the German 'machen;' it also lengthens the preceding vowel. **I, ı** are unstressed and sound like 'u' in 'fur;' **İ,i** are as in 'lit;' look for the dots to know one eye from another. The **ö** is as the French 'eu'; **ş** is as 'sh;' and **ü** is as 'ew' in 'few,' or in the German 'über.'

Cumhuriyet Caddesi is pronounced *Jum-hurry-et Ja-dessy* and means 'Republic Street;' it's a common name in Turkey. Kaleiçi, the old walled city of Gazimağusa (Famagusta), is pronounced *Kah-lay eechee* and means 'within the castle.' And Gazimağusa is pronounced *Gazee-mah-hoo-sa*.

Turkish place names are usually descriptive. Küçükerenköy, on the north coast, means 'village of the little rocky headland;' *küçük* is 'small,' *kerempe* is the rocky point, and *köy* is 'village;' *köy* is a common way to end place names.

Kale means 'castle,' *güzel* (pronounced 'goo-*zell*) is 'pretty,' and *ak* is 'white, clean,' which praises *Akdeniz*, the Mediterranean Sea.

Basic vocabulary. You won't find many Turkish-English phrase books, but this list has the bare essentials, bearing in mind that English is widely spoken around the tourist areas.

yes evet
please lütfen
hello merhaba
good night ıyı geceler
happy journey güle güle
no hayır
thank you teşekkür ederim (mersi)
good morning günaydın
goodbye allah ısmarladık
English Ingiliz.

açık **open**
büyük **big**
kapalı **closed**
küçük **small**
bahşiş **tip, gratuity**
camii **mosque**
kebapçı **kebab restaurant**
lokanta **restaurant**

RELIGION

The events of July 1974 have totally separated the two religions. Few mosques in Cyprus have congregations large enough to support them, with Lebanese and Egyptians outnumbering the Turks, while in North Cyprus the population is 98.7 Moslem, with only a few old women in Apostolos Andreas monastery at the tip of the Panhandle left to represent the Greek Orthodox Church.

Maronites. The Turks had no quarrel with the Maronites of Karpasha village and they have stayed on undisturbed, with their village now called Karpaşa: look for it in the north-west, not in the Panhandle.

In the Greek south, visitors are free to enter any Orthodox church at any time, but should dress modestly and show respect for any service they may interrupt. There are no admission charges, but offertory boxes are always prominent. Most churches are very well maintained, with elaborate decoration and dozens of icons.

By contrast, mosques in Greek Cyprus are near derelict, offering the non-Moslem one of the best opportunities in the world to visit a mosque during Friday prayers, to climb a minaret — normally reserved for the muezzin when he summons the faithful to prayers — and to inspect the *mihrab*, the focal point of the mosque, symbolising Mecca.

Islam. Anybody who has visited north Africa or the Arab world will remember the near-total ban on non-Moslems entering mosques at any time. North Cyprus comes as a complete contrast, with Islam no more intrusive into daily life than is Christianity in southern Cyprus; no woman wears a veil and very few wear the Islamic-style headscarf; men do not prostrate themselves in public on their prayer-mats; and you will not hear the muezzin making his call to prayer from the top of the minaret unless you happen to be in the centre of a large town.

Islam is in its mildest form in North Cyprus. Non-Moslems may wander into the major mosques at any time, though courtesy suggests they stay out during prayers or other services; they even keep their shoes on provided they don't walk on the carpets.

In hardline Islamic states the womenfolk are not tolerated in mosques, but in North Cyprus they are welcome, though they have their place at the back of the prayer-hall, behind the men.

The blurring of the religious divide is most noticeable in the Selimiye Mosque in Lefkoşa and the Lala Mustafa Paşa Mosque in Gazimağusa, for both were built as Gothic cathedrals and have minarets so small they are almost symbolic.

6: GETTING TO CYPRUS

Air or sea

CYPRUS IS SUCH A POPULAR HOLIDAY DESTINATION that the main problem is getting a flight reservation, with or without accommodation, in mid or high season. As North Cyprus is still a newcomer to the tourist industry you can make short-notice bookings even into peak season.

No land crossing. Relations across the Green Line are so tense that there is no possibility whatever of tourists splitting their holiday between Greek Cyprus and Turkish Cyprus.

BY AIR.
CYPRUS

Nicosia Airport was put out of action within the first two days of the Turkish intervention in July 1974, and was officially closed a month later; the runway now lies in the Buffer Zone.

Larnaca Airport: the background. Cyprus's first airfield was a gravel strip at Larnaca, opened in 1930, which received only a few flights. Governor Sir Richard Palmer approved the building of a hard-runway airport if Larnaca Municipality would build the link road, and this new airfield opened in 1935 with scheduled flights to Syria, Lebanon, Palestine and Egypt.

The Royal Air Force used the base during World War Two, but the post-war colonial government abandoned Larnaca as soon as it had opened its new airport at Nicosia. The old airfield slumbered until the Suez crisis of 1956, when British troops, evicted from Egypt, dumped their stores on the runway. Tons of equipment stayed on the tarmac until Cyprus was about to taste independence in 1960, when the British moved everything to their retained bases at Episkopi and Dhekelia.

Larnaca gained nothing; the council used the empty runway as a dumping-ground for the the town's rubbish until the Turkish Army sent paratroops into north Nicosia on 20 July 1974, so closing the island's only civilian airport.

Larnaca Airport's runway was cleared and repaired as quickly as possible, reopening for comercial flights in February 1975, since when it has been Republican Cyprus's main gateway to the world.

Larnaca Airport today. Small by international standards, Larnaca Airport (LCA on your baggage labels) is 5 miles (8km) from the town at the end of a mile-long spur road. It has two banks sharing the same office, four car-hire offices, telephones, toilets, CTO office and a small restaurant, all accessible to arriving and departing travellers. The taxi rank is 200ft (60m) from the main door, with the coach park for package tourists and the rental-car park beside.

The **bus service** between the airport and Larnaca town is unreliable and not to be trusted when you have a plane to catch. Independent travellers' options are to take a taxi (C£1.50 per person), or to walk the spur road and catch a bus coming from Kiti to Larnaca. These are also your options for your return; see Chapter 7 for bus timetables.

Paphos Airport. Paphos Airport (PFO), which opened in 1983, is mainly involved in charter traffic, having just three scheduled flights in an average week; one to Athens, two to Heathrow. It is compact, offering a car park, phone, toilet, CTO office, Hertz and Petsas auto-rental offices, the Popular Bank, and a small restaurant. Taxis take you the 9 miles (14km) into Paphos for C£3, or to Kato Paphos for C£4; there is no pretence at a bus service.

Cyprus Airways: flight confirmation. Passengers travelling on Cyprus Airways should note that they must confirm their return flight at least three days in advance or risk losing their booking. Package tourists should make certain their courier does this, or preferably do it themselves. Offices are in Nicosia (✆02.441996), Larnaca (✆04.654294), Limassol (✆05.373787), Paphos (✆06.233556), Ayia Napa (✆03.821265).

NORTH CYPRUS

The North Cyprus tourist map marks three airfields. Pinarbaşı, south—west of Girne, is a small base for military craft and helicopters, while Geçitkale, near Gazimağusa, was the original civilian airfield. It's now used as a standby for Ercan but there are plans to reintroduce it for commercial traffic when demand increases.

Ercan Airport. Ercan Airport, pronounced 'erjan,' opened in 1986 on what had been the RAF's Tymbou airfield. It has offices for Roots Holidays of Germany, Kings Travel and Tri Sun Travel, four car rental companies, and the local taxis. And there is a branch of Türk Bankası, a souvenir shop and an information desk. *But all these offices keep normal business hours and ignore out-of-hours air movements.* As the post office is also closed, late evening arrivees cannot even buy jetons to use in the airport's one telephone. The WC stays open, but take your own paper.

Bypassing politics. As the Turkish Republic of North Cyprus does not legally exist, it's impossible to fly there. All flights to and from Ercan therefore make an intermediate stop somewhere in Turkey. Your airline ticket will say which airport, and will add 'Ercan,' but be prepared for your airport of departure to ignore the place: if this happens, check your flight number and the Turkish stopover. Ercan's airport designation is ECN but be prepared for some strange labels on your baggage, including ERZ for Erzurum.

Ercan has scheduled connections only with the Turkish airports at Adana, Ankara, Istanbul and Izmir.

Airlines using Ercan. At the time of writing, the airlines using Ercan are Cyprus Turkish (Kıbrıs Türk Hava Yolları), İstanbul Airlines, Noble Air, and Turkish Airlines (Türk Hava Yolları)

KTHY is at Bedreddin Demirel Cad, Yenişehir Lefkoşa; ✆020.73820-1, 081.52313, 036.67999.

İstanbul is on ✆020.77140-1, 081.53413, 036.62950.

Noble Air: 45 S Audley St, Mayfair, London W1Y 5DG, ✆071.495.2535; Belgium: Brussels, ✆230.4728; Germany: Düsseldorf ✆211.161055; München ✆012.697138; Lefkoşa ✆081.53076.

THY: 11 Hanover St, London W1, ✆071.499.9240; Lefkoşa ✆020.71061.

BY SEA
CYPRUS

To Egypt and Israel. The *Princesa Marissa* and the *Princesa Cypria* operate a complex schedule from Limassol; the **winter schedule** goes to Port Saïd every Mon, returning on Wed; then sailing to Haifa (Thurs), Port Saïd (Fri), returning Limassol Sat; then sailing to Haifa (Sun) and back to Limassol to start the cycle again. Bookings through Louis Tourist Agency, 63B Gladstone St, PO Box 100, Limassol, ✆363161.

To Greece and Israel. This ferry service, for anybody taking a car from Europe, is operated by Arkadia Lines with the *Silver Paloma*, carrying 827 passengers, and the *Paloma*, carrying 396. The year-round schedule has a Thurs sailing from Piraeus (Athens) at 1500, calling at Rhodes (Fri 1300, sailing 1500) and docking at Limassol Sat, 1000. The return leaves Limassol Mon 0700, calling at Rhodes (Tues 1100, sailing 1600) and docking at Piraeus Wed 0900.

A shady path in Ayios Herakleidios Monastery.

UK agent is Golden Sun Holidays, 15 Kentish Town Rd, London NW1 8NH, ✆071.485.9555; in the Netherlands, Travel Air Shipping, Kapelstraat 22, NL 1404 HX Bussum, ✆02159.15590; in Germany, Viamare Seetouristik, Apostelnstr 9, D5000, Köln 1, ✆(0221).23491; in Greece, Afroessa Lines, 1, Charilaou Tricoupi St, Piraeus, ✆418.3777; in Cyprus, Salamis Tours, 28 October Ave, PO Box 531, Limassol, ✆355555.

To Lebanon. Because of its location in the eastern Mediterranean, Cyprus acts as an escape hatch for Lebanese Christians fleeing their war-torn homeland. The *Larnaca Rose* car ferry sails from Larnaca at 2200 on alternate days to Jounieh, north of Beirut, returning at 0600.

CRUISES

To Israel and Egypt. Vergina Lines operates the *Queen Vergina* year-round from Limassol to Israel and Egypt:

Limassol,		dep Sat 1500
Port Saïd	arr Sun 0700	dep Sun 2000
Limassol	arr Mon 1100	dep Mon 2000
Haifa	arr Tues 0700	dep Tues 2000
Port Saïd	arr Wed 0700	dep Wed 2000
Limassol	arr Thur 1100	dep Thur 2000
Haifa	arr Fri 0700	dep Fri 2000
Limassol	arr Sat 0700.	

Fares range from C£43 (low season return Haifa, couchette) to C£184 (high season Haifa-Port Saïd, suite); any Cypriot travel agent will book a passage.

Ambassador Cruises operates the 24,000-tonne *Vasco da Gama* and the *Sun Ambassador,* calling at Ashdod instead of Haifa. These are genuine cruise liners with casinos, night clubs, cinemas, and high-class restaurants where guests dress for dinner. Schedules and fares available from Ambassador's agent, Paradise Cruises, PO Box 157, Limassol, ✆369000.

NORTH CYPRUS

North Cyprus has had a passenger ferry from Girne to Taşucu near Silifke, Turkey, since November 1987, and car ferries from Gazimağusa (Famagusta) to Mersin (Turkey) and Latakia (Syria).

Girne–Taşucu. Depart Girne 1430, arrive Taşucu 1630; depart Taşucu 1130, arrive Girne 1330, daily. Fare around £7.20 one way, £13 return; around $11.50 one way, $21 return.

Gazimağusa–Mersin. Depart Gazimağusa Tues, Thur, Sat at 2200 for Mersin; arrive 0800. Depart Mersin Mon, Wed, Fri 2200 for Gazimağusa; arrive 0800. Fare, around £6.60 ($10.50) each way; cars start at the same price.

Gazimağusa–Latakia. Depart Gazimağusa Sat 2300, arrive Latakia Sun 0800; depart Latakia Sun 1300, arrive Gazimağusa Sun 1930. Fare, around £6.60 ($10.50) each way; cars start at £7.30 ($11.60).

OVERLAND: The Ledra Palace Crossing.

There is only one crossing point open to tourists between the Republic of Cyprus and the TRNC. This is outside the original Ledra Palace Hotel on Drakos (Drake) Avenue, Nicosia; the Turkish part is now Selim Caddesi (Selim Ave). The Ledra Palace was unfortunate enough to come in no-man's-land during the intercommunal riots of the early 1970s, and became UNFICYP headquarters. The Turkish troops stopped here in 1974 as well, leaving the hotel in today's buffer zone, and it is *still* in UNFICYP occupation, this time housing the families. The new Ledra Hotel is on Grivas Dhigenis Ave, south Nicosia.

The crossing point is for anybody who qualifies to use it, but tourists may go through only on foot, beginning their journey only on the Greek side, and they must return by a set time that same day, usually 1800; check the cut-off time as you go through.

The Turkish north imposes no controls apart from a normal customs check; the Greek south has decreed that no tourist who enters the island through what it sees as enemy-occupied territory may use the crossing.

If you try the crossing you must present your passport at the Greek side, and on the Turkish side pay a nominal charge for a day visa: *do not have your passport stamped as this bans you from re-entry to the south.*

The crossing is closed without warning at the slightest diplomatic upset, with the risk that you may be caught in the north and need an UNFICYP escort to take you back.

A sign beside the crossing on the Cypriot side reads: *Beyond this checkpoint is an area of Cyprus still occupied by Turkish troops since their invasion of 1974. (They) expelled 180,000 Cypriots of Greek origin . . . and brought over colonists from mainland Turkey to replace them. Enjoy yourself in this land of racial purity and true apartheid; enjoy the sight of our desecrated churches. . . .*

It's not easy, as a visitor to the south, to walk past Greek Cypriots standing by the checkpoint handing out hard-hitting Interior Ministry leaflets such as *Cyprus: a few facts to remember.*

Political bypasses. British and other non-Greek expatriates who took Cypriot residence before the summer of 1974 and who have continued to live in what is now the TRNC, have unlimited access through the Ledra Palace crossing by car – but with a sheaf of documents. Each person needs a North Cypriot identity card as well as the original Cypriot one; in addition every car, which must have been registered before July 1974, must have dual road taxation discs (£58 ($93) for a small car of this age in Cyprus, plus £15 ($24) for TRNC taxation), dual insurance, and dual number plates, which must be changed in the buffer zone.

The advantages are the cheaper living in the north plus the greater range of goods in south Nicosia's shops, as well as access to Larnaca Airport.

7: TRAVELLING IN CYPRUS

Car hire, bus or taxi.

CYPRUS WAS MADE FOR THE TRAVELLER. The country is large enough to offer you something different each day, but not so large that travelling becomes a bore. From Paphos to Limassol and on to Ayia Napa is only 160 miles (256km) on perfect roads; in North Cyprus, Lefke is only 112 miles (180km) from Dipkarpa (Risokarpason) on the Kırpaşa Peninsula, also on good roads.

Car hire and petrol are reasonably cheap on each side of the Green Line, and there are good bus, shared taxi and private taxi services. But the railway no longer runs.

CAR HIRE
CYPRUS

All rented cars in Cyprus have registration numbers beginning with Z — Latin characters are used — mounted on distinctive blood-red plates. Thus identified, visiting motorists receive more consideration from the police and the locals, as I can testify.

The CTO lists 62 rental agencies, including branch offices, in Cyprus, plus those at Larnaca Airport, and there are probably one or two smaller agencies not registered with the CTO. This is the list:

FAMAGUSTA district, AYIA NAPA:
Airtour Cyprus, 18 Dionysios Solomos Ave, ✆03.721718; **Avis,** 17a Nissi Ave, ✆03.721884; **Holiday Tours,** (main road to Fisherman's Harbour) ✆03.721031; **P. Melissas,** 4b Krio Nero St, ✆03.721836; **Panipsos,** Nissi Rd, ✆03.721634; **A. Petsas,** (near Grecian Hotel), ✆03.721260; **A. Spyrou,** 5 Katalymata St, 2A Christodoulou Bldg, ✆03.721690.

LARNACA:
Avis, 43, A'bish Makarios Ave, ✆04.657132;
Eurodollar, 50, A'bish Makarios Ave, ✆04.657585;
Executive Auto Rentals, 5, JGL Constructions, Larnaka-Dhekelia Rd, ✆04.624145;
G.D.K. Rent a Car, 52, A'bish Makarios Ave, ✆04.629170;
Kyprocars, 10 Ermlu St, PO Box 293, ✆04.652241;
Melissas, 1, Karouana Ct, 38, A'bish Makarios Ave, ✆.04.655145;
Omonia, 24, Pierides St, ✆04.62222;

Panipsos, 25, Galileou St, ✆04.656014;
Phoenix, 65, A'bish Makarios Ave, ✆04.623407;
Theodoulou, 117 Stadiou St, ✆04.627411;
Thrifty Rent-a-Car, 8g, Aradipioti St, ✆04.625177.

LIMASSOL:

Avis, Kean Factory, Limassol-Nicosia Rd, ✆05.324192;
Eurodollar, 167, A'bish Makarios Ave, ✆05.381676;
Hertz, G3, Anna Ct, Limassol-Nicosia Rd, ✆05.323758;
Holiday Tours, 4b, Blue Sea House, 28th October Ave, ✆05.324025;
Kyprocars, 57, Sp. Araouzou, PO Box 3321, ✆05.363890;
Manchester Car Hire, (Limassol-Nicosia Old Road), ✆05.329300;
A. Petsas, (Limassol-Nicosia Rd), ✆05.323672;
St. George's Car Hire, St George's Ho, 62, A'bish Makarios Ave, ✆05.336007;
A. Spyrou, 38-40 Ominia Ave, PO Box 1623, ✆05.371441;
Vintage Car Rentals, 3, Vasileos Georgiou St, ✆05.322050.

NICOSIA:

Airtour Cyprus, 87, A'bish Makarios Ave, ✆02.450403;
Ansa International, Eleftherias Sq, PO Box 1186, ✆02.423920;
Anneli, 17c Prince Charles St, ✆02.475025;
Avis, 2 Homes Ave, PO Box 2276, ✆02.472062;
Europcar, 7e and 7z Santa Rosa St, PO Box 1915, ✆02.445201;
Kyrenia Car Hire, 87 Athalassa Ave, ✆02.432858;
A. Manolis, 42, Thermopyles St, PO Box 8518, ✆02.421924;
A. Petsas, 24, Pantelides Ave, ✆02.462650;
A. Spyrou, Modeas & Esperidion Sts, Acropolis, PO Box 8608, ✆02.494701.

Several agencies operate from Eleftherias Sq, sharing PO Box 1186, Telex 2628 and Fax 357.2.311293: American International, Ansa International, Autohansa International, Bricar International, Car Hire Centre, Carop, and Odysseos Panayiotis.

PAPHOS:

Avis, 87 St Paul's Ave, ✆06.243231;
Bella Rentals, 20, Poseidonos St, ✆06.236909;
Geko Tours, 8, Dionysos St, PO Box 24, ✆06.232848;
Holiday Tours, 77 Poseidonos St, ✆06.234149;
Melissas, 54a St Paul's Ave, ✆06.233985;
P&A Car Hire, 86, St Paul's Ave, ✆06.242794;
A Petsas, Green Ct, St Paul's Ave, ✆06.235522;
A. Spyrou, 19 Natalia Centre, Poseidonos Ave, ✆06.236944.

And at **Polis:** Fontana Rentals, PO Box 12, ✆06.321555.

International agencies. Budget Rent a Car is represented by A. Petsas; Eurodollar by Glamico; Europcar by Holiday Tours; and Hertz by P. Melissas.

What does it cost? These prices are daily rates in sterling with US dollar equivalents for 7-14 days in summer (April-Oct) and winter (Nov-March): **Group A: 1,000cc:** £14 ($21), £11.50 ($19); **Group D: 1,600cc:** £22 ($36), £18.50 ($30); **Group E: 1,000cc, 4WD:** £24 ($40), £17.

Extras. In addition, you have the option of paying for Collision Damage Waiver (CDW) at C£3 daily for average-sized cars, or agreeing to pay for the first C£400 ($800) of damage. Personal Accident Insurance, (PAI), is another optional extra. You pay for a full tank of petrol, around C£12 to C£14 (around $25); when you return the car you get a refund for all the petrol left in tank, judged by guesswork.

Payment. You can pay by credit card (Visa, Access, DC or AE), by cheque if the account is at a British bank, by cash or by travellers' cheques.

Special clauses. The rental agreement excludes any driver who has been convicted of drunken driving, and restricts the use of the car to hard-surfaced roads. If you have an accident or breakdown when you're on a dirt track in the Troodos Mountains, you're on your own.

MOTOR-CYCLE HIRE

In the coastal resorts — Paphos, Polis, Limassol, Kyrenia and Ayia Napa — two-seater Yamaha mini-motor cycles are available for hire

St Paul's Pillar — but was the saint whipped at this post?

at around C£3 a day for up to 3 days and C£2.50 a day for longer. Insurance is included but crash-helmets are not, as these machines' engines are less than 50cc capacity and may not be driven outside the immediate area.

MOTORING REGULATIONS

Motoring regulations are similar to those in Britain. Drive on the *left*, give way on roundabouts to traffic from the right. **Speed limits** are 50km-hr (31mph) in towns, 80km-hr (50mph) in the countryside, and 100km-hr (62mph) on the Highway (it's not a motorway, and has no other concessions or restrictions). The standard of driving is good — and courteous.

The breathalyser was introduced in March 1990, and it's now an offence to drive with more than 32mg of alcohol in 100ml of blood: this is less than half the tolerance in Britain and virtually means no drinking at all. The penalty is up to three years in prison or a C£1,000 fine, or both. The penalty for not wearing a **seat belt** is a fine from C£5 to C£300; drivers of hire cars — 'Z-cars' — get a first warning. Children from five to ten may use the front seat only if a special belt is fitted, and children younger than five may not sit there at all.

Super grade **petrol** (gasoline) costs around 29c a litre (C£1.32 per gallon, £1.03 per gallon, 52¢ per US gallon), before the Iraqi invasion of Kuwait. Unleaded petrol was introduced in late summer 1990. Diesel (gas oil) costs 9.2c a litre (32 pence a gallon, 16¢ per US gallon). Petrol stations are not open in the evenings: see 'business hours' in Chapter 4.

NORTH CYPRUS

The car rental business in North Cyprus lacks organisation. None of the international firms has an agency here, leaving the way open to small businesses, sometimes with just one car whichcould have spent its first years in Turkey. Strangely, all rented cars have red number plates as in Greek Cyprus, and all have Z registrations. A ZZ registration on a white ground shows a car under temporary import licence.

North Cyprus drives on the *left*, but there are many left-hand-drive vehicles around, notably the Turkish-built Murats or the Renault 12s assembled in Turkey, the latter being the cheapest new cars available in the TRNC. They seldom have rear-view mirrors on the passenger's side.

Airlines aren't interested in arranging hire for anybody not buying a full package, and as the rental offices at Ercan Airport operate normal business hours, passengers on evening arrivals are stranded — unless they have made their own arrangements.

Rental agencies. This means knowing in advance who has a car for hire. My list contains most of the rental firms; call one from home, using the special telephone code for North Cyprus, and arrange for a car to be at the airport.

GAZIMAĞUSA (Famagusta):
Atlantic, Sinan Paşa Sok, Adatae Tourism, ℘036.63277; **Deniz,** Yenibo-
ğaziçi village, ℘036.65510; **Oyo,** 3 Fevzı Çakmak Cad, ℘036.64507,
67712; **Sur,** Ismet Inönü Bul, ℘036.65600; **Zetcar Rentals,** 28a Ismet
Inönü Blv, ℘036.62153 (home, 036.62154); **Zodiac Travel & Deniz Rent-
a-car,** 15 Polatpaşa Blv, Eski Polis Binası, ℘036.64717.

GIRNE (Kyrenia):
Atlantic, Dome Hotel, Kordonboyu, ℘081.53053; **Aydın Çanlıbarık,**
Kordonboyu, ℘081.52182; **Oscar,** Kordonboyu, ℘081.52272; **Pacific,**
Ecevit Cad, ℘08218.712; **Salahi (Dervs),** Ecevit Cad, ℘081.54276; **Yeni
Kartal,** nr Denizkızı Hotel, Alsancak, ℘08218.644.

GÜZELYURT (Morphou):Özdeş, 21 Ecevit Cad, ℘071.42765; **Pacific,**
Ecevit Cad, ℘071.42225; **Sişman,** 27 Alemdar Sok, ℘071.43326.

LEFKOŞA (Nicosia):
Capital, Sehit Ulu0amgil Sok (behind Orient Hotel), ℘020.78172; **Elite,**
103 Girne Cad, ℘020.73172; **Huzur,** Nalbantoğlu Cad, 11 Ogretmen
Apartaman, ℘020.32879; **Sun,** Ahmet Kahveci, ℘020.78787, 72303.

What does it cost? Prices are slightly lower than in Cyprus, and
are usually quoted in sterling. These are sample daily rates, with
dollar equivalents, for 9 to 28 days in **low season** (Nov-Mar), **mid
season** (Apr-Jun and Oct), and **high season** (Jul-Sep): **Group 1
(1,000cc):** £7 ($11.50); £8.50 ($14); £9.50 ($15.50); **Group 4 (1,600cc):**
£9.50 ($15.50), £11 ($18), £12.50 ($20.50); **Group 5 (1,000cc, 4WD):** £10
($16.50), £12.50 ($20.50), £16.50 ($27).

You may need to shop around a little, and you will find some firms
offering a slightly higher rate for right-hand-drive cars.

Confirm your method of payment, which will usually be by cash or
by cheque on a British bank, less frequently by credit card; you'll
probably be expected to call in at the firm's office a day or so later to
make the payment. Insurance extras are negotiable.

MOTORING REGULATIONS

Motoring regulations are the same as in Greek Cyprus, but **speed
limits** are 30mph (48kph) in urban areas, 40mph (64kph) in the open
country and 60mph (96kph) on the Girne-Lefkoşa-Ercan Highway.
Note that speed limits and distances are still posted in miles although
car speedometers register kph, and there is no indication where
urban areas merge with rural. Occasional police radar checks ensure
some compliance with the speed limits.

The breathalyser was introduced in 1989, with the same blood-
alcohol limits as in Britain: 80mg of one in 100ml of the other. **Seat belts**
must be worn out of town; within the town you have the option. Your
normal **driving licence** is acceptable.

Super grade **petrol,** known as 'benzin,' costs around 27 pence (43¢)
a litre (£1.22 per gallon, $1.63 per US gallon), with diesel, 'motorin,'
costing 13 pence (21¢) a litre (59p per gallon, 80¢ per US gallon).
Unleaded petrol has yet to arrive.

BUSES
CYPRUS

Cyprus's bus services are smart and efficient, using the latest vehicles — but on some of the local routes in the Troodos you may find yourself on a restored 1930s charabanc.

These timetables list the majority of the services:

LARNACA

to and from **Airport.**
Service 2: departs Marina. Service unreliable: use Kiti bus or take taxi.

to **Nicosia.**
Lefkaritis Bus Co: (Marina)
0600, 0630, 0700, 0800, 0900, 1030, 1200, 1300, 1405, 1500,
([1600]S, [1630]M-F)
from **Nicosia** 🚌A (Stasinos Ave)
0615, 0730, 0900, 1000, 1100, 1200, 1300, 1345, 1415, 1530,
[1600]S (S only), 1700, 1745, (1830)
Fare 70c

to **Limassol**
Lefkaritis Bus Co: (Marina)
0545, 0730, 0815, 0945, 1145, 1245, 1345, [1445]S (S only), 1545
from **Limassol** 🚌E
0600, 0730, 0830, 0930, 1100, 1200, 1400, [1500]S (S only), 1600
Fare 80c

to **Ayia Napa**
Eman: (Marina)
Mar-Nov: 0830, 0930, 1030, 1130, 1300, 1400, 1530,
1630, 1730, 1830
Dec−Feb: 0930, 1030, 1300, 1530, 1630
from **Ayia Napa** (bus stn)
Oct-Apr: 0630, 0800, 0900, 1000, 1100, 1200, 1400,
1500, 1600, 1700
May-Sep: 0715, 0800, 0900, 1000, 1100, 1200, 1400,
1500, 1600, 1700
Fare 60c

to **Kiti Village**
Service 6: 🚌B
0630, 0745, 0845, 1000, 1100, 1200, 1315, 1400, 1500, 1600, 1630,
1700, 1800, (1900)
from **Kiti Village**
0600, 0630, 0700, 0815, 0915, 1030, 1130, 1230, 1430, 1530, 1630 (1730)
Fare 20c

to **Perivolia & Cape Kiti**
Perivolia Bus Co: 🚌B
0800, 1000, 1200, 1300, 1345, 1630, 1745, (1800)
from **Perivolia & Cape Kiti**
0830, 1030, 1230, 1530, 1700
Fare 30c

to **Paralimni**
(via Frenos & Dherinia)
Paralimni Bus Co: (Marina)
0630, 0900, 1100, 1300, 1330, 1400, ([1500]S), 1630, 1730 (1800, 1900)
from **Paralimni** (west of St George's Church)
0800, 0900, 1030, 1600, (1730)
Fare 60c

NICOSIA
(see also Larnaca timetables)

to **Limassol**
Kemek Bus Co: ⛟C, Leonidou St
0600, 0700, (0730) (0800), 0900, 1030, 1200, 1430, 1600.
from **Limassol** ⛟E
0600, 0630, (0700), (0730), 0900, 1030, 1200, 1330, 1415, 1630
Fare C£1

to **Limassol & Paphos**
Costas Bus Co: ⛟H
1200, 1600
from **Paphos & Limassol** ⛟G
0800, 0900
Fare all way C£2, half way C£1.
to **Paralimni** ⛟C
1315
from **Paralimni** (west of St George's Church)
0700
Fare C£1.50 (reservations needed, ✆031.21318)

TROODOS MOUNTAINS services:

to **Platres**
Zingas Bus Co: ⛟C
1215
to **Hill resorts**
Solea Bus Co: ⛟D
1200

from **Platres**
0600
Fare C£1
from **Hill resorts**
0600
Fare 80c

to **Kakopetria**
Solea Bus Co: ⛟D
0615, 1020, 1200, (1300), (1330), 1400, 1530, (1600), (1640),
1730, 1800, (1900)   S 0745, 1700
from **Kakopetria**
0530, 0545, 0610, 0630, 0800, 1315, 1515 ⚘ 0545, 1515

to **Ayia Napa**
Eman Bus Co: (Eleftheria Sq) ⛟J
1500, 0800
from **Ayia Napa** (bus stn)
0800 (mid June-mid Sep   ⚘ 1600
Fare C£1.50

LIMASSOL
(see also Nicosia and Larnaca tables)

to **Paphos**
Kemek Bus Co: 🚌E
0700, 0915, 1230, 1530

from **Paphos** 🚌F
0600, 0900, 1230, 1530
Fare C£1

TROODOS MOUNTAINS services:

to **Platres**
Karydas Bus Co: 🚌F
0900, (1300), 1800

from **Platres**
(0700), 1000, 1600
Fare C£1

to **Platres**
Platres Bus Co: (50 Eleftheria St) 🚌J
1400

from **Platres**
0600
Fare 60c

to **Prodhromos**
Gero Demos Bus Co: 🚌E
1300

from **Prodhromos**
0600
Fare 75c

to **Agros Hill resort**
1300

from **Agros Hill resort**
0600
Fare 75c

Local buses: Limassol's town buses, E.A.Λ. ΛΕΜΕΣΟΥ operate from the market behind CTO office; Route 6 serves the seafront hotels; Rte 16 serves Kolossi Castle; in high summer an extra service to Lady's Mile Beach, dep 0800, 0915, 1030, 1145, 1600; ret 0845, 1000, 1115, 1235, 1530, 1700.

Kykko, the most impressive monastery on the island, sheltered Makarios during EOKA days.

PAPHOS
(see also Limassol tables)

Local buses: A. Le. Pa. (ΑΣΤΙΚΑ ΛΕΩΦΟΡΕΙΑ ΠΑΦΟΥ) has frequent services to Kato Paphos (27 buses each way from 0630 to 1915), Coral Bay, Yeroskipou, from 🚐G; less frequent to other local villages from 🚐F.

to **Kato Pyrgos**
Pyrgos Bus Co: (Evagoras Pallikarides Ave)
1230, 1600

from **Kato Pyrgos**
0500
Fare C£1

to **Polis**
Amoroza Bus Co: 🚐F
0645, 0900, 1000, 1100, 1200, 1300, 1400, 1500, 1600, 1700, 1800
(1900)   S, 1000, 1200, 1300, 1600
from **Polis**
0600, 0615, 0645, 0715, 0800, 0900, 1015, 1200, 1300, 1330, 1400,
1515, 1700, (1800, 1900), 0700, 1300, 1500
Fare 50c

AYIA NAPA
(see also Larnaca and Nicosia tables)

to **Paralimni via Protatas**
(Asterias Beach Hotel)
0900, 1000, 1100, 1200, 1300, 1400, 1600, 1700, 1800,
(1900)🐚, 1000, 1200, 1400, 1700, (1900)
from **Paralimni via Protaras** (west of St George's Church)
0900, 1000, 1100, 1200, 1300, 1400, 1600, 1700, 1800, (1900),
🐚 0900, 1100, 1300, 1600, 1800
Fare 25c

KEY TO BUS TIMETABLES
Times quoted are for Monday to Saturday inclusive. 🐚 denotes Sunday schedule.

Brackets ( ) indicate summer schedules only. Summer is considered 1 May to 30 September, but this does not always match the summer schedule exactly.

Brackets [ ] indicate the last bus on the stated day, e.g. [1800]S, with days indicated M Tu W Th F S 🐚.

NORTH CYPRUS
The people of North Cyprus are more dependent on their bus services, which run with the efficiency of those of Turkey. In addition to the timetables that follow, there are bus or dolmuş (minibus) services linking almost all the remote villages with at least one of the larger towns; these buses set off from 0600 carrying workers, and spend the day parked in some backstreet before heading home around 1700.

Each town has consolidated its public transport to operate from one site, and all but Girne have the various companies' offices gathered in a small block, Turkish-style. At Girne you have to ask.

GIRNE

to **Club Acapulco**
1000, 1100, 1200, 1330, 1530, 1800, 1900
from **Club Acapulco**
0900, 1030, 1130, 1300, 1500, 1830

to **Gazimağusa**
0630, 0700, 0830, thence hourly to 1730, 1900.
from **Gazimağusa**, same times.
Fare 95p, $1.50.

to **Güzelyurt**
0630, 0800, hourly to 1200, 1245, 1315, 1400, 1500, 1600, 1630,
1715.
from **Güzelyurt**, same times.
Fare 35p, 56¢

to **Lefkoşa**
0600 to 1800 at 15-minute intervals

from **Lefkoşa**, same times.
Fare 23p, 37¢

GÜELYURT

to **Lefkoşa**
0600 to 1740, with 36 services

from **Lefkoşa**
0700 to 1840, with 36 services.
Fare 22p, 35¢

to **Lefke**
0715 to 1830, with 21 services

from **Lefke**, same times.
Fare 22p, 35¢

GAZIMAĞUSA

to **Lefkoşa** by bus
0700 to 1730, with 28 services, up to 36 on Tu, Thur, Sat when Mersin
ferry is in port.
from **Lefkoşa**, same times.
Fare 68p, $1.10.

to **Lefkoşa** by Itimat dolmuş
0615 to 1715 (1800 on Mon), with 16 services
from **Lefkoşa**, same times.
Fare 37p, 60¢

LEFKOŞA

to **Lefke**
0600 to 1730, with 6 services

from **Lefke**, same times.
Fare 65p, $1.

YENIERENKÖY

to **Lefkoşa**, 0600; from **Lefkoşa**, 1100, fare 58p, 93¢

to **Gazimağusa**, 0600, 1400; from **Gazimağusa**, 1100, 1600, fare 35p, 55¢

A last relic of the Cyprus Railway stands in Polatpaşa Bulvarı, Famagusta.

TAXIS
CYPRUS

Cyprus has two kinds of taxi. The **service taxi** is an improved version of the bus with smart cars, often Mercedeses, operating set routes at set times for set fares, but with the advantage of collecting passengers from their hotel. Services operate only between Nicosia, Larnaca and Limassol, and on to Paphos and Polis by the main road,

The service taxis start at 0600 and run through until 1800 or 1900 hours, with departures every half hour. Fares are from 50% to 80% higher than on the buses.

From LARNACA
to **Nicosia**: (Acropolis) Afxentiou St—Archb. Makarios St (✆041.55555); (Makris) 13 King Paul St (✆041.52929); (Kyriakos) 2c Hermes St (✆041.55100)
to **Limassol**: (Acropolis) as above; (Makris) as above.

From NICOSIA
to **Larnaca**: (Acropolis) 9 Stassinos Ave (✆02.472525); (Kyriakos) 27 Stassinos Ave (✆02.444141); (Makris) 11 Stassinos Ave (✆02.466201).
to **Limassol**: (Karydas) 8 Homer Ave (✆02.462269); (Kypros) 9a Stassinos Ave (✆02.464811).

From LIMASSOL
to Nicosia: (Karydas & Kyriakos) 21 Thessalonikis St (✆051.62061); (Kypros) 49 Sp Araouzos St (✆051.63979).
to Larnaca: (Makris) 166 Hellas St (✆051.65550); (Acropolis) 49 Sp Araouzos St (✆051.66766).
to Paphos: (Karydas & Kyriakos) 21 Thessalonikis St (✆051.62061); (Kypros) 49 Sp Araouzos St (✆051.63979).

From PAPHOS
to Limassol: (Karydas & Kyriakos) 9 E. Pallikarides St (✆061.32459); (Kypros & Nea Paphos) 21 E. Pallikarides St (✆061.32376).

Names in brackets are the taxi operators.

Other taxis. The **rural taxi** is a modified service taxi operating in the Troodos Mountains, and in the rural areas which have no other form of public transport.

The **urban taxi** is the more conventional taxicab, fitted with a meter and taking one passenger (and all companions) to the required destination.

Urban taxi fares. Hiring charge: 35c; thereafter 27c per mile (17c per km) for a single trip (tariff 1) or 20c per mile (13c per km) for a return trip (tariff 2); the minimum charge is 60c. The first 13kg (28lb) of luggage is free; thereafter 20c per 13kg, with the driver guessing the weight. Between 2300 and 0600 the fare is increased by 15% with the minimum charge being C£1.

You can engage an urban taxi driver to take you anywhere in the republic; the tariff 1 fare between Paphos and Ayia Napa of C£32 being a guide.

NORTH CYPRUS
North Cyprus just has the private taxi, available in the main towns and at the airport, for destinations anywhere. Most are smart Mercedes saloons; all are distinguishable by the word TAKSI. Sample fares? Gazimağusa to Lefkoşa, or Ercan to Girne, £10 ($16), which includes all passengers and their luggage.

8: EAT, SLEEP, WINE and DINE

And see the nightlife

THERE IS A VAST DIFFERENCE in the tourist capacity on each side of the Green Line. Cyprus's tourist office lists 213 hotels, 18 guest houses, 242 hotel apartments (apart-hotels or self-catering apartments), and 5 tourist complexes. North Cyprus promotes 29 hotels, and 19 hotel apartments, motels and camping sites, but ignores the *pensions*.

HOTELS and other accommodation
CYPRUS

Outside Nicosia, virtually all the hotels from 5-star down to 2-star are involved in the package holiday business, a few of them dealing exclusively with tour operators; Cyprus is also heavily involved in self-catering apartment holidays.

Standards are high, and maintained at that level by strict checking by CTO staff; tariffs are set by the CTO and the Ministry of Commerce, and Industry, are displayed in every hotel room, and may not be exceeded. Service charges and an allowance for staff tips is included.

Extras. You may be charged up to C£2 extra per day for air-conditioning, but only if you ask for it; room service can cost up to 50c, but heating is not an extra.

Costs. Hotel prices are always per *room,* not per person, with single-occupancy costing 80% of double; the fourth adult in a three-bed hotel apartment gets a 50% discount. Tariffs range from C£79, bed only, at the 5-star Cyprus Hilton in Nicosia, and C£88 full board at the Amathus Beach, Limassol, to C£7.91 at the city's no-star Cottage Hotel and C£5 at the Akamis in Polis. Guest houses range from C£12 at the Pelican Inn, Paphos, to C£4 at the Kypros in Nicosia.

Hotel apartment tariffs depend on the number of beds; in Ayia Napa prices range from C£48 to C£12, with beds for two.

Other accommodation. The bargain hunter can find cheaper rooms, though they won't be CTO-approved. R&T Travel & Tours of Ayia Napa (PO Box 20, ✆03.721580, fax 03.721583) is one of several agencies in the resort for apartments not listed by the CTO, and if you walk the backstreets you can find others, though these will probably be lacking some basic requirement.

Polis, north of Paphos, has plenty of people willing to rent out a room or an apartment for as long as you want, and by asking you'll be able to find basic accommodation in the mountain villages far from the tourist trail.

Youth hostels in Limassol and Paphos provide rock-bottom basics: the Limassol hostel has around 40 bunk beds in five rooms and charges C£1.85 for the first night, including breakfast, and C£1 thereafter, with breakfast at 60c. The Paphos hostel has 20 beds in three rooms. There are **camping sites** at Polis, and near Paphos, Larnaca, Ayia Napa and Troodos, but there's no restriction on camping anywhere, provided you're not on military land, nor private land without permission, and that you take away your rubbish.

But what about the **monasteries?** Here is an excellent opportunity to sample the monastic life without taking holy orders. Accommodation is simple, and you're not presented with a bill: give what you think the service was worth. The only problem is that some monasteries will not open their doors to women.

NORTH CYPRUS

North Cyprus's hotel industry is virtually a copy of that in the south, but on a much smaller scale. Hotels' star rating is awarded by the government which also sets the maximum prices and threatens prosecution if they are exceeded; hotels may offer discounts of up to 15% in April and October, and up to 30% from November through March. Hotel-apartments — call them apart-hotels or self-catering establishments — come under government control but don't get a star rating: most are squeaky clean but there are a few exceptions.

Extras. A 10% service charge and a 3% municipal tax are additional to prices quoted by the tourist office.

Standards are equal with the south, but you should expect occasional power failures until the hotel generator takes the load; additionally, the Palm Beach Hotel and Laguna Bay Apart-hotel in south Gazimağusa are victims of the erratic water supply from across the Buffer Zone, and the pensions in the city's Kaleiçi and some way to the north have undrinkable water.

Pensions. Pensions — *pansiyonlar* — are controlled by the municipality, the *belediye*, which is the place to go for more information, although you may be told that these are 'for Turkish visitors, not for Europeans.' Standards do indeed vary, as there is nothing to prevent anybody opening a pension, though the owner will eventually need to apply for a licence.

Other accommodation. There are no youth hostels, no monasteries, and few camping sites — but there's no restriction on bringing your own tent and camping in the countryside.

Do-it-yourself booking. If you contact any hotel direct, don't forget the special postal and telephone codes for North Cyprus.

RESTAURANTS

Cyprus is not a gourmet's paradise, but it has some excellent restaurants on each side of the Green Line, those in the south obviously specialising in Greek dishes but with French, Italian, Lebanese and Arabic menus available – and there are plenty of Turkish-style *lokantas* serving şiş-kebaps. Turkish, French, Greek and what passes for British, and the main themes of restaurants in North Cyprus.

CTO approval. The Cyprus Tourism Organisation of the south has its list of approved restaurants and tavernas, each of which carries on its door the CTO symbol of six breaking waves; here the prices and the size of servings is also controlled, and the 10% service charge and 3% CTO tax are included in the bill.

Sample menu. Menus vary enormously, but this is a selection from Maryland at the Mill in Kakopetria, one of the most distinctive restaurants in Cyprus; see Chapter 17 to learn why.

Appetizers, cold:

Melon	65c, **85p** $1.35
Lounza	C£1 **£1.25** $2
Smoked trout	C£1.75 **£2.25** $3.55
Avocado vinaigrette	120c **£1.55** $2.45
Crab cocktail	C£2 **£2.50** $4.05

Appetizers, hot:

Grilled trout	C£1.60 **C£2.05** $3.25
Halloumi	75c **95p** $1.55

Soups:

Avgolémoni	70c **90p** $1.45
Mushroom soup	70c **90p** $1.45

Omelettes:

Spanish or seafood	C£1.20 **£1.55** $2.45

Side orders:

Tahini	40c **50p** 85¢
Talatouri	40c **50p** 85¢
Taramas	40c **50p** 85¢
Fetta	50c **65p** $1

Main course:

Maryland trout with French fries, salad	C£3.25 **£4** $6.55
Steaks, T-bone or fillet	C£3.25 **£4** $6.55

Desserts:

Creme caramel	60c **80p** $1.10
Choc sundae	75c **95p** $1.55

Tea:

Earl Grey or Jasmine	50c **65p** $1

Cypriot cuisine. The Cypriot cuisine aims to enhance the flavour of foods, with *mezé* among the most popular and surprising of dishes. A mezé – or mezedakia in Greek – comes in anything from 12 to 20 small dishes, each with something different. Sample from cheeses, *houmous* (ground chick peas in oil and garlic), seafoods (octopus, shrimps or *barbouni* (red mullet)), meats (turkey, chicken, *șeftalia* (salami-like sausage), smoked ham), vegetables and salads, and pickled olives.

A typical Greek Cypriot main course will be *moussaka* or *tavva*, or perhaps a *souglakia* which is often a meal in itself.

Moussaka is a local casserole, a dish of minced meats and herbs covered with aubergines, sliced potatoes and marrows; tavva is veal and onion, flavoured with herbs and spices and served as it is cooked, in individual dishes. Souglakia is a Greek kebab (*kebap* in Turkish) eaten with *pitta*, the local unleavened bread.

Cypriot specials. In the menu given above, lounza is smoked pork, halloumi is an ewe-milk cheese while fetta is from goats' milk. Avgolemoni is rice soup with chicken and eggs, tahini is based on sesame, and talatouri is yoghourt with cucumber – and you can find most of these specialities on both sides of the Green Line.

And then there are *patcha*, a lamb stew with lemon – lemon goes with so many meat dishes in Cyprus – *fasolada*, pork marinated in wine and fried in oil and wine with coriander spicing, and *zalatina*, a well-spiced potted meat. *Keftedes* is a spiced meat ball, the *köfte* you will see in Turkey. There is little scope for vegetarians.

Desserts include *gliko*, fruit preserved in syrup, *loukoumades* which look like doughnuts, *souzoukko*, nuts boiled in grape juice, *loukoumi*, alias Turkish delight, and several rich cakes such as *baklava* and *kadeifi*. And don't forget the honey: the island's bountiful and unspoiled meadows yield vast amounts of this soft, golden bounty.

Wines and spirits. Cyprus was one of the first places in the world to produce wines, probably as early as 1600BC, and its solera wine, Commandaria, is one of the oldest in the world – but more of that in Chapter 14. Today's Cyprus wines include red, rosé (blush) and white, dry or sweet, and Cyprus sherry-type wines such as Emva Cream.

Keo of Limassol, the biggest producer, also distils grape juice as the base for spirits such as rum, brandy, Cossack vodka, and ouzo. My palate suggests that the wines and fortified wines are good, but I find the rum and brandy are indistinguishable and not worth more than their local cost of C£1.25 (£1.50, $2.50). Keo also brews the south's lager which I find refreshing, a rival to the Efes Pilsen of the north.

The following menu comes from one of several restaurants to be found in the charming harbour at Girne in North Cyprus. It is not in the same class as Maryland at the Mill so comparison is not possible, but it gives an idea of the range and price of an average meal.

Fish mezze	**£4.18**	$6.70
Red mullet (about 4in (10cm) long)	**£3.25**	$5.40
Vlagos (a meaty-textured fish)	**£3**	$4.80
Şiş fish (small fish on a skewer)	**£3.50**	$5.60
Fish fillet	**£3**	$4.80
Squid kalamar	**£3**	4.80
Octopus (small sections)	**£2.80**	$4.50
Şeftali (minced meat in goat stomach)	**£2.80**	$4.50
Kebaps (meat pieces on skewer)	**£3.50**	$5.60
Fillet steak	**£2.80**	$4.50

NIGHTLIFE

Cyprus is a quiet island. Before the coming of mass tourism, Greeks and Turks would spend their evenings in the taverna or the lokanta, where there might occasionally be some spontaneous dancing.

The situation is similar today, but it has adapted to modern demands, particularly in the south. The taverna is a little more sophisticated, and the better-class restaurant with evening trade may stage a show of dancers in national costume, be they Greek or Turkish.

All other entertainment is put on especially for the tourist trade, and includes the ubiquitous disco, the night-club, and the bar. The larger tourist hotels, particularly those in Limassol, Larnaca and Ayia Napa, manage their own programmes.

Culture. Opera? Orchestral concerts? Republican Cyprus has a limited offering of classical entertainment, mainly in summer and much of it from Britain or Greece, with prices ranging from free entry to a modest C£2 (£2.60, $4.20).

Casinos. North Cyprus has several casinos, but none can begin to approach those of the world's major resorts.

Some of the minor roads are axle-breakers, like this cobbled track near Lythrodhonda.

9: MOVING IN

Retirement or holiday homes

THE CLIMATE, THE SCENERY AND THE COST OF LIVING make Cyprus a popular place for retirement — and for owning a holiday home. North or south of the Green Line, you are welcome to come and buy a home, provided you don't want to look for work and you have an adequate income from abroad.

CYPRUS

The Migration Officer of the Ministry of the Interior issues immigration permits; he's at the Department of Aliens, Nicosia, ✆(02)303138. He may want proof that you have an income of at least C£4,000 (£5,200, $8,300) a year for a single person, or C£6,000 for a couple, available from pensions or investments abroad.

Property. Property in Cyprus ranges from cheap to moderately-expensive; you can find an acceptable house in the foothills of the Troodos for C£7,000, but one in the conservation-conscious village of Kakopetria in need of extensive renovation will cost C£35,000 (£43,000, $70,000). Even in Pano Lefkara, noted for its lace, a new three-bed house sells for C£12,000 (£15,000, $25,000) — but smart tourist-style villas range from C£40,000 to C£80,000.

Foreigners are restricted to one property, which must not exceed two donums (3,200 sq yds or 2,676 sq m), and they need the Council of Ministers' approval before buying. Houses are sold freehold — you own the land in perpetuity — and the law of 'horizontal freehold' will soon allow apartments to be owned outright, rather than on leasehold. Property taxes were greatly increased in 1990 but are still low by western European standards. Capital gains tax applies on profits from the sale of property.

Cars. You may import one *right-hand-drive* car, regardless of its age, and any household goods and furniture, without paying any duty except the 5.5% Temporary Refugee Levy; the Department of Customs and Excise (✆(02)402795) has the application forms.

Work permits. Your prospective employer must apply for your work permit before you arrive in Cyprus, and it will be granted only if there is no suitably-qualified person already available; there are occasional union disputes about Egyptians and Lebanese being granted work permits.

NORTH CYPRUS

The Girne area is popular with Britons and Germans seeking holiday or retirement homes in the sun, and there is a better chance of getting a work permit in North Cyprus, particularly if you can contribute to the growth in tourism; your prospective employer applies for the permit before you start the job, and the six-month licence is renewable. Residence permits, which don't carry the right to employment, are available from the Aliens Department in Lefkoşa. For either, you must be certified free from tuberculosis and the aids virus.

Property. Look around in the villages on the north slope of the Kyrenia Mountains − the views are wonderful − and you can find a plot or a ruin at a ridiculously low price: *but make absolutely certain it's owned by a Turkish Cypriot, not a Greek; under no circumstances should you buy a Greek Cypriot property, even if dealing directly with the legal owner on neutral territory, as your title deeds will be defective.*

A completed apartment in Girne itself sells from around £35,000 ($55,000), with a two-bedroom villa costing from £80,000 to £120,000 ($125,000 to $190,000), with the prospect of renting the property through local estate agents or through tour operators. As a customer you could expect to pay a weekly rental equal to the market value, less the three zeros; as an owner you could expect to receive half this figure from the tour operator.

Avoid leasehold property: you may find, too late, that the lease is broken into five-year renewable periods. When you've done the restoration, the freeholder may decide not to renew.

North Cyprus has no property tax at all. The Belediye makes a charge for collecting rubbish in the urban areas, but householders in the countryside must make their own disposal arrangements. Electricity (which includes the television licence) is ridiculously cheap by western European standards.

Cars. Retired expatriates may import one car duty-free, but other people must pay a duty of 128% of the car's agreed value.

If you decide to move in you qualify to join the British Residents Society, established in 1975; its office is behind the Post Office in Girne and its address is PO Box 167.

10: CYPRUS DOWN THE AGES

From Neolithic to Independent

THE NEW STONE AGE PEOPLE who built the first known community on Cyprus were better organised than their contemporaries in the Near East. Their settlement, now known as Khirokitia, was on a low hilltop half-encircled by a river which probably flowed all year, and with a stone wall to protect the vulnerable rear.

Khirokitia, called Choirokoitia on CTO maps, was built around 5800BC on a steep hillside looking southwards towards the sea. Its inhabitants grew wheat and barley which they harvested with flint tools; they ground the grain between simple millstones; they herded sheep, pigs and goats; and they buried their dead in the floors of their tiny roundhouses, whose ruins were discovered in 1934 and are now open to the public.

Other Neolithic settlements have been found at nearby Kalavasos, and at three sites now in North Cyprus: the island known to Greeks as Petra tou Limniti, near Yeşilırmak; at Troulli, east of Girne; and at Zafer Burnu, formerly Cap Andreas at the tip of the Panhandle, but only Kalavasos is open to the public.

Copper ingot. Neolithic Man landed here around 7000BC, his culture fading around 3900BC as Chalcolithic Man began replacing his stone ware with copper. We can speculate that these early people had used a lump of one of the copper-bearing rocks in their fireplace, and the heat released the metal. The Cyprus Museum in south Nicosia has a gallery devoted to these early islanders, and elsewhere it displays a copper ingot weighing around 90lb (40kg).

Raw copper was more plentiful in the Troodos area, where Copper Age Man began beating the metal into ornaments long before developing copper cooking pots. By 2500BC, zinc had been discovered on the island, and the mixing of the two metals yielded not only bronze but introduced the Bronze Age, taking the islanders one more step towards civilization.

Engomi. Between 2000 and 1700BC the community of Engomi or Enkomi was created, north-west of today's Famagusta; by 1550 it was a leading producer and exporter of copper and, under the name of Alasia, it was mentioned in correspondence between its king and Pharoah Amenophis IV of Egypt; it was abandoned in the 11th cent BC.

Bronze Age Man had become a miner and a trader: the Cyprus

Museum is again your guide on seeing what an early copper mine may have looked like. This soft, non-rusting metal was now shipped east, south, and west, bringing wealth to Cyprus. Around 1400BC the Mycenaeans, from what is now Peloponnesus in Greece, found the island and in the next two centuries boatloads of settlers from the Greek kingdom of Achaea settled in Cyprus, bringing their language and culture: it was the beginning of the Hellenisation of the island.

These early Greeks built the cities of Paphos, Kition, Curium and Salamis, their culture gradually absorbing the cruder Late Bronze Age civilization of the original peoples.

Ten kingdoms. By 1000BC Cyprus was one of the most important points of call in the eastern Mediterranean, and certainly the most important island in that sea. Ten kingdoms shared the territory in what historians call the Geometric Period; in addition to **Paphos, Curium** and **Salamis,** the Phoenicians had settled in **Kition** (Larnaca) and traded from the island until they lost their domination of the sea routes. **Amathus** (east of Limassol) was thriving, and **Tamassos** was established on the north-east foothills of the Troodos. **Idalion** was on the plains at Dali, 12 miles (19km) south of today's Nicosia, and much of the city has still to be excavated. **Soli** and nearby **Vouni** were ruling the area now dominated by Gemikonağı, known to the Greeks as Karavostasi; and **Lapitos** was on the coast near Alsancak, which the Greeks called Karavas. The name has transferred to the adjacent village of Lapithos, now Lapta, west of Girne (Kyrenia).

Assyrians. Beginning in 709BC the Assyrians conquered the Ten Kingdoms one by one, making them vassal states rather than destroying them, but the Assyrians were defeated in 612BC by a re-emergence of power from some of the ten. The Egyptians came in 565BC but stayed a mere quarter-century, then in 525BC the Persians arrived as the new overlords. In 411BC the young man Evagoras seized the throne of Salamis, formerly ruled by his ancestors, and in 20 years had restored the city's prosperity and managed to unite the island under his rule. He became over-ambitious and in 380BC had to surrender everything except Salamis to the Persians.

Alexander the Great. Alexander the Great, King of Macedonia, led his armies eastward from Greece into Asia Minor and on to Persia, which he defeated in 331BC, and Cyprus therefore fell into his empire without a struggle.

Kyrenia shipwreck. Around this time a ship that had called at Samos, Kos and Rhodes, journeyed on to Cyprus where it was wrecked outside Kyrenia harbour. The bottom of its hull was raised in 1969 and went on display in the Kyrenia Shipwreck Museum in 1976.

Meanwhile, Alexander had died in 323 at the age of 32, with no successor, and his empire crumbled as his generals fought for their share of the spoils. Cyprus eventually emerged in the control of the Ptolemaic dynasty of Egypt, then under Hellenistic (Greek) influence and, with Paphos as its capital, the island again prospered.

Aphrodite. The Paphians had inherited the belief in the ancient gods of Greece, but they added their own deity, Aphrodite, Goddess of Love and Beauty, who they believed emerged from the sea (*aphros* means 'foam,' as on the shore) at Petra tou Romiou, one of the most beautiful stretches of coast on the island and just a few miles east of Paphos; another belief claims she was the daughter of Zeus, known as Jupiter to the Romans.

Aphrodite was typically seen in a chariot drawn by swans or doves, and carrying fruits and flowers, but sculptors and artists soon began showing her nude, as she is now seen in the famous statue of the Venus de Milo and the Botticelli painting of the Birth of Aphrodite; Venus is the name the Romans bestowed on her.

According to ancient beliefs, the Goddess of Love married the god Hephaestus (Vulcan), but was the mistress of Aries, Dionysus, Hermes and Poseidon among the deities, and Adonis and Anchises on the mortal level, and she was the mother of Cupid. Her lower abdomen had the miraculous gift of exciting male passions, which soon led to sexual excesses among mere mortals who saw her as an excuse for their orgies.

Aphrodite had several places in Cyprus venerated in her honour, apart from Petra tou Romiou; her bath is on the western tip of the island, her temple is in Paphos, her sacred gardens are at nearby Yeroskipios (the name means 'sacred gardens'), and her name is used to promote business and tourism across the southern part of the island and even in the Moslem north.

Roman rule. The Romans came in 58BC, ruling Cyprus as a part of the province of Syria until the island became a separate province. The Latin for 'copper' was *aes cyprium,* later reduced to *cuprum;* as *aes* meant 'copper ore' and later 'bronze' and 'brass,' and *cyprium* meant 'of Cyprus,' there is speculation that the metal took its name from the island during the Roman era. There is equal speculation that the island took its name from the metal, as earlier names had included Acamantis, Aerosa, Alasia, Amanthusia, Aspelia, Cythera, Paphos and Salamis.

Biblical Cyprus. Christianity arrived early in Cyprus, as the Bible itself testifies:

And Joses, who by the apostles was surnamed Barnabas (which is, being interpreted, the son of consolation), a Levite, and of the country of Cyprus [Barnabas was born of Jewish parents in Salamis], having land, sold it, and brought the money, and laid it at the apostles' feet. (Acts IV, 36,37.)

Now they which were scattered abroad upon the persecution that arose about Stephen travelled as far as Phenice, and Cyprus, and Antioch, preaching the word to none but unto the Jews only.

And some of them were men of Cyprus and Cyrene, which, when they were come to Antioch, spake unto the Grecians, preaching the Lord Jesus. (Acts XI, 19,20.)

Now there were in the church that was at Antioch certain prophets and teachers; as Barnabas, and Simeon that was called Niger, and

Lucius of Cyrene . . . As they ministered to the Lord, and fasted, the Holy Ghost said, Separate me Barnabas and Saul [Paul] for the work whereunto I have called them. . . .

So they, being sent forth by the Holy Ghost, departed unto Seleucia [Silifke]; and from thence they sailed to Cyprus. And when they were at Salamis, they preached the word of God in the synagogues of the Jews . . . And when they had gone through the island unto Paphos, they found a certain sorcerer, a false prophet, a Jew, whose name was Bar-jesus . . . (Acts XIII, 1,2,4-6.)

And Barnabas determined to take with them John, whose surname was Mark. But Paul thought not good to take him . . . And the contention was so sharp . . . that they departed asunder one from the other; and so Barnabas took Mark, and sailed unto Cyprus. (Acts XV, 37-39.)

There went with us also certain of the disciples of Caesarea, and brought with them one Mnason of Cyprus, an old disciple, with whom we should lodge. (Acts XXI, 16.)

First Christian. St Paul's first missionary journey took him from Antioch to Salamis, overland to Paphos, and then to Perge, just north of Antalya, Turkey. While in Cyprus in 45, Paul and Barnabas converted the Roman proconsul Sergius Paulus to Christianity, although Barnabas was murdered soon after, and thus this island was the world's first territory to be ruled by a Christian. Paul's later journeys covered much of Asia Minor and Greece, and on his fourth mission he was wrecked in what is now St Paul's Bay, Malta (see *Discover Malta* in this series) on his way to Rome. Lazarus, the 'friend of Christ,' came over to preach at Kition, now Larnaca.

Earthquakes. Earthquakes had shaken much of the eastern Mediterranean in the last century BC and the first of the new era, destroying the cities of Asia Minor and, in 76 or 77AD, laying waste to Salamis and other cities on Cyprus.

There is historic evidence that many Philistines (Palestinians) had left the Holy Land for Cyprus in the last centuries before Christ. After the Crucifiction, Stephen began preaching the new religion with such fervour that the Jews in Jerusalem put him on trial – his evidence forms Acts VII – and stoned him to death. Christians now fled the Holy Land for Cyprus where they had a warmer welcome, though there was conflict with the Jews on the island, particularly in 116 when the Jews of the rebuilt Salamis slaughtered many Christians; some figures claim around 200,000 victims across the island, which seems grossly inflated. Soon after, the Roman Senate expelled all Jews from Cyprus, which helped Christianity to expand. Then in 164 bubonic plague, to be known in the Middle Ages as the Black Death, struck Cyprus and reduced the population still further.

Edict of Milan. The Edict of Milan of 313 granted freedom of worship within the Roman Empire, and in 325 bishops from Cyprus attended the Council of Nicaea (east of the Sea of Marmara) which, among other things, decided how Easter would be determined.

The Roman Empire collapsed in 330, with the eastern part becoming the Byzantine Empire based on Constantinople, named from Constantine the Great. Constantine's mother, Helena, is credited with founding the hilltop monastery of Stavrovouni as well as having an Atlantic island named from her.

Further earthquakes in 332 and 342 destroyed much of what remained of the early cities of the island, though Salamis was rebuilt on a smaller scale and named Constantia in honour of Emperor Constantius II.

Red ink. Bishop Anticitus had a dream; he dreamed he knew where the body of St Barnabas, murdered in Salamis in 45, had been buried. When the bishop and his team found the grave in the indicated spot, they recognised Barnabas's body from the Gospel of St Matthew, in Barnabas's own writing, which had been buried with him. In recognition of this miracle, the Byzantine Emperor Zeno granted independence to the Church of Cyprus, allowed its archbishop to wear an imperial purple cope − an ecclesiastical cloak − to carry a sceptre instead of a staff, to sign in red ink, and to carry the title which in English translation is 'His Beatitude.' All these privileges survive today, and His Beatitude Archbishop Makarios, as President of the Republic of Cyprus, signed the independence documents in red ink.

Monastery of St Barnabas. Emperor Zeno also gave enough funds for the building of a monastery on the site where Barnabas had been buried. The monastery, a mile west of the coast road north from Gazimağusa (Famagusta) in North Cyprus, is now empty but open to view as a museum.

Independence? Mahomet died in 632, and within two years the Islamic conquest had begun. The Arabs invaded Cyprus in 647 while their caliphs − successors to Mahomet − surged across north Africa and by 711 had landed in Gibraltar (see *Discover Gibraltar* in this series) and were invading Europe through Spain and threatening it through Asia Minor. Emperor Justinian II and the caliphs agreed a pact in 688 to neutralise Cyprus, while both sides demanded a tribute from the island. Arab raids continued intermittently until 965 when Emperor Nicephoros Phocas drove the last Arabs from the island. During these 277 years, Cyprus was nominally in the Byzantine Empire but was in effect out in the cold, pray to any passing pirate; it was independence − of a kind.

Emperor of Cyprus. Cyprus remained in Byzantium while the Seljuks invaded Asia Minor from the east, but in 1184 the governor of the island, **Isaac Comnenus,** rebelled against the weak Andronicus I in his second year as emperor and declared himself Emperor of Cyprus; Andronicus was deposed and murdered the next year, but his successor was unable to unseat Comnenus.

Richard the Lionheart. That task fell to King Richard I of England, Richard the Lionheart, who, with King Philip Augustus of France and Emperor Barbarossa of Germany, was on the **Third Crusade** to the Holy Land.

Richard's fleet had sailed from England in 1189 and had overwintered in Messina where Richard was betrothed to **Berengaria,** daughter of King Sancho VI of Navarra. The fleet sailed again in April but storms drove Richard and some of his ships to seek safety in Rhodes while three others were wrecked off Cyprus and a fourth, carrying Berengaria and Richard's sister, Joanna of Scily, ran aground off Amathus, Cyprus.

Emperor Comnenus ordered that Berengaria and Joanna be thrown in prison and all flotsam be seized; for the sake of his own salvation Comnenus had agreed with **Saladin** of Syria not to help the Crusaders in any way. On 6 May 1191, Richard arrived with his fleet at Amathus, learned what had happened to his future queen, and demanded Comnenus be the gentleman; Comnenus refused, so Richard decided his only course of action was to seize Cyprus.

It was probably on 8 May that Richard landed his troops at Limassol and within a few hours seized the tiny city, forcing Comnenus to pull back to Kilani in the Troodos Mountains. King Richard and Emperor Isaac met, probably on the 11th, at **Kolossi** village — there was no castle here yet — and agreed that Richard should vacate Limassol in return for Isaac's giving 20,000 gold marks to the Third Crusade, sending 500 men, and helping all future passing crusaders; Isaac even pledged his only daughter as hostage. But when Comnenus learned how few troops the English had, he demanded Richard pull out at once, or fight.

Queen Berengaria. On that same day Richard landed his cavalry of 110 knights and his 500 foot soldiers, defeated Isaac and forced him to flee. Richard then went back to Limassol and on 12 May 1191, he married Berengaria in the Chapel of St George in the town's castle; in the same ceremony Bishop Jean of Evreux crowned her Queen of England.

Kingdom of Jerusalem. Saladin had been winning the Holy Land bit by bit, reducing the Kingdom of Jerusalem (which had earlier held roughly the area occupied by modern Israel) to the single town of Tyre by 1187 and seizing that soon after. The deposed King of Jerusalem, **Guy de Lusignan,** met Richard in Limassol and pleaded for help. Richard loaned Guy his fleet then led his little army in pursuit of Emperor Isaac.

Cyprus under the English Crown. The crusaders marched eastwards, seizing the undefended Kiti (Larnaca) and Famagusta, then turned west for Nicosia, meeting Isaac at Tremetousha (or Tremithoussa, but now Erdemli in North Cyprus). Although Isaac was defeated he managed to escape, but he had lost control of Cyprus. Richard took Nicosia then turned north and picked off the mountaintop castles of **St Hilarion, Buffavento** and **Kantara,** while Guy de Lusignan sailed round to Kyrenia (now Girne) and seized the castle there. As a bonus he found Emperor Comnenus, his wife, and daughter sheltering in **Kyrenia Castle;** once more Isaac Comnenus escaped, but Guy caught him as he made his way to Kantara Castle,

Bellapais Abbey.

already in Richard's hands. By late May 1191 — the actual date seems to have been lost — Cyprus was under the English Crown.

Richard redistributed the lands, replaced Greek garrison commanders with his own men, appointed his own administrators and, on 5 June 1191, sailed for Acre to resume the Third Crusade. He took Isaac Comnenus in chains and handed him to the **Knights Templar,** the Knights of the Order of St John, who incarcerated him in the Castle of Marcab, south of Lattakia in Syria, where he died of starvation in 1195.

Berengaria? She saw the Third Crusade recapture Acre but she probably never set foot in England, dying at Le Mans in 1229. Richard? He returned overland to England, was captured in Austria, saw England briefly in 1194, and was killed in Aquitaine in 1199.

Hire purchase. Cyprus didn't stay in English hands for long. A monk on the island stirred up a revolt and as Richard had no soldiers to spare from his siege of Acre, he sold the problem isle to the Knights Templar for 40,000 gold besants cash and 60,000 to be paid in instalments from taxes.

The Knights couldn't hold the island either. After a further revolt on 6 April 1192 they sold Cyprus on the same terms to Guy de Lusignan, who had not gone back to Acre to reclaim the crown of the Kingdom of Jerusalem. The Knights? They moved on to Rhodes and eventually to Malta (see *Discover Malta*).

Lusignans. The Lusignan era, from 1192 to 1489, was the golden age for medieval Cyprus. Catholicism replaced Greek Orthodoxy and, although the feudal system oppressed the peasantry, it helped the merchants and the ruling classes who made fortunes from the increasing trade. Famagusta became one of the richest cities in the Near East, its splendid architecture including St Nicholas's Cathedral (now the Lala Mustafa Paşa Mosque) where the Lusignan monarchs were crowned as 'King of Jerusalem.' Other Lusignan buildings of renown include St Sophia's Cathedral in Nicosia (now the Selimye Mosque) and Bellapais Abbey near Girne.

Feudal system. The Lusignans realised they needed a strong defence force to keep the Cypriot peasantry under control. The answer was to offer castles and estates to Europe's middle-ranking aristocracy in return for feudal services, particularly the immediate call to arms when required. The turcopiles, non-aristocratic holders of smaller fiefs who would form the light cavalry when called, were mostly foreigners, but *not* Turks, who were yet to migrate down from the Aral Sea.

The Knights Hospitaller and the Knights Templar – the former having taken their name from the Hospital of St John the Baptist they had created in Jerusalem, and the latter from the Temple of Kuvat es Sahra where they had settled in that same city – pulled back to Cyprus in 1291 as the Mameluke sultanates recaptured Palestine, and they joined the upper levels of the Lusignans' feudal system despite having their own social order.

Knights of St John. The hospitaller knights of St John of Jerusalem, for example, whose modern descendants are the St John Ambulance Brigade and an aristocratic system still surviving in Malta, were governed by their Grand Commander who ranked equal to a prince, and back in 1148 the Pope had given them their own special cross, that eight-pointed symbol still worn by the St John Ambulance Brigade and now known as the Maltese Cross. The Knights of St John moved to Rhodes in 1310, with a short-lived enclave in Bodrum Castle, Turkey (see *Discover Turkey*), before pulling out to Malta in 1530.

Genoa or Venice? The Lusignans found distinct problems arising from the policy of bringing in foreigners; as an example of the difficulties of protocol, a Genoese held the reins of the king's horse on the right, while a Venetian held them on the left, but during the coronation of King Pierre II in 1372 in Famagusta a Venetian tried to take the *left*-hand reins. The resulting riot turned into a minor battle, with the Genoans seizing Famagusta and holding it for exactly a century, when the charms of Queen Cathernie Cornaro regained the city for the Venetians.

Venetian. The Cornaro incident happened this way. James (Giacomo) II of Cyprus, son of King John (Giovanni) II and his mistress Marietta, had seized the throne from his sister Charlotte, who then took refuge in Kyrenia Castle. James already had mistresses and, by them, two sons and a daughter, but he wanted a queen, and in 1468 he was married by proxy to Catherine Cornaro, a 15-year-old Venetian beauty whose uncle was a courtesan in Cyprus. The marriage also included an undertaking for Venice, which ruled the Adriatic coast and down to Crete, to protect Cyprus from the Ottoman threat.

Catherine came in triumph to Cyprus in 1472, but within a year she was a widow. Anti-Venetian factors then tried removing her in favour of James's bastards, and Charlotte even came back from Kyrenia to try her luck, but Venetian influence kept Catherine on the throne. Finally, the Ottoman Sultan Bajazet II threatened Cyprus and Alfonso of Naples proposed marriage to Catherine, forcing Venice to act. In 1488 it demanded Catherine's abdication, though it had to appear voluntary; Catherine obliged by signing away her throne in St Nicholas's Cathedral on 26 February 1489, and Cyprus became part of the Venetian Republic.

The Venetians were poor overlords, looking at the island more as a military outpost against encroaching Islam than as a community in its own right. In that first year they tore down Famagusta's high and thin walls to replace them with the still-standing lower walls, averaging 60ft (18m) high and up to 100ft (30m) thick.

Othello's Tower. In 1492 they remodelled the citadel, which has long been known as Othello's Tower because of a single line in Shakespeare's play *Othello*.

Venetian walls. And in Nicosia they destroyed the old city walls, nine miles around, plus many temples, palaces and other buildings, to provide masonry for their one great monument, the new Venetian walls, three miles in circumference and forming a perfect circle, with eleven triangular bastions projecting into the moat. The walls, built between 1567 and 1570, were to protect Nicosia against the Ottomans — but the Ottomans came in 1570 and swept right over the defences.

Ottoman dominion. The Moslem invaders slaughtered the 20,000 inhabitants of Nicosia; the population didn't reach that figure again until just before World War Two. Famagusta held out for a year, but when the Turkish pasha saw how few people had defied him he had the Venetian leader, Marc Antonio Bragadin, skinned and quartered and all his followers slaughtered.

The Ottomans gave the Venetian population the choice of conversion to Islam or expulsion, and banished the Catholic Church, but Greek Orthodoxy, which had been on the verge of extinction since the end of the Byzantine era, was restored to favour at a tolerably low level — for example, Ayia Napa Monastery was handed over to a few Orthodox priests, but the large St Nicholas's Cathedral became the St Sophia Mosque of Famagusta, changing in 1954 to Lala Mustafa Paşa in honour of its Ottoman captor.

The Ottoman Empire expanded to reach Austria at one extreme and Egypt at the other, but a gradual contraction began in 1683 with the withdrawal from Vienna. By 1820 Greece was able to make its first attempt at gaining independence from the Turks; its failure had severe repercussions in Cyprus where Archbishop Kyprianos, three bishops and scores of other people were executed in reprisal. Most of Greece gained its freedom at the second try, in 1827.

British occupation of Cyprus. The Ottoman decline continued, though Turkey tried to regain its Russian territory in 1877. Defeated, Turkey was forced to accept the loss of more lands at the Congress of Berlin in 1878, including Rumania, Yugoslavia and Bulgaria — and Cyprus, which came under British administration though still remaining legally Turkish territory. And the *British* paid the *Turks* £92,800 a year!

Greece attacked crumbling Turkey in 1897, but lost; the 'sick man of Europe' wasn't quite on his deathbed.

British annexation. Turkey sided with Germany at the start of World War I, so prompting Britain to annexe Cyprus on 5 November 1914; from that day on the island was no longer part of the Ottoman Empire. At the war's end, a defeated Turkey saw Greece and Italy share the Aegean islands then, on 15 May 1919, Greece attacked once again, landing at İzmir and sending its troops deep into Anatolia, aimed for Ankara: this was vengeance for the years of suppression under the Turks.

The Turkish War of Independence began in 1920 at the gates of Ankara, with Mustafa Kemal, soon to call himself **Kemal Atatürk,** 'father of the Turk,' fighting for the homeland and **İsmet İnönü** driving the Greeks back to the coastline. But Turkey had to accept the loss of all its offshore islands and, at the Treaty of Lausanne in 1923, it renounced all claim to Cyprus.

British Crown colony. On 16 August 1925 the island became a British Crown colony and therefore a member of the British Empire. Its head of state was George V, represented in Nicosia by a governor. For the first time, Turks and Greeks were British citizens — and with their ethnic motherlands at relative peace with each other for the first time in history, Turkish Cypriots and Greek Cypriots could try to find common ground on their island home. But it was not to be: the campaign for *enosis,* union with Greece, which in Greek eyes was integral with the demand for independence from Britain, made the events of 1974 inevitable.

The mighty columns of once-mighty Salamis.

11: POLITICAL BACKGROUND

EOKA, Enosis, UNFICYP and the Green Line

THE TURKISH ARMY LANDED on the small beach at Ayios Yeroyios (now Karaoğlanoğlu, from the general of that name who died in the operation) west of Kyrenia at 0400 on 20 July 1974. To the Greek Cypriots it was an invasion; to the Turkish Cypriots, the long-awaited liberation.

Within two days the Turks had seized Kyrenia, a dozen villages, and had taken the north-west suburbs of Nicosia. The attack was a severe shock but in view of Greek and Turkish relations over the previous years, it was not unexpected.

Second Plebiscite. Back in 1950, when Cypriots were demanding independence in return for having helped Britain during World War Two, they held a plebiscite − a petition − on the emotive subject of enosis, union with Greece. According to sources in southern Cyprus, around 96% of the population signed, including a few Turkish Cypriots, but sources in North Cyprus deny that any Turk would ever vote for Greek citizenship.

One copy of the plebiscite was sent to the Cypriot Parliament, another to the British Government in London, but when the Westminster Parliament refused to accept the plebiscite it was handed to the Greek Cypriot community in London, which still has it. The third copy went to the United Nations Secretary General who accepted it but did not act upon it. The organisers kept the master copy which is now on display in the National Struggle Museum in Nicosia along with the First Plebiscite of 25 March 1921.

EOKA. On 7 March 1953, General Yeoryiou Grivas, born in Trikomo (now İskele in North Cyprus) and a prominent World War Two general in the Greek Army, with Archbishop Michael Makarios III, and ten other Cypriots, signed an oath in Athens to fight for the freedom of Cyprus, and on 1 April the National Organisation of Cypriot Combatants, Ethnikis Organoseos Kyprion Agoniston, better known as EOKA, began its guerilla war against British rule, with Grivas and Makarios as its joint leaders, one skilled in military tactics, the other prepared for diplomacy. Both had the overwhelming support of the Greek Cypriot community, but there was growing concern among the Turkish Cypriots about what enosis may hold for them.

Execution. The Greek Cypriots already knew what the EOKA campaign was costing them. Of nine men who were hanged on one day in 1956 in the Central Prison, Nicosia, for crimes of terrorism, one was a student of 17 who was convicted of being in possession of a gun; Cypriots claim he had picked up the gun in the street and it was incapable of firing. More men were due to die but Governor Sir Robert Armitage was suddenly recalled and his successor, Sir John Harding, stopped the executions.

Seychelles. Meanwhile, on 6 March 1956 Makarios, Bishop Kyprianos of Kyrenia and two others had been seized and exiled to the Seychelles, and Governor Harding later offered £10,000 reward for Grivas. The general, who was usually hiding out in Kykko and other monasteries, replied with leaflets stating that *he* didn't offer *any* reward for Harding.

The British repealed Makarios's exile on 17 April 1957 and brought him to London where he defiantly argued Cyprus's case in the protracted negotiations for independence, as he no longer wanted union with Greece. The archbishop worked with British, Greek and Turkish representatives in forming the Zürich and London agreements, published on 23 February 1959, which laid the basis for the new constitution and contained several vital treaties. EOKA ceased its campaign of terrorism on 13 February, though its last victims had been three British soldiers injured by a land mine the previous December.

Sovereign bases. The size of the sovereign bases was a major problem as Makarios refused to concede more than 36 square miles (93sq km) to Britain's demand for 120sq miles (310sq km). With agreement on this vital point yet to be reached, Makarios returned to Cyprus on 1 March 1959 still working for independence. Grivas, a naturalised Greek who continued to demand union with Greece, left Cyprus 14 days later to a hero's welcome in Athens. The rift between him and his former comrade was now beyond repair.

EOKA death toll. The EOKA camaign had done its job, though 218 Greek Cypriots (and 142 Britons) were among the 391 killed during the four-year struggle with the British — and 60 other Greek Cypriots had died in disputes with Turkish Cypriots, whose own death toll was 55.

Elections. The first presidential election was held on 13 December 1959, with Makarios polling 144,501 votes to Glavkos Klerides's 71,753. Only the Greeks could vote, as Dr Fadil Küçük had been unopposed as candidate for the Turkish-held vice-presidency.

Turkish praise. After the election Küçük said that Turkish Cypriots "had full confidence in the future of the Republic of Cyprus as long as Makarios is in office and there is no outside influence."

Independence. The Republic of Cyprus became independent on 16 August 1960, delayed from the original target of 19 February because of disagreements over the size of the British bases; the final compromise was 99 square miles (256sq km). The republic was quickly elected a member of the United Nations, and was voted into the Commonwealth on 14 March 1961.

First disagreements. Only a month later the Turkish and Greek Cypriots in the new parliament failed to agree on taxation. Before this was settled they were disagreeing over the composition of the Army, with the Turks wanting separate batallions and the Greeks insisting on total integration. The problem was sufficently serious for Makarios to suggest, in January 1962, that the constitition be revised. And then, in February, the Minister of the Interior, dedicating a building to the fallen EOKA fighters, said "Cyprus has always been Greek." Turkey, which had signed the Treaty of Guarantee with Britain and Greece, protested vigorously.

Major rioting. Early in December 1963 some Turkish Cypriots damaged a statue of EOKA leader Markos Drakos. On the twelfth, Greek vigilantes demanded that Turks show their identity cards in Nicosia. In another incident on 21 December, Turks fired on two Greek policemen in the capital, and the police, returning the fire, killed two Turks.

On that same day, Greek police fired at Turkish boys who jeered them, then a crowd of Turks pulled Greeks from their cars and beat them up; things were indeed deteriorating rapidly. The next day a Turkish couple were shot dead in the streets of Nicosia, leading to two days of bitter street fighting in the already-divided capital. Fighting broke out in Larnaca on 22 December, and at Skylloura (now Yılmazköy), north of Nicosia, 11 Turks were murdered at night.

Worst of all, a thousand Greek vigilantes besieged the 6,000 Turks in Lefka (Lefke), and Greek Cypriot police seized Kyrenia, holding 12 Turks as hostage and promising to kill all Turkish Cypriots in the town if Turkish Army troops, in barracks outside the capital, attacked.

Denktaş appears. In the Christmas troubles nearly 200 people were killed, and British troops were called from the sovereign bases to help. Rauf Denktaş, president of the Turkish Cypriot Communal Chamber, was exiled for four years because of his involvement.

Britain and Cyprus put the problem to the United Nations Security Council on 15 February and on 4 March the council passed a resolution to create the UN Peacekeeping Force in Cyprus, to be known as UNFICYP. But by then heavy fighting had already broken out in Paphos, forcing Turkey to threaten intervention to protect its own kinsmen. Turkey nullified its Treaty of Alliance with Cyprus, introduced conscription at home and put troops and landing craft on standby in Mersin. It was the first hint of major military action.

UNFICYP arrives. The UNFICYP troops, recognised by their blue berets, came for a trial three months to separate Greek and Turk, beginning on 27 March when enough British and Canadian troops had arrived; they were followed by Swedes, Irish, Finns, Austrians and Danes, and by civilian police from Australia, Austria, Sweden, New Zealand and Denmark. The three-month mandate was renewed, extended to six months, and renewed again as the blue berets kept

Greek and Turk apart in Kyrenia and Lefka, and patrolled the so-called Green Line which had been drawn across the centre of Nicosia in December 1963.

The Turks were excluded from political equality by the constitution, so the Cypriot Government created a separate legal and administrative department for Turkish Cypriots, which still exists today.

But skirmishes continued. Turkish Cypriots seized St Hilarion Castle, giving them control of the Kyrenia—Nicosia road and the centre of the Kyrenia Mountains. UNFICYP moved in, but from then on Greek Cypriots could travel that road only in a daily convoy guarded by UN trucks. Other disputes broke out in Paphos, where a third of the population was Turkish and where many of the outlying villages were totally Turkish; soon Paphos town had its own Green Line surrounding a bullet-scarred enclave.

Kokkina. President Makarios introduced conscription to strengthen Cyprus's only defence, the National Guard, and General Grivas came over from Greece to train it. There were rumours that up to 5,000 Greek troops were smuggled into the island and hidden in the Troodos, and soon there were counter-rumours that Turkish troops had been landing by night at Kokkina, the only Turkish Cypriot village on the north coast that had direct access from the sea; the Turks knew the village as Erenköy.

The Greeks blockaded Kokkina with National Guardsmen backed up by light artillery, and when the beleaguered villagers called for help, Turkish Cypriot students in İstanbul, Ankara and Britain

Aphrodite's Baths — but there's only this one pool.

demanded to be sent to Kokkina. The first arrived in March 1964 and soon there were 500, living in crampled conditions with the villagers. One of the students recalled that the Greeks allowed in just enough food for the villagers, so one loaf was shared by 65 people.

On 5 August, Grivas ordered a major offensive against Kokkina with – according to Turkish Cypriot claims – up to 20,000 men. Three days later jet fighters from Turkey attacked the Greeks, killing or injuring 300 and destroying several Turkish-Cypriot villages. These Turks were among the first refugees in the conflict, who fled to overcrowded Kokkina for relative safety.

The United Nations intervened, creating yet another Green Line, and talks at international level prevented the Kokkina skirmish from becoming a full-scale war. And the students left on 19 February, 1966.

Ayios Theodoros. Then came the Ayios Theodoros incident. This village, midway between Limassol and Larnaca, had 680 Turks and 520 Greeks at independence, and was now controlled by the Greek-Cypriot National Guard. The September summit talks had failed, Denktaş had been caught after landing on the Karpas Peninsula (he was quickly sent back to Turkey), Grivas's supporters were openly talking of enosis, and the Greeks of Ayios Theodoros decided to use an access road through the Turkish sector. Four convoys went along it before the Turks, who had earlier agreed to open the road at a specified time, blocked it with a tractor and plough. When the Greeks tried to clear the obstruction the Turks opened fire, and soon a small war was raging with machine guns and artillery deployed.

The Kophinou Affair. Greek armoured cars and infantry surrounded the next village, Kophinou, which had 700 Turks and just 18 Greeks. Bitter fighting broke out until the blue berets managed to intervene.

war with Greece; Turkey sent fighter planes over the Mesaoria lowlands and had warships within sight of Kyrenia – and on Cyprus the fear of invasion was so great that British residents moved to the sovereign bases, and package tourists landing at Nicosia were sent straight back home.

Greece recalled Grivas to Athens, the UN arranged a cease-fire for 16 November 1967, and the dead were counted: 25 Turkish civilians in Kophinou, where almost every house was damaged and the mosque's minaret was in danger of collapse. There were no dead Greeks.

Kophinou today. There was little incentive to rebuild Kophinou, and after the 1974 intervention all its Turkish inhabitants fled to the north. Today the old village still has many derelict houses and, though the mosque is repaired, it stands locked and neglected, with graffiti spray-painted on its walls. But the village has a smart new Orthodox church.

Stalemate. Cyprus entered a period of uneasy stability while larger powers debated a possible new constitution. The Greek Cypriots wanted a unitary state, but the Turkish Cypriots would settle for nothing less than a federation, possibly combined with partition.

Meanwhile, both Greece and Turkey sent military aid to the island.

Cypriots still recall this period of 'phoney war' with trepidation, remembering the mysterious traffic accidents on lonely stretches of road, and the fear on setting out for the daily journey to work, be it in the factory or the field. Many Cypriots on both sides already had stories to tell of friends and relations who had disappeared without trace over the past decade.

Grivas came back in 1971, revived EOKA and began campaigning again for enosis, this time working against his former comrade, President Makarios, who insisted that Cyprus remain independent. Greece, now ruled by a military junta — the so-called 'Generals' — supported enosis, but the country's internal troubles were mounting and few Cypriots wanted unity under those terms.

Grivas died in January 1974. Makarios began purging his administration of EOKA supporters, clearing them from the police, the National Guard, and the civil service, and accusing Greece of subversion.

Makarios deposed. This was too strong for former EOKA terrorist Nikos Sampson and several Greek and Greek-Cypriot officers in the Guard, who would accept union with Greece on any terms, and on 15 July 1974 they deposed Makarios.

Church bells ring. In many villages across the island the church bells rang out on 16 July to celebrate Makarios's death, and Greek tanks appeared on the streets to keep the peace. But Greek now fought Greek over the issue of union with Greece or continued independence.

Makarios, meanwhile, fled from Nicosia to his friends in Kykko Monastery and so down to Paphos, from where the British airlifted him to Akrotiri and flew him out to London.

Sampson as president. Sampson had now declared himself president, and Denktaş, the leader of the Turkish Cypriots, saw the imminent threat of Greek intervention with ultimate control of Cyprus. He called for Turkish help: nothing less than a full-scale military operation.

Turkey invades. On 20 July, Turkey responded, bringing ashore 40,000 men with heavy guns and tanks from 30 troopships and landing craft that had been waiting in Mersin and İskenderun. Paratroops dropped on St Hilarion Castle, on Turkish Cypriot strongholds in the Kyrenia Mountains, and in northern Nicosia.

Britain helps. On that first day, Turkish Cypriots in the south fled to the British sovereign bases for safety, while in Limassol all Turkish Cypriot males were rounded up in the stadium. On the following day British armoured cars escorted a convoy of 4,500 stranded tourists from Nicosia to Dhekelia and, during an agreed cease-fire, a fleet of small boats ferried British residents in Kyrenia to the Royal Navy's *Hermes* and so to the cruiser *Devonshire*, which took them to Dhekelia. In the next 11 days the RAF flew 11,000 refugees, service families and stranded tourists out of Akrotiri to Europe, in the biggest operation since the Berlin airlift.

In their ten-day operation the Turks had taken 15 miles of the north coast, 26 villages, and the town of Kyrenia. There was heavy fighting around Nicosia Airport and UNFICYP headquarters, and with the agreement of both sides the UN declared the airport a protected area and occupied it. They're still there today.

Sampson resigned as president on 23 July, allowing Glavkos Klerides, president of the House of Representatives, to become acting head of state. And on that same day the military regime in Greece collapsed, leaving the country without a government.

Talks. Despite that, Greece joined Turkey and Britain, the three guarantors of Cypriot independence, on 25 July in talks on the troubled country's future. Negotiations collapsed on 14 August and within hours Turkey's troops occupied more of Cyprus, pushing west beyond Morphou but stopping at Amadhies (now Süleimaniye), a village that had just 141 Turks, and reaching the far tip of the Karpass Peninsula in the east.

Greeks stay. The Turks bypassed Rizokarpasa, now called Dipkarpaz, and at later negotiations agreed to let the Greeks stay. They're still there, living on food and essentials brought in by a weekly UNFICYP convoy; their children are educated in the village by a Greek Cypriot to the age of 11, but if they want to continue their learning they must go to Cyprus – and never come back. Any future meeting with their family would be at the Ledra Palace, arranged by UNFICYP.

Kokkina to Yenierenköy. Meanwhile, a landing party consolidated the Turkish hold on Kokkina (the Turkish Erenköy), still occupied by a few Turkish Cypriot students. Kokkina never surrendered and was therefore excluded from the Population Movement Agreement signed in 1975; finally, on 8 August 1976 the Turkish Cypriot authorities rescued the villagers and students, 13 years to the day after the Turkish air force had attacked the area, and the survivors were resettled in the former Greek village of Yialousa in the Kırpaş Peninsula, now renamed Yenierenköy – 'new' Erenköy. The old Kokkina is still part of North Cyprus but is inhabited only by soldiers and is out of bounds to tourists.

Taşkent. All the Turks who took over the Greek village of Sykhari, near Buffavento Castle, and renamed it Taşkent, came from the same southern village. They still maintain that all their menfolk of military age were murdered en masse by the Greeks, and they keep photos of the missing generation in the former Greek church.

You'll not fail to recognise Taşkent; it's where the North Cyprus flag has been created on the hillside from white-painted rocks, visible from south Nicosia.

Cease-fire. A cease-fire had been agreed for 1800 hours on 16 August – it has not been broken to this day – but as there were still appeals for help from beleaguered Turkish Cypriots the Turkish troops pushed forward in the final hours, seizing a few villages south of Morphou (now called Güzelyurt), thrusting down to the village of Louroujina which had 1,500 Turks — it's now called Akıncılar — and trying to consolidate their hold on Famagusta.

Famagusta. Famagusta had 6,120 Turks and 24,500 Greeks (plus 4,000 others) at independence; the Turks had sole occupation of the old walled city and were in strong numbers in the north-west suburbs. During the troubles of the past 11 years they had dug tunnels under the medieval walls and, from the news of the landing on 20 July, had been bringing in their fellow Turks by night. The tunnels are still there, but not open to visitors.

A leader of the Turkish resistance in Famagusta told me that the Turkish community found themselves in control of Famagusta docks, the biggest on the island, and therefore of the vast amount of food and other merchandise in store — but they were surrounded by Greeks. But on 15 August the Turkish Army appeared and the Greeks fled from the city, abandoning their weapons.

The next day the Turks pushed on south, reaching the northern boundary of the British Sovereign Base of Dhekelia and trying to take the Maraş district, the smart new town to the south of the old walled city. The Greeks had not defended it, but the deadline expired before the newcomers could take occupation, and the line of earth-filled oil drums and rusting barbed wire today marks the Turks' positions at cease-fire — leaving south Famagusta and its once-smart tourist hotels as a ghost town, patrolled only by UNFICYP troops. And somewhere

From such humble beginnings: Archbishop-President Makarios was born here.

in Nicosia's buffer zone is a motor showroom, with 50 cars new in 1974 and now covered in dust.

Green Line. The Turkish cease-fire line is now the Green Line, sometimes called the Atilla Line, the southern boundary of the Turkish Republic of Northern Cyprus. The area between this and the Greek Cypriot line is the Buffer Zone, 3% of the island that's accessible only from the south — with the exception of the Maraş district of Gazimağusa, accessible to nobody.

Buffer Zone. The United Nations, and UNCIVPOL, the UN's civilian police helpers, patrol the Buffer Zone, determined that life there must go on — except in the urban areas of Nicosia and Famagusta, where hundreds of buildings stand empty and neglected. The villagers tend their fields right up to the Green Line, but not one step beyond it, and while there is no visible barrier marking the Greek Cypriots' front line of 1974 — the southern border of the Buffer Zone — tourists are not encouraged to cross it. Any person found in the zone without a good reason is asked to leave, and photography is totally banned.

UNFICYP today. The soldiers in blue berets are not only peace-keepers; their role includes maintaining power lines and water pipes that cross the zone, evacuating anybody in need of medical care, and helping the few remaining Greeks and Maronites in the north.

Over the years Ireland and Finland have reduced their troops, Sweden's army has pulled out altogether, and only Australian and Swedish police remain. The UN is still here on a six-month renewable mandate, and its soldiers are on six-month tours of duty with all but the British being volunteers. There is no military connection with the sovereign bases although Britain's UNFICYP troops draw their rations from Episkopi — and it's not a posting where wives and families go along; the occupants of the Ledra Palace Hotel are families of UN civilian staff.

Makarios returns. Makarios came back to Cyprus in December 1974 as president of a country that had lost 37% of its area. The following February the north declared itself to be the Turkish Federal State of Cyprus, with Denktaş as president. Makarios died on 3 August 1977, to be succeeded by Spyros Kyprianou, who continued to urge for reunion with the north.

Both parties maintained their contacts in the negotiations but their terms for reunion seemed to move ever slowly further apart. In August 1981 the north offered to return 4% of the land and resettle 40,000 refugees, in return for equal status for both communities, equal representation in government, strong links with Turkey, and a presidency that alternated between Greek and Turk. Cyprus agreed only to the last condition, arguing that equal status was wrong when the population was still split 80:20.

The UN General Assembly voted in May 1983 for the Turkish Army to pull out, but Denktaş could not agree. He vowed he'd seek international recognition, and he introduced the Turkish lira as the north's currency.

Turkish Republic of North Cyprus. On 15 November 1983 Denktaş declared himself the president of the new Turkish Republic of Northern Cyprus, which failed to win recognition from any country except Turkey. And so talks continued. In May 1984 North Cyprus offered to take 40,000 Greeks back into Famagusta under UN control, but Cyprus said no. Public opinion changed so that in January 1985 Kyprianou was being criticised for not responding to the north's concessions, but it was too late.

Then the UN suggested a bizonal federal state on an 80:20 basis, with a Greek president and a Turkish vice-president, a 50:50 Upper House and a 70:30 Lower House, with the USA offering to finance its setting up. This time the Greeks agreed but the Turks didn't; above all, they wanted Turkish troops to stay as peace-keepers.

After elections on both sides of the Green Line the UN repeated its suggestion, and now the north was in favour — but the south wasn't.

Sweden pulled out of UNFICYP in January 1988, feeling that the stalemate could continue indefinitely, a sentiment voiced by many Cypriots; the Greeks who feel that the longer their country is partitioned the less chance there is of reconciliation, and the Turks who feel that partition is the only acceptable answer. Some people want the blue beret soldiers to be withdrawn so Cypriots can find their own solution — but would that again involve violence?

Kyprianou lost his Presidency to Yeoryious Vassiliou in the elections of February 1988, and on 6 May 1990 North Cyprus re-elected a government firmly committed to the principles of guaranteeing Turkish Cypriot independence and freedom, and pledged to campaign for international recognition of the Turkish Republic of Northern Cyprus. It seems that a solution to the Cypriot problem may still be years away.

The Amathus Beach hotel is the smartest place on the Limassol tourist strip.

DISCOVER CYPRUS

THE BRITISH DIVIDED CYPRUS into the administrative districts of Famagusta, Larnaca, Limassol, Nicosia and Paphos. The independent Republic of Cyprus saw no reason to chance the system, and the government of the Turkish Republic of Northern Cyprus has retained those boundaries that run through it s administration.

This book, therefore, follows the same boundaries, with the districts listed alphabetically in English. I have made just three amendments: the Troodos Mountains defy the logic of the district boundaries so they form a separate chapter; the British Sovereign Bases, which straddle the boundaries (Dhekelia base is in both Larnaca and Famagusta districts), have a chapter to themselves; and the tiny part of Larnaca district that is in North Cyprus has been included with north Nicosia.

As the visitor to the Turkish Republic of North Cyprus will find *all road signs and place names* using the Turkish version instead of the Greek, I have done the same, keeping the Latinised version of the Greek names only for cross-reference.

ADMINISTRATIVE DIVISIONS

Kyrenia

Famagusta

Nicosia

Paphos

Larnaca

Limassol

Abbreviations and symbols. These symbols are used on the maps and in the hotel listings in the following chapters and are based on information supplied by the tourist offices or hotels:

❶ CTO or TRNC information office.

♿ The hotel concerned caters for disabled guests; visitors in wheelchairs can see some or all of the tourist attraction.

⚑ Camping information; location of camping site on map.

🚌 Bus (and dolmuş in North Cyprus) station; a letter following refers to information in Chap 6.

✗ The hotel concerned offers full board; location of restaurant on map. Not given for hotel apartments.

≈ The hotel has a pool; location of beach on map.

☎ Phones are in hotel rooms; location of telephone office on maps.

T The hotel is in town.

❀ The hotel is by the beach.

🛏 Number of beds in hotel (Cyprus).

r Number of rooms in hotel (North Cyprus).

t s The hotel is shown on the town (t) or tourist strip (s) map.

Pano Lefkara's church door featuring in an advertising promotion.

THE REPUBLIC OF CYPRUS

12: FAMAGUSTA

The South-east Corner

FAMAGUSTA DISTRICT COVERS 762 square miles (1,973sq km), the second largest district on the island, but as most of it is in Northern Cyprus, including Famagusta city itself, Republican Cyprus has just the tourist hotspots of Ayia Napa and its neighbouring villages around the rugged cliffs of Cape Greco. To the east and south is the sea; to the west the British base of Dhekelia; and to the north, just 6 miles (10km) from the centre of Ayia Napa, is the barbed wire fence that marks the beginning of no-man's-land.

AROUND THE DISTRICT

AYIA NAPA

Ayia Napa is the obvious destination for package-holiday tourists looking for a good beach backed up with gift shops and restaurants, and not far from the hotel. Add a picturesque fishing harbour, some interesting countryside, and you have the setting for the average family holiday.

The village is a picture-postcard place, but it is not typical of Cyprus: it exists solely for the foreign tourist trade and even the ambiance of the harbour and the monastery has been influenced.

Beaches. The beaches are good. Ignoring Lady's Mile Beach south of Limassol which has no services, the sands of Ayia Napa are the best in the Republic of Cyprus, reaching from the Sovereign Base boundary almost to Cape Greco, but with many interruptions for small headlands and cliffs. The sand is fine, though the grains are too smooth for perfect sandcastles. On the east coast the main beach is at Fig Tree Bay, supplemented with many small patches of sand in the tiny coves.

Ayia Napa Monastery. ♿ The monastery in the centre of Ayia Napa village dates from the 16th cent, with tasteful restoration in the 1960s immediately before the derelict building was reoccupied. The courtyard garden is open all day, with a prominent notice on the door asking visitors to wear suitable dress; sadly, too many people come in

HOTELS

The figures in **bold type** refer to the hotel's location on the Ayia Napa area map; the grid reference is in brackets.

Five-star:

1 Grecian Bay, 470🛏, ☎ ⌣ ✕ & ✿ (G7);

Four-star:

   Adam's Beach, 312🛏, ☎ ⌣ ✕ B;

3 Asterias Beach, 336🛏, ☎ ⌣ ✕ ✿ (B6);

4 Capo Bay, 280🛏, ☎ ⌣ ✕ & ✿ (M5);

5 Dome, 410🛏, ☎ ⌣ ✕ & ✿ (B6);

6 Florida, 256🛏, ☎ ⌣ ✕ & (G7);

7 Golden Coast, ☎ ✕ & ✿ (L2);

8 Grecian Sands, 264🛏, ☎ ⌣ ✕ & ✿ (G7);

9 Nissi Beach, 540🛏, ☎ ⌣ ✕ ✿ (C6);

10 Pavlo Napa, 196🛏, ☎ ⌣ ✕ & (D6);

11 Sunrise Beach, 408🛏, ☎ ⌣ ✕ & ✿ (L5);

   Tsokkos Protaras, 246🛏, ☎ ⌣ ✕;

13 Vrissiana Beach, 276🛏, ☎ ⌣ ✕ & ✿ (L5);

Three-star:

14 Anesis, 130🛏, ☎ ⌣ ✕ (F7);

15 Anonymous Beach, 112🛏, ☎ ⌣ ✕ & (D6);

16 Bella Napa Bay, ☎ ⌣ ✕ (G7);

17 Christofinia, 131🛏, ☎ ⌣ ✕ (C5);

18 Crysland Cove, 218🛏, ☎ ⌣ ✕ (E6);

19 Kapetanios Bay, 175🛏, ☎ ⌣ ✕ (L4);

16 Marina, 192🛏, ☎ ⌣ ✕ (G7);

16 Napa Mermaid, 247🛏, ☎ ⌣ ✕ & (L6);

20 Nappa Tsokkos, 76🛏, ☎ ⌣ (F7);

   Napia Star, 412🛏, ☎ ⌣ ✕;

22 Nissi Park, 152🛏, ☎ ⌣ (C5);

23 Sunwing Beach, 380🛏, ☎ ⌣ ✕ & ✿ (G7);

24 Vassos Nissi Plage, 171🛏, ☎ ⌣ ✕ & ✿ (L4);

Two-star:

25 Chrysland, 87🛏, ☎ ⌣ ✕ (D5);

26 Cornelia, 49🛏, ☎ ⌣ (F7);

27 Cristalla, 40🛏, ☎ ✕ (M5);

28 Pambo's Magic, 160🛏, ☎ (F6);

29 Pernera Beach Sunotel, 289🛏, ☎ ⌣ ✕ & ✿ (L3);

30 Voula, 28🛏, ☎ ✕ (B5);

One-star:

31 Napa Sol, ☎ ⌣ ✕ & (C5);

32 Leros, 45🛏, ☎ ⌣ (F7);

33 San Antonio, 34🛏, ☎ ⌣ (F1);

See map on pages 106 – 107

HOTEL APARTMENTS

34 Adams Beach, 52🛏, ☎ ⌣ & ✿ (C6);

35 Alexia, 28🛏, ⌣ (F7);

26 Androthea 64🛏, ☎ ⌣ (F7);

36 Anthea, 258🛏, ☎ ⌣ (F7);

with shorts and flimsy shirts and blouses. As in all monasteries there's no fee, but another notice suggests a 20c donation. Not surprisingly in the midst of so many tourist hotels, the monastery does not offer overnight accommodation.

Beginnings. The first known inhabitants of this corner of Cyprus lived in the area of the present village during the time of Alexander the Great and began building an aqueduct in the Greek cut-and-cover style. Later occupants added to the channel in the open-topped Roman style before the community faded into extinction probably around the 3rd cent. Ruins of their houses, and of the four-mile-long aqueduct they built, were lost in the scrubland and open forest of the area for more than a thousand years. But wait: a major revelation was to come.

Other early sites. A few other signs of early occupation have been found in recent years, such as the man-made cave north of the Romulus Apart-hotel, whose builders may also be responsible for the rock tombs on Makronisos Point. A six-foot (2m) standing stone by Ayia Mavri Church in the modern village has defied explanation for generations though it became involved in local marriage customs. And at Fig Tree Bay, Protaras Hill — the headland on which the Nausicaa Beach Hotel stands — has some evidence of pre-Christian dwellings, with a few tombs carved from the solid rock of the tiny headland to the south.

Icon of Virgin Mary. A seemingly unconnected argument broke out during the latter part of the Venetian rule of the island over the role of icons in the church, with one faction claiming they were 'graven images' and as such forbidden by the Bible. An unknown supporter of the opposite faction, living in some unknown village at some unknown time took his church's most precious icon, believed now to be that of the Virgin Mary, and hid it in a small cave in the juniper woods at the south-east tip of the island — and never came back for it.

Years later, a group of huntsmen in the woods had a dog suffering from skin disease. The dog's owner noticed that the animal disappeared several times, always coming back wet and with a progressive improvement to its coat. The man followed his dog and so discovered not only the cave where the icon had been hidden, but also discovered a steady flow of water at the end of that ancient Greco-Roman aqueduct.

And now legend takes over. Make your choice from either of these:

First Legend. As the Venetian hunters knew of a merchant in Famagusta whose daughter suffered from skin disease, they told him about the mysterious improvement to the dog's coat. The merchant took his daughter to the cave with its curative spring, and when he saw his child was also cured he built a church on the spot, incorporating the cave and its icon. He gave the church two altars, one dedicated to the Orthodox faith and the other to his own Catholic belief.

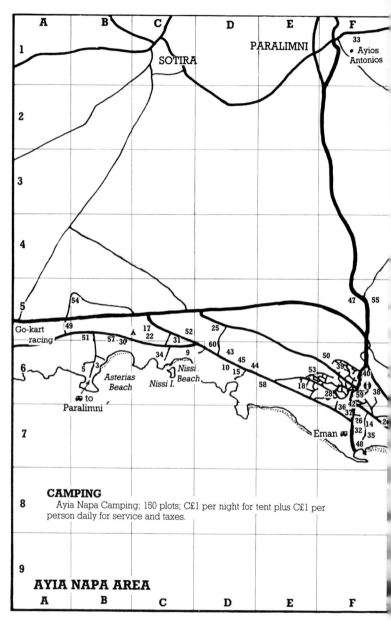

CAMPING

Ayia Napa Camping; 150 plots; C£1 per night for tent plus C£1 per person daily for service and taxes.

AYIA NAPA AREA

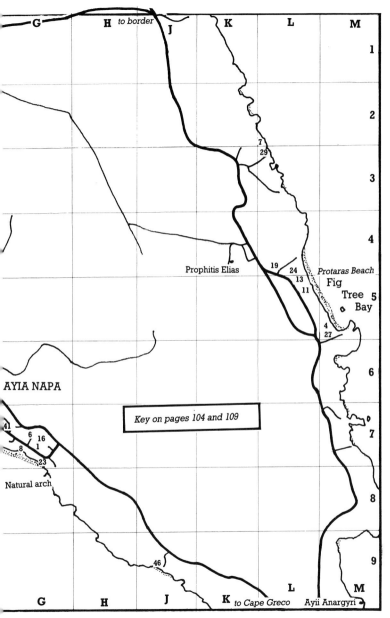

Then he built the monastery around the church, its four outer walls thick and windowless as a defence against possible pirate raids. And the spring was diverted to a more convenient spot, emerging under a domed roof, which still stands in the monastery courtyard. The finished building was dedicated to the Virgin Mary, but it was given the name of Ayia Napa — Holy Forest.

Second Legend. With the discovery of the healing spring and its miraculous icon, a young Venetian noble lady from Famagusta whose father had forbidden her to marry the commoner she loved, left home and established a church on the holy spot, later adding a few monastic cells until she had established a religious order for monks and nuns.

Ottoman invasion. Fact replaced fiction when the Ottoman Turks seized Famagusta in 1571. They massacred the Catholic Venetians but left a few Greek Orthodox priests in the monastery, which had already begun returning slowly to mother earth.

By the end of the 17th cent the monastery was derelict, but a small band of Greeks, having fled from the plague ravaging their native city of Salonika, landed near Cape Greco and put up a few shelters near the ruins of Ayia Napa, probably relying on the water supply they found in the courtyard. These were the first recorded non-religious buildings in the neighbourhood, the beginning of Ayia Napa village.

Dilapidated. Early in the 19th cent the Bishop of Tremithus and Archbishop Kyprianos ordered the monastery to be repaired, but when both men were executed in 1821 at the start of Greece's struggle for independence from Turkey, work instantly ceased and soon the monastery's hulk became a shelter for the homeless. Louis Palma di Cesnola, the United States's consul from Dec 1865 to July 1876, who plundered the ancient city of Idalium, wrote in 1877 that "there is a small village of about 50 houses inhabited by Greek peasants," adding that the convent "belonged to the Latin Church before the [Ottoman] conquest by Selim II, and was given to the Greeks by Mustafa Pasha, but is now in a dilapidated condition. . . ."

Restored. With the coming of British rule the old church became the parish church for the village of Ayia Napa, but the final restoration of the monastery had to wait until 1967, by which time the village was becoming a minor attraction for that late-20th-cent phenomenon, the package tourist.

The monastery now has a beautiful vegetable and flower garden, a simple museum whose main exhibits are an ancient mule-powered olive press and a baker's board with space for ten loaves. There's a small library and a conference room — but this is the only working monastery or convent in Cyprus where I have never seen any of its residents.

The new church of Ayia Napa, with roofs barrel-vaulted outside as well as in, has replaced the monastery's church for parochial needs, and the icon of the Virgin Mary is alleged to be a modern replacement. The giant tree outside the monastery door? It's a sycamore fig believed to be 600 years old, which makes it one of the

37 Antia-Maria, 28🛏, ☎ (F7);

38 Aphelandra, 100🛏, ☎ ⇌ (F6),

18 Castalia, 36🛏, ☎ ⇌ ♿ (F6);

39 Christabelle, 94🛏, ☎ ⇌ (F6);

20 Christatsos, 46🛏, ⇌ (F6);

40 Efi, 26🛏, (F6);

See map on pages 106–107

41 Eleana, 42🛏, ☎ ⇌ (G7);

42 Eligonia, 48🛏, ☎ (F6–7);

18 Euronapa, 140🛏, ☎ ⇌ (E6);

43 Florence, 20🛏, (D6);

28 Green Bungalows, 166🛏, ⇌ (F6);

44 Kallenos, 40🛏, ♿ (D6);

45 Kaos, 28🛏, ☎ (E6);

18 Karousos, 97🛏, ☎ ⇌ (E6);

45 Karystos, 58🛏, ⇌ ♿ (D6);

46 Kermia Beach, 242🛏, ☎ ⇌ ✿ (J9);

41 Kharas, 52🛏, ⇌ ♿ (G7);

47 Lambriana, 56🛏, ☎ ⇌ (F5);

48 Limanaki Beach, 85🛏, ⇌ ♿ (F7);

49 Makronissos Village, 248🛏, ⇌ (A5);

40 Magdalini, 40🛏, (F6);

39 Mastronapa, 30🛏, ☎ ⇌ (F6);

1 Melissi, 64🛏, ⇌ (G7);

37 Melpo, 30🛏, ⇌ (F7);

18 Mike's 40🛏, (E6);

50 Mirabella, 98🛏, ⇌ ♿ (F6);

40 Napa View, 48🛏, ☎ (F6);

51 Mon Repos, 42🛏, ☎ ⇌ (B5);

50 Napa Prince, 84🛏, ☎ ⇌ (F6);

14 New Famagusta, 40🛏, (F7);

18 Nick's, 40🛏, (E6);

52 Nissiana Hotel Bungalows, 69🛏, ☎ ⇌ (C5);

28 Paul Marie, 32🛏, (F6);

20 Pavlinia, 58🛏, ⇌ (F6);

53 Petrosana, 50🛏, ☎ (E6);

39 Philippiana, 62🛏, ☎ ⇌ (F6);

54 Romulus, 114🛏, ☎ ⇌ (B5);

53 Salmary, 48🛏, (E6);

55 Savvas, 22🛏, ☎ (F5);

56 Senator, 72🛏, ⇌ (F6);

57 Sun Fun, 80🛏, ⇌ (B5);

16 Sunside, 60🛏, ☎ ⇌ (G7);

58 Sunwing Sandy Bay Village, 616🛏, ☎ ⇌ ♿ (E6);

59 Takkas, 112🛏, ☎ ⇌ (F6);

39 Tasiasun, 58🛏, (F6);

16 Ttofinis, 90🛏, ☎ ⇌ ♿ (G7);

20 Tsokkos Holidays (One, 64🛏, Two, 110🛏), ☎ ⇌ (F6);

26 Vias, 88🛏, ⇌ (F7);

60 White Mountain, 28🛏, ♿ (D6).

oldest living things on the island.

Natural Arch. Ayia Napa also has the island's only natural arch, much photographed for promotion purposes but with no signpost to show that it is at the base of the cliff south of the Sunwing Beach Hotel near the eastern end of the tourist strip. Access from the clifftop is only for the nimble; it's safer to come by pedalo from the main beach.

Ayia Napa Festival. The Ayia Napa Festival is the village's major tourist event of the year, held in the last week of September since it was first staged in 1985, and so popular that you may need to book your hotel at the start of the season if you want to come at this particular time.

The festival covers every aspect of folk art, from painting and photographic exhibitions to theatre, light opera, traditional dances, and displays of national and regional costume.

The village makes every effort to entertain its visitors on the national public holidays, particularly on Green Monday, Easter Sunday and Monday, and Kataklysmos.

Mary and George. Ayia Napa has two other churches with interesting backgrounds. The Church of Ayia Mavri in the western part of the village, honours the saint who refused to stop preaching the word of Christ though her Roman persecutors tortured her and finally plunged her in boiling water. When the water had no effect the Roman governor poured it on his own arm with disastrous results; in his anger he crucified Ayia Mavri, but legend claims she and her

The natural arch at Ayia Napa.

husband lived on the cross for nine days.

The Church of Ayios Yeoryios by the harbour is dedicated to a Roman officer who refused an order to round up Christians for execution. When he admitted to being one himself, he was beheaded.

Pelican. You want to see a pelican? Several white pelicans have realised there's a better living to be made by hanging around the tourists than by going fishing. You'll see one or two on the beach, or maybe meet the overweight bird who patrols the open-air restaurants facing the harbour.

Cape Greco. Cape Greco, the south-eastern tip of the island, is accessible along a dirt road and offers good views of the immediate hinterland and, at night, the lights of Ayia Napa. Neither the lighthouse nor the Monte Carlo radio transmitter is open to the public, there are no beaches on the headland, and nothing remains of Aphrodite's Temple which stood near where the coast road takes a sharp bend to the north.

Ayii Anargyri. The isolated church of Ayii Anargyri standing on a small promontory north of the cape was built in 1952 to mark the memory of the brothers Damianos and Kosmos who travelled the island in Roman times, healing and preaching Christianity but not accepting any payment. When they refused to obey the order to stop preaching, the Roman district officer beheaded them.

Until the church was built, a mass was held on 1 July in a cave beneath the headland in honour of the 'saints who never took money,' the Ayii Anargyri.

FIG TREE BAY

A wide beach of fine sand, cleaned of weed each morning and free from shingle, an interesting island around 100m out, and a range of watersports all make Fig Tree Bay, also known as Protaras, a popular mini-resort. The area still has a welcome rustic appearance but the string of white hotels stretching up the coast could be anywhere from California to Kenya.

The island shelters the bay, making this a perfect spot for children, and the water is shallow enough for weak swimmers. Building is continuing along the main road, with independent restaurants and souvenir shops slotting between the hotels, but as this stretch of the coast caters exclusively for the package tourist market you will need to take the bus 4 miles (7km) into Paralimni village to see the real Cyprus.

Watersports. Tony's Watersports offers everything from canoe rental at C£1.50 an hour to parascending at C£10 for half an hour. There's also the tempting offer of a boat trip to see Famagusta's derelict hotels from just south of the border, for C£15 shared among five passengers.

Prophitis Elias. Just north of the Flora apart-hotel you'll see the small Church of the Prophet Elias standing on a little mound of rock and with a flight of steps up to the door. Elias had been a sailor all his life but, wanting to spend his final years away from nautical folk, he carried an oar as he walked inland from Fig Tree Bay where he'd come ashore. When people saw his oar merely as a piece of wood he stopped to build his church − but chose this hillock so he could still see his beloved ocean. The legend has one great fallacy: the church is less than a mile from the shore.

The northbound coast road passes through a cluster of small windvanes, drawing water for irrigating the fields, but the second turning on the right past the Windmills Hotel offers an optional route down to the Golden Coast Hotel and a splendid but tiny bay, almost landlocked and with two small beaches. A dirt road follows the cliff edge north but is asphalted before it passes the Mykonos hotels.

Both roads meet at an intersection east of Paralimni, from where you have a choice. East, a dirt road leads to the uninspiring Church of the Holy Trinity and a picturesque fishing harbour; north, you pass the Dickens Inn with its wide selection of British beers and quickly come to a dirt road that ends in the barbed wire of no-man's-land. And west takes to you Paralimni.

PARALIMNI

Paralimni, the largest village in this corner of the island, is genuine Cyprus and full of charm, but lacking in character. The new Church of Ayia Varvara, on the road from Fig Tree Bay, remembers a young woman who was beheaded by her father because she turned to Christianity; the village-centre Church of Ayia Anna is in honour of the Virgin Mary's mother; south-east lies a church dedicated to Ayios Thomas, 'Doubting Thomas;' and north is the Church of Ayios Demetrios who was strangled because of his faith.

OTHER VILLAGES

Dherinia is well-endowed with churches but as it stands on a slight rise its main interest is the view to the north, showing the ghost town of Famagusta; the barbed wire begins at the edge of the village. Liopetri continues an ancient basket-making tradition but also has an unusual church to offer: that of Ayos Andronikos which has an eight-sided dome.

Potamos-tis-Xylophagou, part surrounded by the Dhekelia base, stands on the 'river' − *potamos* in Greek − Xylophagou which sees water upstream only during winter, though the village is at the head of a narrow estuary which harbours a small fishing fleet. The French poet Jean Arthur Rimbaud worked as a quarry foreman here in 1879 and later helped build the British Governor's summer residence in the Troodos.

RESTAURANTS and NIGHT LIFE

Ayia Napa village has a good selection of independent restaurants, snack bars and tavernas, with a few British-style pubs selling British beer and several *Bierkellern* catering for the large German market.

St Hilarion, the craggy castle guarding the north coast.

Beşparmak or Pentadactylos, the Five-Fingered Peak in the Kyrenia Mountains.

Kyrenia Harbour and its majestic mountain background.

Sunshine over Polis, with a distant view of the Troodos.

The *Cape Greco News*, a free monthly newspaper published in English and German, keeps you up to date with the latest in eating-houses and nightlife, but as Ayia Napa is so compact you can amble around the village in an afternoon and make a note of the places that appeal to you.

Here's a small selection: Nautilus, a pub and spaghetti house; Oasen, an ice-cream and salad bar catering for Germans; Patio Mazery, a smart restaurant-bar; Taverna Napa, which sells food as well; and the Venetia, typical of the snack-bars as it's open all day.

Night-life is reasonably lively and varied, but targeted at the younger generation. Among a good selection of options are the Babylon Disco, the Cave Rock Club, and the Pzazz Disco, the latter claiming the only video wall in Cyprus.

SPORT

Virtually all water sports are available in Ayia Napa or Fig Tree Bay, with contacts either from notices on the beaches or in hotels. Speedboats and spear fishermen are strictly segregated from swimmers, and CTO staff are usually on duty; the major beaches have lifeguards but there is no risk from currents provided you keep clear of the headlands.

The Go-kart track to the west of the village is open daily; May-Sep 0800-2400, Oct, Mar, Apr, 1000-2100; C£1 for one minute or C£5 for 10 minutes.

Backgammon is a favourite game for Turks. Here it's played in İskele, birthplace of George Grivas who wanted Cyprus to become part of Greece.

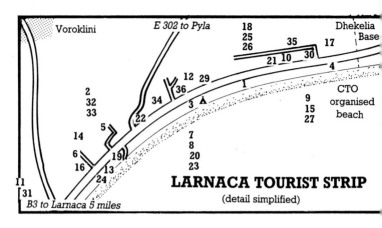

LARNACA TOURIST STRIP

(detail simplified)

KEY TO HOTELS & APART-HOTELS

1 Beau Rivage	19 Michael's Beach AH
2 Boronia AH	20 Palm Beach
3 Chrystoula Beach Gardens	21 Paschalis AH
4 Corinthia Beach AH	22 Patsalia AH
5 Daniandry AH	23 Philippou AH
6 Destalo AH	24 Princess
7 Eva	25 Protea AH
8 Frixos AH	26 Royal
9 Golden Bay	27 Sandy Beach
10 Golden Day Original AH	28 Socoriky Sea Gardens AH
11 Henipa	29 Stavros AH
12 Ioanna	30 Sussex AH
13 Karpasiana Beach Sunotel	31 Sveltos
14 Kasapis AH	32 Tanamara AH
15 Lordos Beach	33 Themis AH
16 Lucky	34 Tofias AH
17 Lysithea AH	35 Tsialis AH
18 Mariandy	36 Vergi

13: LARNACA

Here lies Lazarus

LARNACA IS A SMALL BUT BUSTLING town that has the island's busiest airport, a smart marina, a good chunk of the tourist trade — and strong associations with the birth of Christianity.

Old city, or oldest? Some authorities, perhaps relying more on the Bible than on archaeology, claim that modern Larnaca may stand on the site of one of the world's oldest cities, Kition: spell it how you please, including Chittim, Citium or the Latin Kitium. But if you opt for Kittim you can then quote Genesis X, 4-5: **And the sons of Javan; Elishah, and Tarshish, Kittim, and Dodanim. By these were the isles of the Gentiles divided in their lands . . .**

On this evidence you may argue that the great-grandsons of Noah divided the world among themselves, with Kittim taking Cyprus.

Kition. Archaeological evidence can take Kition back no further than the Mycenaean era, 14th to 12 cents BC, from a find made in 1959; before that Kition was presumed to be Phoenician, no older than 900BC.

Little of the ancient city can be excavated as modern Larnaca sits on top of it, leaving access only at the occasional open plot. The British administration in 1879 must also take the blame for demolishing much of Kition that was then exposed, in order to dump the rubble in the malarial marshland to the north.

The Swedes began excavations in 1930, finding statues of Hercules (Heracles to the Greeks), but the main area of modern digging is centred on a short section of Kition's northern wall, built of mud brick, and exposing the foundations of 13th cent BC temples, and some copper slag which must rate among the world's oldest surviving evidence of mankind's smelting of metals.

Archaeologists have noted that doors connect the copper foundries and the temples, suggesting that metalworking was rated as important as religion: the discovery of a bronze statue of a warrior god standing on a copper ingot traced to Enkomi, near Famagusta, and a bronze goddess similar to Astarte, strengthen this belief. The warrior god is now in the Cyprus Museum and the goddess in the Ashmolean, Oxford.

Elsewhere, there is evidence which suggests an earthquake severely damaged Kition around 1075BC, with rebuilding beginning in the 9th cent BC by Phoenicians: history records that Kition then remained a Punic city until 312BC when Ptolemy I of Egypt seized the island.

Access and hours. Kition is of major importance to archaeologists, but the average tourist will probably find it not worth a visit. The site described above, known as Area II, lies in the city's backstreets and is open during museum hours for 50c.

Lazarus. The Gospel according to St John XI, 1-44, tells the story of Jesus going to the grave of Lazarus, four days dead, and calling him back to the living. Longstanding tradition in Larnaca completes the story, claiming that the resurrected Lazarus came to Cyprus and preached Christianity in the town, St Barnabas of Salamis ordaining him as the first bishop of Kition. When he died a second time, permanently, he was buried in the floor of the church named from him, and tradition adds that in 890 his tomb was discovered and identified by the inscription *Lazarus, friend of Christ*. The tomb is still in the crypt of the present church and may be inspected.

Tradition continues with the account of the Byzantine Emperor Leo VI taking most of Lazarus's remains to Constantinople in 901, from where they were stolen, coming to light again in Marseille Cathedral.

Church of St Lazarus ♿. A few relics stayed in Larnaca, to be housed in the Church of St Lazarus, a triple-aisled building that was begun around 900 and which is now the city's most important medieval church, despite its numerous restorations, principally in the 17th cent, and its late 19th cent belfry. The 17th cent also saw the addition of the wooden screen by the altar, the *iconostasis,* one of the most impressive features inside any Greek Cypriot church, but here an acknowledged masterpiece.

The icon showing Lazarus emerging from his grave in Bethany (now El Eizariya, 2 miles east of Old Jerusalem) also dates from the 17th cent, and forms the focal point of the annual **Procession of St Lazarus** through the streets and back to the church, on the evening of the Saturday before Easter. The current Bishop of Kition leads this parade commemorating the first bishop, who is surprisingly not the city's patron saint.

A small section of St Lazarus's cemetery holds the graves of English travellers who died in the town between 1685 and 1849.

The Big Mosque. The church is 600ft (200m) from the Big Mosque, Cami Imamliği, whose tiny congregation is now drawn from Lebanese visitors and migrant workers from Egypt. A notice on the door details the seven times for daily prayer — five is the normal number throughout the Islamic world — with variations of up to two minutes a day, governed by the moon's phases; the first prayer is around 0600 with the last around 2100.

Before the Turkish intervention of 1974, Islam in Cyprus was probably less regimented than anywhere else. Now, the Big Mosque presents non-Moslems with one of their best opportunities to explore a mosque that is still functional: it's open daily, including Friday, 1500-2200, for 75c. This is one of only two consecrated mosques in Cyprus (the other is the Omerieh Mosque in Nicosia) in which the 'infidel' may climb the minaret — 52 steps with room for just one person, and you needn't take your shoes off — for a view over the city. Don't pay too much attention to the dry rot on the lower wooden stairs, or to the cracks in the minaret.

Larnaca Castle ♿. The minaret offers an excellent view down into the grounds of Larnaca Castle, built in 1625 and open standard museum hours for 50c.

During the early years of Ottoman rule, every visiting Christian man-of-war fired a salute as it dropped anchor. The captain then waited for a messenger to be sent to Nicosia to inform the paşa of his arrival, and if the paşa ordered Larnaca Castle to fire a salute in reply, the visting vessel was welcome. The ceremony obviously took up to a day.

The castle, which stands with one wall on the beach, holds a small archaeological museum with relics from Kition and the Hala Sultan Tekke.

Pierides Museum ♿. The main shopping street, Zinonos Kitieos, leads north for 1,800ft (600m) to the Pierides Museum, housed on the ground floor of an elegant white Florida-style timber building. The museum is privately owned and open Mon-Sat 0900-1300 for 50c; the first floor is the residence — not the office — of the Swedish consul-general. The exhibits are mainly archaeological, ranging from Neolithic to Byzantine, and represent the work of Dimitrios Pierides who saw the island's ancient treasures being looted in those pre-conservation days. He began his collection in 1839 and the museum opened in 1974 in the family home.

With captions in English and Greek, the 3,000 items on display include several unique specimens, ranging from a nude male figurine from the Chalcolithic period and a 5th cent BC model of a wine cart to the most surprising exhibit — a 5-in (13cm) jug, dated to between 750 and 600BC and decorated with what can best be described as a stylised modern astronaut in a space suit.

At the end of your tour you may meet and talk to Mr and Mrs Pierides in their private room lined with diplomas.

Archaeology Museum. In a city with a history going back at least 3,000 years, the Larnaca District Archaeology Museum caters not only for ancient Kition but for the entire administrative district, including the Bronze Age site at Khirokitia. The museum is open Mon-Fri 0730-1400, Sat — 1300; winter Mon-Sat 0730-1330, for 50c.

More tombs. Less than a mile away, the church of Ayia Phaneromeni is a conventional Byzantine building that stands on a large boulder whose centre has been carved away to create a catacomb or a secret chapel, or maybe both. Four paces square, the cave is believed to date from Phoenician times, and may possess magical qualities. Headache? Walk three times round the church and catacomb and leave a piece of your hair in the church's south window.

The church is usually locked, but the catacomb is open most of the day. There's a donation box.

To north of town centre: Elysso, Fairways, Filanta, Kallithea, Sunflower, Tsokkos No 7.

AROUND THE TOWN

The city's name may have been corrupted from the Greek *larnax,* a sarcophagus, but modern Larnaca is a vibrant and pleasant city that is still comfortably small. Surprisingly there is very little of architectural interest apart from church, fort and perhaps the mosque. The centre has a maze of narrow streets, some pedestrianised, making a good shopping district though with some parking problems.

Beach. The beach, running between the modern marina and the fishing harbour to the south, is the best to be found *within the town*

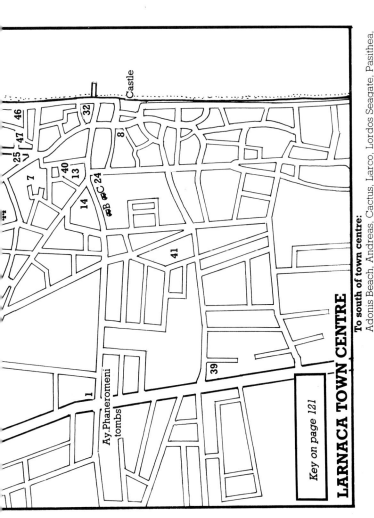

To south of town centre:
Adonis Beach, Andreas, Cactus, Larco, Lordos Seagate, Pasithea, Sandbeach Castle, Seagate, Sea 'n Lake View, Sveltos Beach.

Ay.Phaneromeni
tombs

Key on page 121

LARNACA TOWN CENTRE

itself anywhere in Cyprus, starting at around 350ft (100m) wide at the north, narrowing to 20ft by the castle, and widening again thereafter. The sandcastle zone is about 20ft (7m) wide with the upper beach becoming more hardpacked and eventually having a salty crust; the water is shallow for 80ft (25m) near the marina, narrowing to 20ft (6m) by the castle. Parking is difficult north of the castle, where you will find pleasant gardens and some open-air restaurants, but is easy to the south where ordinary houses and shops face out to sea.

The beach in the tourist strip fronting the old Larnaca-Dhekelia

Road is, on average, reasonable, but with local variations to good and to poor, though nowhere does it rival the sands of Ayia Napa.

Zeno ♿. Larnaca is proud of its most famous son, the philosopher Zeno, born in 326BC and founder of the stoic school of philosophy which divided the subject into logic, physics and ethics. He argued that pleasure is more evil than good, that a person must be either virtuous or vicious, and that suicide was an acceptable route to independence. Zeno's statue, erected in 1921 in the city's park, is not worth visiting.

Aqueduct ♿. Just beyond the city limits on the Limassol road stand the renovated arches of the Kamares Aqueduct – *kamares* is Greek for 'arches' – built in 1745 in the Roman style to bring water from some six miles (10km) away. The aqueduct was the personal gift of Alhajj Abu B'kir, the pasha of Cyprus, and it was in use until superceded by a pipeline in 1939.

Marina. The marina can berth 210 yachts either stern-on to the quay or moored fore-and-aft to jetties; they all have access to the full range of piped services, including television – and a permanent guard on the gate keeps undesirables away.

Salt. The squat peninsula on which the airport is built forms the eastern side of a long salt lake covering 2.4sq miles (6.2sq km) and with a shoreline of 14 miles (22km). Sea water infiltrates from the south and evaporates during the summer, leaving a crust of salt four inches (10cm) thick. Until the Second World War around 50,000 tons were raked up each summer and exported, but modern yields are far less, and the export trade finished long ago.

Hala Sultan Tekke. ♿ in part. The road across the salt lake gives an extremely good view of the Hala Sultan Tekke, literally the 'convent of the sultan's paternal aunt.' Umm Haram, allegedly Mahomet's foster mother, is supposed to have died here in 647 during an Arab raid on the island, and the Ottomans built this mosque on the spot. The mosque – it's not a convent – is at the far end of a small car park which it shares with a restaurant; it's open daily 0730-1930 and usual mosque rules apply: take your shoes off and don't try going up the minaret. You may inspect the mihrab (the focal point of Moslem prayers, representing Mecca), and you may use the torch by the donations box to look at Umm Haram's tomb.

The Hala Sultan Tekke is rather austere inside, as are almost all mosques, but it has a splendid setting in a grove of palm and pine trees.

AROUND THE DISTRICT:

AYIOS MINAS

South-west of Pano Lefkara, the 15th-cent Ayios Minas convent is noted for its honey and its icon-painting. The nuns close their convent to visitors 1200-1500 Sun-Fri and all day Sat.

Key to Larnaca map on
pages 118–119

KEY TO HOTELS

20 Arion
21 Four Lanterns
22 Maison Belge, La
23 Palmiers Sunotel, Les
24 Pavion
25 Rainbow Inn
26 Sun Hall
27 Tefkros
28 Zenon the Kitiefs

KEY TO HOTEL APARTMENTS

30 Acropolis
31 Andreas
32 Athene Beach
33 Avenue
34 Chryssopolis
35 Eleonora
36 Eviathe
37 Frangiorgio
38 Kition
39 Layiotis
40 Livadhiotis
41 Onisillos
42 Patsalos
43 Pelagos

MAIN KEY

🚌A Buses: Airport
🚌B Buses: Ayia Napa
🚌C Buses: Kiti
🚌D Buses: Nicosia, Limassol
🚌E Buses: Paralimni
T1 Service taxis: Nicosia & Limassol
T2 Service taxis: Nicosia only
1 Consulate: Denmark
2 Consulate: Netherlands
3 Consulate: Norway
4 Consulate: Sweden
5 Cyprus Airways
6 Cyprus Handicrafts
7 Market
8 Mosque
9 Museum: Archeological
10 Museum: Pierides
11 Police
12 Post Office (Main)
   (& poste restante)
13 Post Office (other)
14 St Lazarus's Church
15 Stadium
🅣 Telecommunications
16 Town Hall

KEY TO APARTMENTS

44 Alexia
45 Hermes
46 Kolonaki Sea
47 Yiota

CAPE KITI

The nearest beach to the south of Larnaca Airport runs north from Cape Kiti, where there is the best access: there are even three tourist hotels here.

The sand is gritty and the sandcastle zone almost non-existent, but there is a gentle ruggedness to the area. The stumpy lighthouse, not open to the public, provides a small landmark.

CHAPELLE ROYALE ♿

Midway between Larnaca and Nicosia, the little-known Chapelle Royale in Pyrga was built by the Lusignan King Janus in 1421, and restored in 1977. Its main appeal is the wall painting of Janus and his queen, Charlotte de Bourbon.

GOVERNOR'S BEACH

There are few beaches in Larnaca District west of Cape Kiti, and Governor's Beach is the only one signposted from the Highway. Most of the access road is unmade and potholed, and at journey's end you have the Andreas Cafe, a restaurant, and several camping spaces. The beach is small, with fine if dark sand, and a few pedalos and small boats for hire, but the Zyyi cement works spoils the view eastwards. The only other beach is at **Mazotos,** but it's tiny and has no comforts.

KHIROKITIA

Khirokitia, mentioned in Chap 10, must be on the itinerary of everybody interested in ancient history, and even the casual visitor may wonder why early man should have built his huts on a one-in-four slope. The site is within 500m of the Highway, with a parking site by the Maroni stream; it's open at normal museum hours, for 50c.

The site was discovered in 1934 and excavations are not yet complete, but Khirokitia raises more questions than it answers. Did these Neolithic settlers build a wall up the slope to defend themselves, or merely to mark their boundary? Why did they then build beyond the wall? Why did they bury their dead in their hut floors — for convenience, reverence, or fear of the spirit world?

It has now been decided that their huts, which are up to 18ft 3in (5.6m) in diameter, did not have domed roofs of stone similar to Byzantine architecture, but had flat roofs of branches covered by brushwood and topped off with earth. This method of roofing was widespread throughout Cyprus until earlier this century, and if you investigate some of the poorer homes among the many thousand that stand in ruins since the happenings of 1974, particularly in North Cyprus, you will see the same method used, with woven bamboo matting and thick layers of dried seaweed as variants of the simple brushwood.

A 35c booklet available at the Khirokitia ticket office gives a fuller story of the excavations.

KITI &

The Angeloktisi Church — the name means 'built by angels' — in Kiti is claimed to have the best church mosaic in Cyprus. Mosaics are rare after the early Byzantine period, and this life-size one in the 11th-cent Byzantine central apse showing the Virgin Mary holding the infant Jesus is believed to have survived from the earlier chapel of Ayii Anargyri, the 'Penniless Saints' Damianos and Cosmos, who healed the sick at no charge and who have a modern church by Cape Greco. Note the Old Greek inscription, **HAΓIA MARIA.**

KOPHINOU &.

Kophinou was one of the villages to be caught in intercommunal fighting before the Turkish intervention of 1974 and subsequent partition; it is described in Chap 11. The village's attraction for the passing tourist is the Skutari Craft Pottery, &, very close to the new church though the signs are difficult to find. You'll be able to throw your own pots here and buy the results, so allow enough time for firing in the kiln.

Kornos's potters turn out amphorae by the lorryload.

KORNOS ♿

Kornos's appeal lies in its pottery industry based in its backstreets. As you enter the village from the Highway, turn right, bear left, pass the post office on your right, and follow the occasional 'pottery' sign until you reach the notice Σ. Ε. ΑΓΓΕΙΟΠΑΣΤΩΝ marking the headquarters of the small co-operative which also employs craftsmen and women working from their cottages. The pots, ranging from hand-held vessels to large amphorae in a design almost unchanged for 3,000 years, are thrown (moulded) on a foot-operated potter's wheel whose design could also be 3,000 years old. Most of the terra cotta from this pottery is functional – a large amphora costs C£15 – but the small items destined for the tourist trade are available from C£1.50. The main problem may be the lack of anybody able to speak English.

PANO LEFKARA ♿

Pano, or 'Upper' Lefkara, is the island's best-publicised lacemaking village, though it is far from being the only place where lace is made in the traditional manner.

The E105 branch road from the Highway has been regraded and widened to highway standards to accommodate the tourist coaches that come to this former summer resort of the Venetian aristocracy, 2,000ft (650m) high on a spur of the Troodos massif. In your hire car, ignore the first entry to the town as this leads through narrow backstreets to the church; the second entry goes to the main street and the car park.

Pano Lefkara, pronounced *Lef*-kara, is a beautiful town with well-preserved medieval houses in many of the sidestreets, some with first-floor (US second-floor) rooms spanning the street itself. The Church of the Holy Cross, usually locked (ask any lacemaker where to find the key), has an 18th-cent iconostasis (a wall of icons), and the 13th-cent silver cross which gave the building its name. The splendid façade has a commanding view across miles of rolling hills.

Lace has been made in Lefkara for centuries, but in recent years the town has sold itself to the tourist market not only because of its unspoiled beauty but also because **Leonardo da Vinci** came here in 1481 and bought lace for the altar cloth of Milan Cathedral. Leonardo, born in the village of Vinci in 1452, entered the service of Ludovico Sforza, Duke of Milan, around the time of his visit to Cyprus, but he is best remembered for his paintings *The Last Supper* and the *Mona Lisa,* known as *La Gioconda* in Cyprus and southern Europe as it represents the wife of Francesco del Giocondo. Leonardo also invented paddlewheels, steam engines and the helicopter, but couldn't transfer his drawings into reality.

The villagers of Pano Lefkara claim he also designed lacework, with his patters still used to this day. As you watch the women sitting in the streets weaving their lace, you will appreciate the delicacy of the craft and the length of time involved in making, for example, a tablecloth. Prices reflect this intricacy and while you are in a seller's market in Lefkara, you can reduce the asking price a little by bargaining.

With lace dominating the economy it's easy to forget the detailed silverware made by some of the men: in the Poli family, as one example, working opposite the church, the wife Polyts weaves while the husband Yioryios produces silverware which he sells direct or through other traders. A few people in the town continue the tradition of making Turkish delight, known locally as *lokoumia.*

The House of Patsalos, currently being restored, holds the Lace and Silverware Museum.

Despite its obvious attraction to the passing tourist, the only **hotel** in town is the one-star bed-and-breakfast Lefkarama Village with 19 beds, nor do the banks offer the tourist afternoon service, but the main street has ample bars, restaurants and souvenir shops.

The church of the Archangel Michael in Kato Lefkara is noted for its late-12th-cent murals of a style found in several old churches on the island.

SKARINOU ♿ (but church has steps).

When you visit Skarinou village, lying a mile or so from the new road to Pano Lefkara, call on Charis (Harry) Papantoniou who sells Lefkara and other lace in a small shop at the end of the village. Charis feels that Skarinou deserves a share of the tourist market, and proudly shows visitors his walnut carvings of village characters, normally kept on display in his shop and not for sale. Charis is also guardian of the church key and, while Skarinou's church, built in 1951, is not exceptional, this is a good opportunity to have Greek Orthodox architecture explained in as much detail as you want. Charis has the key to the much smaller and insignificant 16th-cent church opposite; ♿ to both.

STAVROVOUNI MONASTERY

Stavrovouni ('Mountain of the Cross') Monastery, standing at 2,260ft (688m) on the pointed summit of a spur of the Troodos Mountains, is unique in several respects. The most isolated of the island's monasteries, its peak is visible from Buffavento Castle in the Kyrenia Mountains, and from the monastery itself the view takes in Limassol, Larnaca and Nicosia.

Stavrovouni is also Cyprus's oldest monastery, founded by Helena, mother of Constantine the Great, in 327. St Helena was sailing back to Constantinople from Jerusalem where, according to legend, she had discovered the Holy Cross, one of the nails that were used in Christ's crucifixion, and the cross of the penitent thief who was executed beside Christ.

While Helena was camped at night on the southern shore of Cyprus an angel told her that it was God's will that she build a church on the island and bless it with a fragment of the True Cross. She woke, struck

Harry Papantoniou and the beautiful church of Skarinou.

dumb, and was told that the Holy Cross had gone but there was now a fire burning on one of the island's mountains. Helena mimed for two servants to investigate and they returned with the news that the Cross had been transported up there and was the seat of the fire, yet was undamaged.

Realising that she had now been shown where to build the church she recruited what little labour was available and completed the project in three years, incorporating parts of both crosses and the holy nail near the altar.

Today, the monastery's church has a 4ft (1.2m) high ornately-tooled silver cross dominating the iconostasis, with a fragment of that True Cross said to be hidden inside the vertical bar.

Stavrovouni's isolated position has made it vulnerable to attack over the centuries, and it appears now more like a castle than a monastery, its outer walls dropping precipitously and with traces of a drawbridge visible at the main entrance. The early monks had a secret crypt where they hid from pirates and other raiders, taking the monastery treasures with them, but during the Ottoman rule they were caught unprepared and slaughtered to a man. The crypt is now a private chapel to St Constantine and his mother, St Helena.

The monastery's regime is the strictest in Cyprus, with the 18 or so young monks vowing lifelong celibacy: indeed, no woman is allowed in Stavrovouni for any reason, nor is photography permitted — my photo of the exterior was allowed as a special favour and later had to

The old city of Curium has some of Cyprus's most impressive ruins.

be cleared by the civil police (see Chap 3). Perhaps it's no surprise that in the 1980s only two elderly monks were here; their remains are now in the crypt where all Stavrovouni monks are taken three years after their death.

With the recent revival of interest in the holy order, Stavrovouni has laid a tarmac road from the Highway to its own doorstep, and in 1985 it brought in mains water, electricity and telephone, the water pumped from the tiny satellite monastery of **Ayia Varvara** at the base of the mountain. The monks grow as much of their food as possible, consistent with the climate, which brings frosts and occasional snow in winter, and the need for irrigation: the original rainwater cisterns are still available.

The monastery is open to male visitors from sunrise to sunset, but is closed daily 1200-1300 (1200–1500 in summer) and on Green Monday and the day after; neither does Stavrovouni provide overnight lodging. Be prepared for some confusion as the monks do not put their clocks forward for summertime (daylight saving time), so they actually close the door at 1100 Cyprus time in high summer.

Ayia Varvara — St Barbara — (&) at the base of the mountain and just beyond the army camp, specialises in painting icons for sale, with the aged Father Kallinikos the principal artist. Women are allowed in to watch him . . . and to buy.

ZYYI

The tiny village of Zyyi, Zygi or Zyghi, but pronounced 'zi-hi,' had 84 Turk, 86 Greek and one unclassified resident at the 1960 census, making it the most evenly divided community on the island. Here is the British East Mediterranean Relay Station which receives the BBC World Service via satellite and re-transmits it for normal radio reception. It's not open to visitors.

The road goes on to the Vassiliko cement works, which takes in raw limestone by the lorryload, converts it to cement, and ships it from its own jetties. It's a major contributor to the Cypriot economy but is also a major polluter of the atmosphere.

The beach has sloping shingle 20ft (6m) wide, with thick weed below sea level.

HOTELS:
address given if not shown on either map.
　　Five-star: Golden Bay, 388☎, ☎ ⇌ ✕ ✿;
Four-star: Lordos Beach, 350☎, ☎ ⇌ & ✕ ✿; Palm Beach, 376☎, ☎ ⇌ ✕ ✿; Princess Beach, 247☎, ☎ ⇌ & ✕ ✿; Sandy Beach, 410☎, ☎ ⇌ & ✕ ✿ T; Sun Hall, 224☎, ☎ & ✕ ✿;
Three-star: Beau Rivage, 258☎, ☎ ⇌ & ✕ ✿; Flamingo Beach, 122☎, ☎ ⇌ & ✕ ✿; Four Lanterns, 107☎, ☎ & ✕ ✿ T; Henipa, 165☎, ☎ ⇌ & ✕ ✿; Karpasiana Beach, 200☎, ☎ ⇌ ✕ ✿; Sveltos, 87☎, ☎ ⇌ ✕ ✿;
Two-star: Arion, 26 Galileo St, 59☎, ☎ ⇌ ✕ T; Aris, Pyla Rd, 25b;

Baronet, A'bish Makarios Ave, 89🛏, ☎ ⇌ ✕; Cactus, 106🛏, ☎ ⇌ ♿
✕ T; Eva, 75🛏, ☎ ⇌ ✕ ✿; Faros Village, Cape Kiti, 258🛏, ☎ ⇌ ♿
✕ ✿; Sandbeach Castle, 26🛏, ✕ ✿; Ioanna, 30🛏, ☎ ✕ ✿;
Karpasitis, Tourist Strip, 97🛏, ☎ ⇌ ✕; Larco, Hum Haram St, 104b,
97🛏, ☎ ⇌ T; Les Palmiers, 80🛏, ☎ ✕ ✿ T; Mariandy, 47🛏, ☎ ⇌ ✕;
Onisillos, Onisillos St, 76🛏, ☎ T; Rebioz, 98 A'bish Makarios Ave,
43🛏, ☎ T; Three Seas, Cape Kiti, 99🛏, ☎ ⇌ ✕ ✿; Vergi,49🛏, ☎ ⇌
✕;
One-star: Atalanti, Hum Haram St, 36🛏, ☎ T; La Maison Belge, 30🛏,
☎ T; Pavion, 20🛏, ☎ T; Tefkros, 21🛏, ☎ T; Zenon The Kitiefs, 17🛏,
☎ T.

HOTEL APARTMENTS:

Acropolis, 154🛏, ☎ ⇌ T; Adonis Beach, 80🛏, ☎ T,✿; Andreas,
Varnavas St, 68🛏, T; Antonis, Voroklini village, 56🛏, ☎ ⇌ ♿; Atrium
Zenon, Zenonos Pieride St, 154🛏, ☎ ⇌ ♿ T; Avenue, 62🛏, ☎ ♿ T;
Boronia, 38🛏, ☎ ⇌; Chryssopolis, 48🛏, ☎ T; Constantiana Beach,
40🛏, ☎ ♿ ✿; Daniandry, 22🛏, ☎; Destalo, 54🛏, ☎ ♿; Eftychia
Beach, 24🛏, ☎, ✿; Eleonora, 60🛏, ☎; Elysso, 34🛏, ☎ ⇌ T; Eviathe,
30🛏, ☎ T; Fairways, 44 A'bish Makarios Ave, 18🛏, ☎ ♿ T; Kallithea,
70🛏, ☎ T; Filanta, 72🛏, ☎ T; Frangiorgio, 54🛏, ☎ T; Frixos, 42🛏, ☎
⇌ ✿; Golden Day Original, 22🛏, ☎; Kasapis, 36🛏, ☎; Kition, 102🛏,
☎ T; Larnaca Alexia, 93 Const. Kalogera St, 16🛏, ☎ ♿ T; Laurana,
Athens Ave, 94🛏, ☎ T; Layiotis, 40🛏, ☎ T; Livadhiotis, 42🛏, ☎ ♿ T;
Lucky, 54🛏, ☎ ⇌; Lysithea, 64🛏, ☎; Michael's Beach, 70🛏, ☎ ✿;
Paschalis, 24🛏, ☎; Pasithea, 4 Michaelangelo St, 60🛏, ☎; Patsalia,
Larnaca-Dhekelia Rd, 32🛏, ☎ ⇌; Patsalos, 60🛏, ☎ ♿ T; Pelagos,
58🛏, ☎ ♿ T; Ph. Achilleos, Mitsi St, ☎ T; Protea, 42🛏, ☎; Seagate,
76🛏, ☎ ⇌ ♿ T; Sea 'n Lake View, 40🛏, ☎; Socoriky Sea Gardens,
Cape Kiti, 136🛏, ☎ ⇌ ✿; Stavros, Larnaca-Dhekelia Rd, 62🛏, ☎ ⇌;
Sunflower, 69 Makarios Ave, 74🛏, ☎ ⇌ T; Sun Hall, 78🛏, ☎ ♿ T;
Sussex, 20🛏, ☎; Sveltos Beach, Piale Pasha St, 76🛏, ☎, T,✿; Tofias,
22🛏, ☎ ♿; Tsialis, 46🛏, ☎ ⇌; Tsokkos, Polygyrou St, T.

GUEST HOUSE:

The Rainbow Inn, 140 Zenonos Kitios St, 15🛏.

CAMPING:

Forest Beach, Larnaca-Dhekelia Rd, 78 sites. Water available but no
shop. Water slide. Unattended out of May-Sep season when you camp
free; otherwise C£1 per night per tent plus C£1 per day per person.

Fig Tree Bay, one of the beauty spots of the south-east.

Hala Sultan Tekke, the mosque beside the salt lake.

The snows of Mt Olympus.

Lone travellers in the Troodos Mountains.

14: LIMASSOL

Ancient cities, Richard the Lionheart, and beer

LIMASSOL, WITH AROUND 120,000 PEOPLE, is the second-largest city and the largest coastal resort on the island. The Turkish intervention of 1974 deprived Cyprus of its major port, Famagusta, which meant the immediate expansion of the tiny ports at Limassol and Larnaca; Limassol's new harbour is squeezed in between the expanding city and the RAF base of Akrotiri, but it now handles the larger share of seaborne trade.

Limassol is a lively, bustling town, home to much of Cyprus's manufacturing and processing industries, including the wineries and breweries, and while it shares with south Nicosia the rank of best shopping-centre of the island, for me its size makes it a little less intimate and relaxing than Larnaca.

What's on offer? Among the luxury goods on sale in Limassol are jewellery, high fashion, leatherware and shoes, but at prices less than you will find in western Europe. The republic is an excellent place to buy spectacles at less than half the British price, but bring your optician's prescription if possible.

Limassol Castle. ♿ The oldest building in Limassol is its 13th-cent castle, successor to the Byzantine fortress in which Richard Coeur de Lion married Berengaria on 12 May 1191 and where she was proclaimed Queen of England. Recent excavations in the basement have revealed part of the original fortress's foundations, including a large hall which might have been the chapel of Ayios Yeoryios where the wedding was held.

Museums. The castle, open Mon-Sat 0730-1700 (-1800 in summer) for 50c, holds the small **Cyprus Medieval Museum,** including several cannons. Elsewhere in town, the **Archaeological Museum,** open Mon-Sat 0730-1700 (-1800 in summer), and 1000-1300 on Sun, admission 50c, takes you on a tour through the island's history from the Stone Age to the Roman era, as seen in Neolithic pot shards and tools, Bronze Age art, Greek ceramics and Roman coinage. The **Folk Art Museum,** (♿ after the initial step) in a 1924-vintage house in Ayiou Andreiou Street, is open in summer Mon-Sat 0830-1300, (plus 1600-1800, Mon, Wed, Fri); in winter afternoons it's open 1500-1700. Admission 30c. Its exhibits span the 19th and early 20th cents, concentrating on national costumes and embroidery, with a section devoted to farming equipment. The **Art Gallery,** (♿ with difficulty) on Oktovriou 28 St east of the Municipal Gardens, has a permanent display of paintings and sculpture by artists of many nationalities. Admission 30c, hours very complex.

Zoo. The municipal gardens, &, are smart and refreshingly green, but the zoo in the eastern corner has a poor display of aviary birds and a few small animals.

WINERIES.

Limassol's most interesting and most popular tourist attraction is undoubtedly a guided tour of any of its four wineries, all of which operate from factories on Fragklinou Rousvelt St, named from the United States president during World War Two.

Keo (✆362053) includes a tour of its lager bottling plant which produces Cyprus's most popular beer, but visitors are also welcome at the Loel plant next door (✆369344), and Etko (✆373391) and Sodap (✆364605) further down the road. All offer free tours year round, Mon-Fri, beginning 10am and lasting about an hour, with later tours depending on demand; if you're travelling independently you can chance arriving unannounced around 0950, or make a booking by phone the previous day. And all offer a free tasting session at the end of the tour, with the chance to buy your drinks at the factory shop.

The best time to come is obviously during the grape harvest from July to November, but there is always something to see.

Keo: a tour. Keo (&) is not only the biggest winery, it is also Limassol's biggest employer, with a permanent staff of 550 and an extra 100 during the grape season. The company's name is made from the initials of the Greek for 'Cypriot Spirits & Wine,' and its products include the well-known Commandaria which is claimed to have been made in the traditional manner for longer than any other wine in the world and dating back to the Crusades; Commandaria St John, Keo's premier wine which takes its name from the Knights of St John who occupied Kolossi Castle, has been made on the solera system since 1927, the year the company was founded, which means that every bottle contains a trace of that original vintage. Commandaria is used in church services throughout Greek Cyprus, and has been exported to the USA since 1947.

Keo also produces Cossack brand vodka, which it sells to Russia; Five Kings brandy; Monte Cristo and Mosaic wine, the latter sold in Britain by the VP wine company – and its neighbour Etko produces Emva Cream sherry-type wine, also well known in Britain. Keo has expanded into the production of so-called whisky, rum and ouzo which, like the vodka, are based on an a distillation of 95% pure alcohol, the 'eau de vie de vin.'

The firm's only brand of beer, a light lager of which 3,500,000 gallons are brewed each year, uses hops from England, Czechoslovakia and Germany, and yeast from Denmark, with only the water coming from Cyprus. And most of its wines are matured in barrels imported from Limoges. The grapes, of course, come from the island's south coast, particularly around Paphos, with up to 100 lorryloads a day − 43,000 tons a season − arriving in late summer.

As Keo produces far more than the island can consume, it exports to Germany, Scandinavia, Britain, Australia, the United States and Japan; and at Burton upon Trent in 1987 Keo won the gold medal for lager, beating 68 brewers around the world.

AROUND THE DISTRICT
AMATHUS

Amathus, one of the original city states of Cyprus, is now a ruin that is only partly excavated; a barbed wire fence surrounds the site and the best viewpoint is from the hillside north of the city. Nothing now remains of the breakwaters which sheltered the small harbour where Berengaria and Richard the Lionheart landed in 1191, but plans have been prepared for a possible reconstruction.

Ancient gods. During its days of power and glory, Amathus was unusual in allowing peoples of many races to settle freely in the city and practise their various religions quite openly; the ancient Greeks claimed that Theseus, who had already slaughtered the Bull of Marathon, left his pregnant wife Ariadne here after he killed the half-bull, half-man Minotaur, an offspring of King Minos of Crete. Poor Ariadne, the Minotaur's half-sister, had given Theseus a ball of thread to help him find the way out of the monster's labyrinth, and you might spot the slender connection between Ariadne and her thread and the Greek *arachne,* 'spider.' Ariadne died at Amathus in childbirth, but her memory lives on in the shrine of Ayia Varvara − the change of name is unexplained − a rock-cut temple east of Amathus to which pregnant women used to come to pray for a safe delivery.

Ancient kings. Aphrodite, who was born of the sea foam 28 miles (45km) west, also had a large cult following in the city, and Androcles, the mortal king of Amathus, sailed with Pasicratus, the last King of Curium, in a fleet to help Alexander the Great besiege Tyre.

Modern looters. Earthquakes helped destroy the city, which lay undisturbed until the early 19th cent when looters raided many of the tombs, and the base rocks were shipped to Egypt for use in the Suez Canal.

Stone jar. In the 6th cent Amathus had two jars or cauldrons, each hewn from a solid lump of stone and measuring around 7ft 4in (2.2m) across by 6ft (1.9m) high, and weighing 14 tons. Legend claims that the cauldrons stood at the entrance to a temple in the Acropolis, holding water for religious ceremonies. The remains of one jar are still on site, but the other was taken to the Louvre in Paris.

AYIOS YEORYIOS ALAMANOS &

The convent of St George Alamanos at the eastern end of the tourist strip is one of the lesser-known of Cyprus's religious houses, and has a more forbidding, prison-like atmosphere than the others. The 30 or

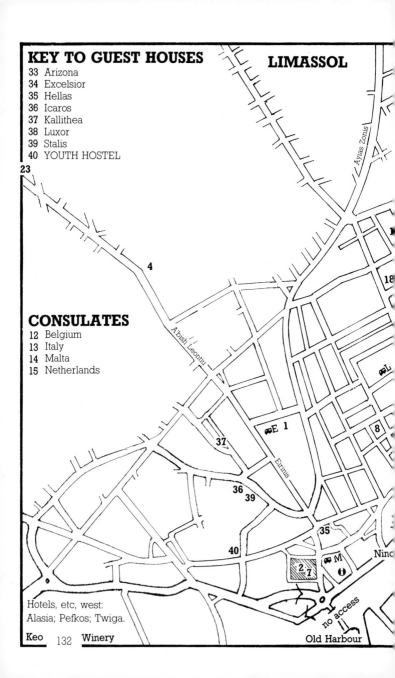

KEY TO GUEST HOUSES

33 Arizona
34 Excelsior
35 Hellas
36 Icaros
37 Kallithea
38 Luxor
39 Stalis
40 YOUTH HOSTEL

LIMASSOL

CONSULATES

12 Belgium
13 Italy
14 Malta
15 Netherlands

Hotels, etc, west:
Alasia; Pefkos; Twiga.

Keo   132   Winery

Old Harbour

no access

Nino

KEY

1　Bishopric
2　Castle
3　Handicrafts
4　Hospital
5　Museum: Archaeology
6　— Folk Art
7　— Medieval
8　Post Office
9　Zoo

KEY TO HOTELS

16　Acropol
17　Aquamarine
18　Astir
19　Astoria
20　Continental
21　Curium Palace
22　Eastland
23　Le Village
24　Limassol Palace
25　Metropole
26　Panorama
27　Rose
28　Vienna

KEY TO HOTEL APARTMENTS

30　Chrielka
31　Mistral
32　Pier Beach　133

so nuns and their one male priest keep bees and paint icons for a living, and welcome visitors around noon.

The convent is modern in comparison with others in Cyprus, although a building was probably on this site in the 12th cent; in 1949, 13 nuns established themselves here with help from the then Bishop Makarios, and though their numbers rose to 60 in the mid-1980s they have fallen again.

There is no entrance fee, but a donation is welcome unless you buy some of the nuns' wares.

CURIUM ♿ (partially)

The remains of the ancient city-state of Curium or Kourion are the most important and impressive of the ruins in the Republic of Cyprus, rivalling those of Salamis in North Cyprus. Herodotus claimed that Curium was founded by Greek immigrants from Argos in 1200BC, but archaeologists have found evidence of Achaean settlements 100 years or so earlier.

Access. The Curium site is open daily in summer 0730-1930, in winter 0730 to sunset, for 50c admission. The **Museum of Kourion** in Episkopi village is open in summer Mon-Sat 0730-1330; in winter Mon-Fri 0730-1400, Sat 0730-1300, for 50c. The museum holds the finds of an archaeologist from Pennsylvania University engaged in the 1930s dig. ♿: both sites are accessible to disabled visitors, but from a wheelchair much of Curium can be seen only at a distance.

The entrance to Curium is from the west of the site, on the main Paphos road; don't be misled by signs to 'Curium' on the east; they lead to the beach. A CTO restaurant on the clifftop is open 0900-2400, and is crowded when coach tours call.

Theatre. Curium's most impressive feature is the theatre, built by Greeks in the 2nd cent BC and enlarged by Romans between 50 and 175AD, to give a seating capacity of around 2,400. It is the setting for the Drama Festival held during the last week in September when Cypriots and British servicemen perform Shakespeare on a stage which would have delighted the bard.

The Baths. The 5th-cent baths were adorned by a mosaic featuring birds, which is among the most impressive of mosaics on an island liberally endowed with them. The building was originally the private house of citizen Eustolios, but the houses of fellow-citizens were similarly decorated, particularly the so-called House of the Gladiators, a 3rd-cent building near the nymphaeum, which is still being excavated.

New York Met. Digging began at Curium in 1865 under the control of the United States's consul, who soon found a large collection of jewellery and other works of art which he sent to the Metropolitan Museum in New York. Later finds have remained on the island, most going to the Cyprus Museum in south Nicosia and, as if to compensate for earlier misappropriation of artefacts, the Pennsylvania Museum carried out a major excavation beginning in 1933 and ending, after interruptions, in 1954.

Early Christian Basilica. The early Christian basilica, between the pay desk and the theatre, was built around 400 on the site of a former pagan temple, and served as the city's cathedral for some 240 years. The single stone column dominates the site of what was probably the largest church built on the island before the Gothic era, a church which, like Curium itself, was battered by earthquakes and ravaged by Arab pirates, forcing the abandonment of the city in the 7th cent: the Bishop of Curium moved his episcopal seat to the nearby village which has ever since been known as Episkopi.

Stadium. A little way west of the Curium site, the stadium has its own access from the main Paphos road. This is the only stadium discovered so far on the island and to the casual visitor it is unimpressive, being merely a flat stretch of open land 600ft (200m) long by 80ft (25m) wide, with the remains of stone seating along its perimeter. But stretch your imagination and picture an audience of 6,000 watching athletes compete in races in the 2nd cent AD. There is no fence around the stadium, so there are no entry fees or times.

KOLOSSI CASTLE

Kolossi Castle, the largest and most impressive fortress in Greek Cyprus, was built around 1454 by the Knights of St John of Jerusalem on the ruins of the original castle of 1210, traces of which can be seen in the east and north walls of the present structure. Almost certainly there was nothing on the site when Richard the Lionheart came to Kolossi village in 1191 in his pursuit of Isaac Comnenus.

That original castle had suffered badly at the hands of the Genoese in 1373 and 1402, and the Mamelukes from Egypt in 1425 and '26. A coat of arms on the east wall is attributed to Louis de Magnac, known to be Grand Commander in 1454 – hence the dating of the rebuilt castle.

Knights Hospitaller. Guy de Lusignan, who bought Cyprus from the Knights Templar in 1192, encouraged Knights Hospitaller and Knights Templar to join him in the occupation and defence of Cyprus as the forces of Islam gradually conquered the Holy Land. The Hospitallers were the older order, having been established by Pope Gregory at the end of the 6th cent; in 1128 they decided to give their senior officer the title of Grand Commander, which Pope Innocent IV ratified in 1252.

From 1210, when King Hugh I of Cyprus built Kolossi Castle and gave it to the Knights Hospitaller, also known as the Knights of the Order of St John of Jerusalem, an uneasy truce bonded both holy orders in the face of their common enemy. The Commander of the Hospitallers decided to occupy Kolossi Castle in 1302, but four years later the Templars took temporary possession after their Grand Master seized the throne of Cyprus from his brother King Henry II.

Downfall of the Templars. The Templars had made a strategic mistake. They were too belligerent in Cyprus, as well as in Europe, and lacked the strength to support their actions, so in 1308 Pope Clement and King Philip IV, 'the Fair,' of France declared them heretic. In Cyprus, Amaury, the Lord of Tyre, imprisoned the Templars at Yermasoyia, east of Limassol, and at Pano Lefkara; they went on trial in May 1310, and in 1313 the Pope decreed their order be disbanded and the remaining knights to be imprisoned for life, their sentences being spent in the dungeons at Kyrenia Castle.

Commandaria St John. But in 1310 Commander Foulques de Villaret had transferred the Order of St John to Rhodes, leaving in Cyprus a military presence, the Commandaria, based at Kolossi Castle. The Commandaria St John at Kolossi was by far the strongest of several such military outposts on the island and it increased its economic strength by continuing the cultivation, production and trade, already long-established, in cotton, cane sugar, wheat and wine – including the brand that is now produced exclusively by Keo.

Kolossi Castle today. The imposing fortress of Kolossi Castle is open daily 0730-1930 in summer, 0730 to sunset in winter, for 50c admission. Its walls are each 53ft (16m) long, forming a square tower with main access from an exposed 23-step stairway, rebuilt in 1933 replacing an earlier ramp, and so bringing you up to the level of the drawbridge.

The first floor has two gaunt rooms each 41ft (12.5m) long, with barrel-vaulted stone ceilings that support the floor above. Two enormous fireplaces stand back-to-back in the centre of the castle, the only other relief coming from a mural of the crucifixion, now protected by glass after the deprivations of modern vandals.

Another 34 steps lead to the second floor, whose matching rooms are 44ft (13.5m) long as the walls need not be so thick. Here was where the Grand Commander or his lieutenant lived, and the ornate fireplace carries the fleur de lys badge of Louis de Magnac, the castle's builder. Look in the north wall and you'll find the G.C's personal toilet inset in the masonry. In 1468 the Englishman John Langstrother succeeded de Magnac as Grand Master, but three years later he was taken prisoner at the Battle of Tewkesbury and beheaded on the orders of Edward IV.

A circular stair with 35 steps takes you to the flat roof, where the machicolis (battlements) protected the original defenders while giving them a perfect view across miles of countryside; three of the four battlements were restored in 1933.

The ground floor, accessible through an exterior door, was used for storage and holds one of the wells, with water now 25ft (7.5m) down.

Look on the outside of the east wall for the large inset cross; the central motif is the Lusignan coat of arms of which the top left quadrant shows the emblem of Jerusalem, a large cross with smaller crosses sheltering between its arms. You'll see this same emblem on the obverse of Cypriot coins of the time, now displayed in several museums. The shields beside the Lusignan motif are the coats of arms of Grand Masters Jean de Lastic (left) and Jaque de Milli.

Sugar. The Arabs introduced sugar cane to the fertile lands of Mesopotamia from its native China, and carried it across the Islamic world; it's still grown today in southern Spain and Tunisia, for example. But the Crusaders took it to Cyprus from plantations they found in 10th-cent Egypt. It quickly became one of the most important crops on the island, sharing the south-west coast with the vineyards, and the Commanderie of Kolossi used the original Arab process to extract sugar from the raw cane, exporting the finished white powder mainly to Venice but also to Beirut and Lattakia in Syria.

Cornaro interests. By the 15th cent the Cornaro family, which produced Queen Catherine, had at Episkopi the island's largest plantations, alongside those owned by the Order of St John. In 1468 the Cornaros and the Order were in dispute over irrigation rights, and in that year King Jacob II's diversion of the vital water to the Order resulted in the Cornaro's loss of thousands of canes. Four years later, Catherine Cornaro married King Jacob in Venice, and by 1488 her brother George was Grand Commander of the Order of St John and so controlled all the sugar plantations in the Kolossi area; a visitor in 1494 reported that the Kolossi and Episkopi plantations had more that 400 labourers.

Martini. Kolossi Castle also had a sugar mill and a refinery which produced sugar exclusively for the Venetian House of Martini, a family now known for its spirits. The 14th-cent mill, with a floor area almost as large as that of the nearby castle, had a nether-stone (the fixed millstone) 10ft 6in (3.2m) in diameter, which is still visible today amid the well-preserved remains of the refinery complex to the east of the castle and overlooking the main road. Waters of the the tiny Kouris river turned the upper millstone then went on to irrigate the plantations.

Written records show that from cutting the cane to producing the refined sugar took a month, with repeated boilings of the black molasses until the final white sugar crystallised out in conical pots. The Venetian customers called the pots *zamburi,* and from their shape the sugar was known as *pan di zucchero,* or 'sugar loaf,' a shape which has given its name to that spectacular mountain by Rio de Janeiro. There were always a few impurities at the bottom of the cone – the top of the *zamburo* – but the Martini family was alone in being allowed to buy *polvere dezamburade,* pure powder sugar.

Downfall of sugar. It was the Genoese-born Christopher Columbus, discoverer of America, who ultimately destroyed the Venetian's sugar bonanza, for the cane grew much stronger in the better-watered Caribbean islands, was tended by slave labour from Africa, and so undercut the price of Cypriot sugar. Production was declining by the late 16th cent and within 100 years had ceased altogether.

The Church of St Eustathios. A short distance from Kolissi Castle stands the 12th-cent Church of St Eustathios, where the Knights of the Order of St John attended mass. St Eustathios, the Great Martyr, was a warrior of Roman origins, with obvious appeal to the warrior knights.

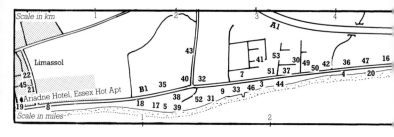

St NICOLAOS OF THE CATS

Your map of Cyprus will show you that the island's southernmost point is Cape Gata, 'Cape of the Cats.' A detailed map shows the monastery of St Nikolaos of the Cats a little to the north; it is, in fact, within the boundary of RAF Akrotiri but is accessible (&).

When the original monks began cultivating the sandy soil at the southern shore of the salt lake and found the area infested with snakes, they brought in a colony of cats. Legend claims that the animals were trained to respond to one monastery bell for their daily food, then another bell would send them back to the fields and their unending hunt for snakes; understandably, many of the cats were killed or wounded.

The monastery fell into decay but has been restored in the past few years, and now holds a few elderly and shabby nuns — and at least 30 cats. But there are very few snakes.

How to get there. From Kolissi, follow the road south to RAF Akrotiri (no access) and turn left just before the main gate down a road poorly signed to Lady's Mile Beach. As you approach the salt lake, look for a sign on the left saying: ΙΕΡΑ ΜΟΝΙ ΑΓ ΝΙΚΟΛΑΟΥ ΓΑΤΩΝ.

Don't go down the track to which it points; take the next one on the right, opposite the sentry box. From the salt lake, look for the sign and backtrack. Entry is free but the nuns welcome a small donation, if only for the cats.

Akrotiri. Akrotiri village is a tiny community with half its buildings appearing to be snack bars.

Bargain shop. The road south from Kolissi brings you to Savvas Ioannides's family shop, standing opposite the Red Seal Phassouri Plantation and offering the cheapest citrus I found on the island, in 4kg (9lb) bags; Savvas has a good selection of UK processed foods as well.

SANCTUARY OF APOLLO HYLATES &

Travel two miles west of Curium and you reach the Sanctuary of Apollo Hylates, the god of the woodland and the protector of Curium.

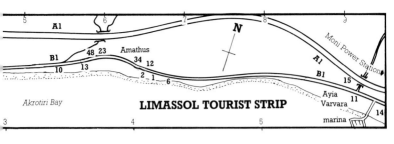

Akrotiri Bay

LIMASSOL TOURIST STRIP

Ayia
Varvara

marina

KEY TO HOTEL APARTMENTS

30 Atlantica
31 Azur Beach I
32 Azur Beach II
33 Balmyra Beach
34 Bertha
35 Bois, Le
36 Caravel
37 Castle
38 Drakos
39 Emitage Beach
40 Estella
41 Flora Maro
42 Lordos
43 Old Bridge
44 Onda Beach, L'
45 Oratos
46 Pegasus
47 Pigeon Beach
48 Renanda
49 Romios Beach
50 Roussos Beach
51 Ser Criso
52 Takelena
53 Tasiana

KEY TO HOTELS

1   Adonia Beach
2   Amathus Beach
3   Apollonia Beach
4   Aquarius Beach
5   Asteria Beach
6   Avenida Beach
7   Chez Nous Sunotel
8   Churchill
9   Crusader Beach Sunotel
10 Elena Beach
11 Elias Beach
12 Golden Arches
13 King Richard
14 Limassol Sheraton
15 Limonia
16 Marathon Beach
17 Miramare
18 Park Beach
19 Pavemar
20 Poseidonia Beach
21 Sunny Beach
22 Sylva
23 Trans

Marked on some maps as the 'Temple of Apollo,' this was the religious and cultural sector of Curium from the 7th cent BC until the old gods were overtaken by Christianity in the 1st cent.

Much of the sanctuary was destroyed by the earthquake of 350 but excavations by Pennsylvania University have given us the ground plan of two temples, a bath complex, and an administration building, with later restorations showing what the corner of the main temple looked like.

Opening hours are the same as for Curium, but you need to pay an extra 50c entry fee.

TOURIST STRIP and BEACHES

Limassol town centre has no beach at all. There is a sandy play area among the gardens on the car-free promenade, and a gravelly beach begins near the municipal gardens, but you need to go to the city limits before you're by a beach of sandcastle quality.

Dhassoudi Beach. A little way beyond the city is Dhassoudi Public Beach, offering the best stretch of sand that has unrestricted public access, and with changing rooms, parking, restaurant and snack bar provided by the CTO.

Beyond Dhassoudi the tourist strip begins in earnest, the largest community of hotels on the island, outranking the tourist development in new Famagusta which has been lost in no-man's-land since 1974. But it lacks that main ingredient of most family holidays — an unreservedly good beach.

Breakwaters built of large boulders are gradually collecting tidewashed sand along this coast, but it takes years for a perfect beach to be formed in this manner when the sand itself is scarce. Meanwhile, each of those hotels on the shore has access to its own small stretch of coastline which it likes to reserve for its guests; a few have perfect sands; some have a good beach, though not always large enough to give every guest space to sunbathe; some have flat rocks with just a few grains of sand.Guests at those hotels and apartment houses with no direct access to the shore must go to Dhassoudi or compete for the limited public sands.

Lady's Mile Beach. Ironically, the largest stretch of sand on the entire island, Lady's Mile Beach, lies just to the south of Limassol and reaches for all of five miles (8km), offering a wide and almost flat beach perfect for sandcastles and sunbathing, with no hint of shingle.

So why wasn't the tourist strip built along here? The answer is simple: Lady's Mile is on Britain's Episkopi base and so outside Cypriot control. While there is no restriction on entry, access is along a track of hardpacked sand which is often under an inch or two of water in winter when the Akrotiri salt lake overflows. Limassol's buses run a limited service to the beach in high summer, but the only other way to get here is by taxi, hire car, or on foot — which guarantees some degree of solitude even on a scorching day in August. Refreshments are available at two or three ramshackle snack bars which don't have permanent status, and beyond the last bar a wire fence runs across the sands marking the no-go area of the RAF Akrotiri base.

Other beaches. All other beaches in Limassol district lie to the west of the Akrotiri Peninsula: **Curium Beach** beneath the ruins of that old city, is enticing, but access is difficult; from the *east* of the Curium site, follow a sign to 'Curium' (it means the beach), go down the steep hill and turn right at a derelict fountain, now following signs to Ayios Ermogenis through an eucalyptus grove. The beach is long but with large pebbles at the top graduating to sand at the waterline, except for a stretch where the pebbles have been bulldozed clear. A sign warns that bathing is dangerous here at any time, but the place is popular with windsurfers prepared to take the risk. A few simple shacks serve refreshments, their lack of permanence reminding us that they, too, are on the British Episkopi base.

Avdimou Beach, usually spelled as **Evdhimou,** is 17 miles (28km) from Limassol at the end of a narrow and winding tarred road signposted to Evdhimou Jetty. The Kyrenia Bar and an unnamed restaurant offer the only services, with fresh fish, landed at the jetty, being top of the menu. The narrow beach is about half a mile long, with some shingle and boulders, and is not suitable for sandcastles.

Turn right along a track to **Melinda Beach,** which has a single restaurant and three military camping-sites; civilian camping is not allowed. The beach is small and shingly.

For something a little special, come to **Pissouri Beach,** 20 miles (32km) west of Limassol and snuggling at the base of Cape Aspro. A good road, signed to the Columbia Hotel, leads through vineyards and passes the Kotzias Hotel Apartments. The beach is narrow and short, with dark sands and a touch of shingle, but the beachfront Columbia specialises in water sports including parascending at C£10 a flight, windsurfing at C£5 an hour, and canoeing, jetskiing, sailing and pedalo at comparable rates. If you go along the main road and turn off to Pissouri village you can walk a mile down a track to a tiny isolated beach on the other side of Cape Aspro.

HOTELS:

Five-star: Amathus Beach, 488◄, ☎ ⌂ ✕ ⅋ ✿ s; Apollonia Beach, 408◄, ☎ ⌂ ✕ ⅋ ✿ s; Meridian Limassol (100m east of strip map), 382◄, ☎ ⌂ ✕ ⅋ ✿ ; Limassol Sheraton, 432◄, ☎ ⌂ ✕ ⅋ ✿ s; Poseidonia Beach, 276◄, ☎ ⌂ ⅋ ✿ s;

Four-star: Ajax, Damonos & Nicolaou, Mesayitonia, 352◄, ☎ ⌂ ✕ ⅋; Churchill Limassol, 28 Oct Ave, 292◄, ☎ ⌂ ✕ ⅋ ✿; Curium Palace, Byron St, opp Art Gallery, 112◄, ☎ ⌂ ✕ ⅋ T; Elias Beach, 346◄, ☎ ⌂ ✕ ⅋ ✿ s; Limonia Bay, 172◄, ☎ ⌂ ✕ s; Marathon Beach, 260◄, ☎ ⌂ ✕ s;

Three-star: Adonia Beach, 60◄, ☎ ⌂ ✕ ✿ s; Alasia, 1 Haydari St, 110◄, ☎ ⌂ ✕ ⅋ T; Aquamarine, 133◄, ☎ ✕ T t; Ariadne, 28 Oct Ave, 133◄, ☎ ⌂ ✕ T; Arsinoe, 224◄, ☎ ⌂ ✕ ⅋ s; Asteria Beach, 152◄, ☎ ⌂ ✕ ✿ s; Avenida Beach, 114◄, ☎ ⌂ ✕ ✿ s; Azur, 160◄, ☎ ⌂ s; Columbia, Pissouri Beach, 258◄, ☎ ⌂ ✕ ✿; Crusader Beach Sunotel, 217◄, ☎ ⌂ ⅋ ✿ s; Golden Arches, 209◄, ☎ ⌂ ✕ s; Kanika Beach, 28 Oct Ave, 145◄, ☎ ⌂ ✕ ⅋ ✿ T; Kanika Twin, Pan Symeou St, 102◄, ☎ T; King Richard, 95◄, ☎ ⌂ ✕ ⅋ ✿ s; Park Beach, on strip, 209◄, ☎ ⌂ ✕ ✿; Pavemar, 28 Oct Ave, 124◄, ☎ ⌂ ✕ ⅋ ✿;

Two-star: Aquarius Beach, 21◄, ☎ ✿ s; Chez Nous Sunotel, 57◄, ☎ ⌂ ✕ s; Continental, 51◄, ☎ ✕ T t; Eastland, 61◄, ☎ T t; Elena Beach, 76◄, ☎ ⌂ ✕ ⅋ ✿ s; Old Bridge, 148◄, ✕ s; Pefkos, 86 Kavazoglu & Misiaoulis St, 152◄, ☎ ⌂ ✕ T; Sunny Beach, 28 Oct Ave, 68◄, ☎ ⌂ ✕ ✿; Sylvia, 124 Gen Dhigenis St, 114◄, ☎ ⌂ ✕ T; Pissouri, 18◄; Le Village, 61◄, ☎ ✕ T t; Limassol Palace, 25◄, ☎ ✕

141

T t; Panorama, 57✉, ☎ ✗ T t; **Unclassified:** Acropolé, 22✉, T t;
Astoria, 20✉, T t; Metropole, 32✉, T t.

HOTEL APARTMENTS:

Agathangelos Court, Kefalinias St, 49✉, ☎ ⟐ T; Atlantica, 156✉, ☎
⌂ ✗ ⟐ s; Azur Beach 1, 48✉, ☎ ✿ s; Balmyra Beach, 102✉, ☎ ⌂ ✗
⟐ ✿ s; Bertha, 40✉, ☎ ⌂ ✗ s; Caravel, 120✉, ☎ ⌂ ✗ s; Castle,
96✉, ☎ ⌂ ✗ ⟐ s; Chrielka, 40✉, ☎ T t; Drakos, 90✉, ☎ ⌂ ✗ s;
Eden Beach, 28 Oct Ave, 336✉, ☎ ⌂; Kotzias, Pissouri, 30✉;
Ermitage Beach, 170✉, ☎ ⌂ ✗ ✿ s; Essex, off 28 Oct Ave, 66✉, ☎
⌂ ✗; Estella, 40✉, ☎ ⌂ ✗ s; Flora Maro, Potamos Yermasoyia, 56✉,
☎ ⌂; Gloria, off 28 Oct Ave, 66✉, ☎ ✗ ⟐; Le Bois, 42✉, ☎ ⌂; Lime
Gardens, strip, 24✉, ☎ ⌂ ✗; Lordos, Andrea Zaimi St, 62✉, ☎;
L'Onda Beach, 100✉, ☎ ⌂ ✗ ⟐ ✿ s; Oratis Beach, 28 Oct Ave, 34✉,
☎ ⟐ ✿; Pegasus, 72✉, ☎ ⌂ ✗ ✿ s; Pier Beach, 126✉, ☎ ⌂ ⟐ T t;
Pollyanna, 22✉, ✗ ⟐ s; Polyxeni, 40✉, ☎ ⌂ ✗ s; Renanda, 48✉, ☎
⌂ s; Romios Beach, 72✉, ☎ ⌂ ✗ ⟐ s; Ser Cristo, 40✉, ☎ ⌂ ✗ ⟐
s; Takelena, 56✉, ☎ ✗ s; Tanta, 44✉, ☎ ⌂ ⟐ s; Tasiana 1, 34✉,
⌂ ✗ s; Tasiana 2, 20✉, ✗ s; Twiga, 114 Makarios Ave, 50✉, ☎.

GUEST HOUSES:

Arizona, 14✉, T t; Excelsior, 29✉, T t; Hellas, 19✉, T t; Icaros, 17✉,
T t; Kalithea, 28✉, T t; Luxor, 25✉, T t; Stalis, 19✉, T t.

RESTAURANTS:

French: L'Onda Beach, in hotel of that name; ✆321821, 1100-2400,
reservations. **Indian:** Taj Mahal, opp Apollonia Hotel, ✆326500, 1800-
2330, reservations.
International: Aristocats, Plaza Complex, tourist strip, ✆ 325427,1900-
2400; Blue Island, 3 Amathountos Ave, tourist strip, ✆321466, 1900-
2330, ex Wed, reservations; Calypso, Amathus Beach Hotel, ✆321152,
1000-2200; Clemmies, Churchill Hotel, ✆324444, 1230-1500; Palladium,
Limassol Sheraton, ✆321100, 1930-2330; Westminster, Churchill Hotel,
✆324444, 2000-0100, reservations.
Italian: Bocconi, Aquamarine Hotel, ✆374277, 1800-2330, reservations.
Oriental, Phoenician, Limassol Sheraton, ✆321100, Fri-Sat 1930-0100,
reservations.

NIGHTLIFE:

Limassol has the best nightlife on the island but, as elsewhere, it is
almost entirely confined to the smarter hotels on the tourist strip and
mostly consists of bars; the Amathus Beach, Churchill, Meridian,
L'Onda Beach and the Sheraton are among those which offer discreet
music most evenings. For livelier entertainment try the few independent discos on the strip, notably Malibu or Whispers or, for more
conventional dancing, the Salamandra. There's always the option of
popping into the Lapponia, which goes Finnish twice a week.

15: NICOSIA

Venetian elegance

THE SOUTHERN PART OF NICOSIA is a smart and bustling city, competing with Limassol for the best shopping district on the island.

Here, particularly around Eleftheria Square (♿) — Freedom Square — the focal point of Republican Cyprus, parking is at its most difficult, and you may find yourself in a traffic jam on Archbishop Makarios III Avenue.

Pedestrians only. Nicosia's Municipality is in the process of excluding vehicles from most of the streets in the western part of the old city, creating a ring road, and locating car parks along it by the Green Line and in the Venetian moat. Phaneromeni Square will replace Eleftheria as the recognised city centre and Eleftheria will be remodelled, with the EEC granting $2,000,000 to help finance the scheme.

Shopping. Nicosia's main shopping district is Makarios Ave north from its junction with Santa Roza Ave, plus Eleftheria Sq and, in the old city, Ledra and Onasagoras streets.

Origins. Nicosia's origins are unknown, but Neolithic man had a settlement here around 5,500BC. The first hint of a civilised community came with the discovery of an inscription acknowledging that King Onasagoras of Lidir was one of 10 kings of Cyprus paying tribute to Esarhadon, the King of Nineveh (Syria), in 673BC.

There were numerous variations on the city's name: take your pick from Ledra, Ledroi, Ledron, Letra or Lidir, then bridge the gap to the Greek version, Lefkosia, and its Turkish equivalent, Lefkoşa.

Landlocked Nicosia has been the island's capital since the 10th cent, an unusual choice for the days when the sailing ship was the quickest form of travel. But Cyprus was open to attack from pirates and every ambitious conqueror, so an inland capital made sense — and Nicosia was within a day's horseback ride from its coastal cities and castles, Kiti (Larnaca), Salamis (Famagusta), St Hilarion (Kyrenia), Soli and Kantara, and a little longer from Curium and Kolossi (Limassol), and Ktima (Paphos). The city also controlled the Mesaouria Plain, the island's granary since the dawn of civilisation.

Venetian walls. The Venetians, who ruled Cyprus from 1481 to 1571, saw the steady advance of Islam, and the Ottoman Empire in particular, and replaced Nicosia's nine-mile (14km) rambling city walls with a more defensible three-mile (4.8km) wall-and-ditch

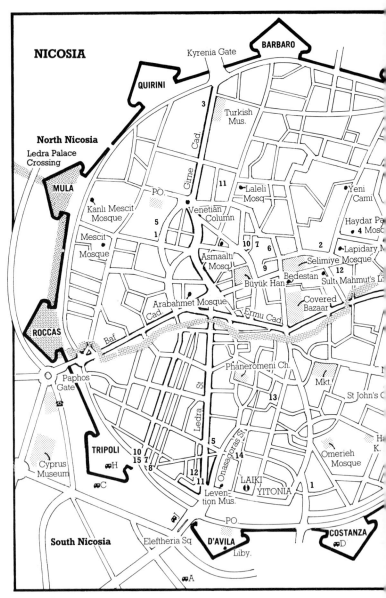

NICOSIA

BARBARO

Kyrenia Gate

QUIRINI

North Nicosia

Ledra Palace
Crossing

MULA

3

Turkish
Mus.

Girne Cad.

11

Laleli
Mosq

Yeni
Cami

PO.

Venetian
Column

Haydar Pa
4 Mosc

Kanlı Mescit
Mosque

5

1

10 7

6

2

Lapidary M

Mescit
Mosque

Asmaaltı
Mosq

9

Selimiye Mosque

12

Büyük Han

Bedestan

Sult Mahmut's Li

Arabahmet Mosque
Cad.

Ermu Cad.

Covered
Bazaar

ROCCAS

Baf

Paphos
Gate

Phaneromeni Ch.

Mkt.

St John's C

Ledra St

13

Cyprus
Museum

TRIPOLI

10
15

5

7

8

Onasagoras St.

14

H

K.

Omerieh
Mosque

C

12

11

Leven-
tion Mus.

LAIKI
YITONIA

1

PO.

South Nicosia

Eleftheria Sq

D'AVILA

COSTANZA

D

Liby.

A

KEY TO HOTELS
and PENSIONS

1 Saray Hotel
2 Aile
3 Altın
4 Anadolu
5 Antalya
6 Bursa Uludağ
7 Efes
8 Gözde
9 Güzel
10 Kurtuluş
11 Side
12 Sönmez

KEY TO HOTELS

1 Alexandria
2 Averof
3 Carlton
4 Churchill
5 City
6 Cleopatra
7 Delphi
8 Denis
9 Excelsior
10 Kennedy
11 Lido
12 Regina Palace
13 Royal
14 Sans Rival
15 Venetian Walls

See also Nicosia area map, pages 152–3.

forming a perfect circle, and with 11 bastions to make the city even more impregnable. Work began in 1567 and was finished in 1570 – but that same year the Ottomans attacked, seized the city, and slaughtered its 20,000 inhabitants.

Almost all the walls and bastions survive today, giving Nicosia a feature that is unique, but each half of the city controls only five of the bastions, the eleventh having the Green Line running through it.

Come to Paphos Gate, one of the original three openings in the walls, and study an anomaly of a divided city: Roccas Bastion is in North Cyprus, with the Turkish and North Cypriot flags flying and with Turkish troops and North Cypriot police standing on top of the parapet while, on the road at the bastion's base, the flags of Greece and the Cypriot Republic fly, Cypriot police are on permanent patrol, and the traffic swirls by.

THE OLD CITY

THE CITY GATES

Paphos Gate. ♿ The Venetians called it Porta de San Domenico from the large monastery which stood here, with one of the Lusignan royal palaces in its compound. The Ottomans decided that the gate itself was such a formidable bulwark that they put their artillery and arsenal on it.

The British, assuming control of the island in 1878, closed the gate in '79 and eventually improved on the Ottoman arsenal and converted it into the headquarters of the Cyprus Police Force; it's now Divisional HQ.

Traffic once again moves through the gate but, following the Turkish intervention of 1974, cannot proceed along Paphos Street which is renamed Baf Cadessi and is in North Cyprus. Wander in through the gate and take a cautious look around at the desolation, where oil drums and barbed wire mark the southern side of the buffer zone which frequently cuts through a house, leaving the front door in Cyprus but the back door in no-man's-land, patrolled only by UNFICYP and inhabited only by weeds. The Holy See Chancellery and the Holy Cross Catholic Church are just in south Nicosia, but elsewhere a church has its front door in Cyprus, its rear door in North Cyprus, and the buffer zone, in effect, running through the middle. The priest has been compelled to fasten the rear door permanently.

Famagusta Gate. ♿ The Venetians' Porta Giuliana, now the Famagusta Gate, was the old city's major entrance and took its name from Count Giulio Savorgnano who masterminded the building of the walls; it was also known as the Porta di Sotto, the 'Low Gate,' because its inner façade was 15ft (3m) lower than its outer.

The passage through the gate is 149ft (45.3m) long by 13ft (5m) wide, though at each end the masonry reduces the width to 10ft 3in (3.12m); a cupola (dome) above the passage lets in daylight at the centre, while rooms on each side were for guards. The gate was closed to wheeled traffic in 1945 and since 1979 has been barred as a pedestrian throughway, but is open Mon-Fri 1000-1300, 1600-1900, Sat 1000-1300, free. Several one-day exhibitions are held here each month.

NICOSIA WITHIN THE WALLS

Laiki Yitonia. ♿ The essence of old Nicosia has been recaptured in Laiki Yitonia, a quarter-acre (1,000sq m) reconstruction of medieval streets and buildings, though tarmac and coloured brick have replaced the cobbles, and the beautiful precinct is obviously a well-designed tourist trap.

Laiki Yitonia − 'folk neighbourhood' is a loose translation − was opened in December 1983 with around 30 small premises. Most of the craftsmen who moved in were refugees from North Cyprus, and their businesses include a tinker, tailor, potter, ironmonger, shoemaker, jeweller, weaver and leather-worker, but there are also a bakery, cafeteria, philatelist, a bookshop, an art gallery, a bank, and the Nicosia office of the CTO: the main office, not for casual tourist inquiries, is on the first floor (2nd floor, USA) of a modern office block outside the walls.

Historical Museum. The small Historical Museum on Hippocratous St, west of Laiki Yitonia, seems to compete with the Cyprus Museum by specialising in artefacts from earliest recorded history to the present − see for yourself. It's open Tues-Sun 1000-1600. ♿

Organised tours. Two guided tours organised by the municipality and starting at the CTO office are aimed at individual travellers. A walk through the old city sets off each Thursday at 1000 and includes a visit to a chairmaker and waxmaker as well as the conventional sights; a bus and walking tour leaving on Mondays at 1000 goes to **Kaimakli,** the Greek quarter north-east of the old city close to the Green Line, and sees the churches of Ayia Varvara and Archangelos. Transport is on an old-style wooden bus with hard seats; both tours are free, but you'll pay to go in places.

Archbishopric. ♿ Probably the most popular and impressive building inside the old city is the new Archbishopric, started in 1956, completed in 1960, and open to the public only on special occasions but nonetheless dominating Kyprianos Square. A marble bust of Archbishop Kyprianou, 51st head of the Church of Cyprus, stands outside the railings; Kyprianou was hanged from a mulberry tree in Atatürk Square, now in Northern Cyprus, in 1821. His statue, and indeed the Archbishopric itself, are overshadowed by an enormous statue of Archbishop Makarios III, 63rd archbishop, and first president of independent Cyprus. If you go to Pano Panayia in the Troodos Mountains, think of this vast building as you explore the humble cottage in which Makarios was born.

St John's Church. ♿ (beware steps). North of the Archbishopric is a cluster of buildings of tourist interest; the first is St John's Church, also known as Ayios Ioannis, the Orthodox Cathedral of the island, open daily 0800-1300, 1400-1700. This church of 1662 incorporates

The lacemakers of Pano Lefkara.

over its west door a few bas-relief carvings from the original Benedictine abbey on the site.

The restored 18th-cent murals show Biblical scenes such as the Creation, and scenes from the island's history such as the discovery of St Barnabas's tomb at Salamis; Barnabas became the island's first archbishop. And in the centre of the cathedral floor is a sculpting of a two-headed eagle, the symbol of the Eastern Orthodox Church since the fall of Constantinople in 1453. This symbol, seen in every Orthodox cathedral, marks the spot where bishops and archbishops stand at their consecration.

Makarios Cultural Centre. The second building in the cluster is the Makarios Cultural Centre, (&. but with front steps), home to the Byzantine Museum and the largest collection of icons in Cyprus, some dating from the 9th cent. It's open in summer Mon-Fri 0900-1300, 1400-1530, Sat 0900-1300; in winter it closes at 1500. Admission is free.

Museum of Folk Art. Beside it stands the Museum of Folk Art (&. but with front steps), open Mon-Fri 0800-1300, 1400-1600, Sat 0800-1300, for 50c. It holds a good collection of artefacts from daily life in the 19th and 20th cents, notably embroidery, delicate woodwork, farm implements and national costume.

National Struggle Museum. The National Struggle Museum, in the *old* Archbishopric Palace, tells with complete frankness the story of

Cyprus's struggle for independence from the British between 1955 and 1959, and has enough material to fill a large book with the Cypriot side of the events.

Open in summer Mon-Fri 0800-1400, 1500-1900, Sat 0800-1300, and in winter Mon-Fri 0800-1800, Sat 0800-1300, with free admission and ♿ access, the museum has many unique documents, foremost being an original copy of the 1921 First Plebiscite, taken on the centenary of the outbreak of the Greek War of Independence which saw, in Cyprus, the execution of Archbishop Kyprianou and others.

One of four copies of the Second Plebiscite of 15 January, 1950, is also here, showing that 97% of Greek Cypriots, and around 400 Turkish Cypriots, favoured total integration with Greece. When Britain was reluctant to agree to independence, EOKA, the National Organisation of Cypriot Combatants, was formed to change Imperial thinking. The campaign for *enosis,* union with Greece, which became part of the EOKA campaign was, in many people's opinion, the cause of the Turkish intervention in 1974.

The museum has actual documents and photographs as well as photocopies, to illustrate this story of the fight for freedom, and a reconstruction of the small gallows and noose on which nine men were hanged in 1956 emphasises the bitterness that existed between Britain and Cyprus in those years. One of the victims was a student of 17, claimed to have been caught up in the dispute by accident.

Statue of Independence. ♿ If Makarios's gigantic statue had the gift of sight it would be gazing in perpetuity on the Statue of Independence, standing in front of the Podocataro Bastion in the city walls. The design of this statue leads one to believe that the British colonialists were brutal oppressors, as it shows 14 people of all ages being released from jail by two soldiers hauling up a portcullis. The 14 bronzes are life-size and lifelike, and so designed that the visitor can take his place among them, as if he is also coming out of prison.

Chrysaliniotissa Church. North of Makarios's statue, past the Taht-el-Kale Mosque (translated from the Turkish as 'throne-castle' or 'lower castle'), stands the oldest Byzantine church in Nicosia, the Panayia Chrysaliniotissa Church, completed in 1450 and today noted for its icons and its gold leaf; its popular name is 'Our Lady of the Golden Flax.'

Other churches. Tripiotis Church, near Laiki Yitonia, in Franco-Byzantine design of 1695, has silver- and gold-brushed icons on its impressively-large iconostasis, showing its early congregation was wealthy. Ayios Antonios Church near the Hadjigeorgakis House, dedicated to a 3rd-cent monk named St Anthony, claims to have a grandfather clock with a ship on its pendulum — but grandfather clocks are in almost every monastery and in many churches as well.

The Phaneromeni Church, the largest in the city when it was built in 1872, holds the remains of most of the churchmen murdered by the Ottomans in 1821.

The Hadjigeorgakis Kornessios House. A house with such a

The most impressive burial chamber at Paphos's Tombs of the Kings.

difficult name should be impressive, and this one is extremely ornate on the inside, though its exterior looks a little drab. The Kornessios family originated in Paphos but came to Nicosia in the late 18th cent and made its name and its fortune in textiles. The son, Hadjigeorgakis, rose in Turkish Cypriot society to the post of Dragoman, the second-in-command of Turkish affairs, and the person who granted or refused audience with the sultan's representative on the island. Taking this office in 1779, he used his power wisely but had to flee from Cyprus at the turn of the century, living in the British and Russian embassies in Istanbul until he was caught in 1809 and beheaded.

His house, built by Venetians but exquisitely furnished by Hadjigeorgakis himself, became a museum in May 1987; it's open Mon-Sat 0800-1330 for 50c, with ♿ access on ground floor only.

Omerieh Mosque. The only mosque of any significance in south Nicosia is the Omerieh (♿ in part), though its Turkish congregation has gone and the dark brown walls look neglected. The original building was the 14th-cent Augustinian Church of St Mary which the later Ottoman ruler, Mustapha Pasha, declared to be on the very spot where the prophet Omer had rested during his travels in Nicosia. St Mary's, already ruined by cannonfire, therefore became a mosque in 1571 — but traces of that original church can still be seen at the east end. Would you like a surreptitious view of north Nicosia? Then climb the minaret and look around.

NICOSIA OUTSIDE THE WALLS

The Central Prison. The Central Prison may seem a strange addition to your tourist itinerary, but the establishment is open to visitors daily 0800-1300, free. If you're not visiting any inmates you can see the gallows, still standing although Cyprus has not had capital punishment for many years. But this is the actual gallows on which those nine EOKA convicts, including the student, were hanged in 1956 by the British. A narrow passage leads on from the gallows to the mens' graves in the prison yard.

The prison is on Iroon St, beyond the Averof Hotel and en route to the British High Commision.

Commission, residence, palace. The British High Commission on Alexander Pallis St is 100m from the Green Line, but the Commissioner's Residence, 300m east in a straight line, is in North Cyprus. It holds the British Consulate and the British Council; details are in Chapter 3. The residence of the Governor in colonial times is now the Presidential Palace, not open to public view.

Cyprus Museum. The most important museum on the island is the Cyprus Museum, sited appropriately enough on Museum St. Hours in summer, Mon-Sat 1730-1330, 1600-1800; in winter, 0730-1400, 1500-1700. Entry costs C£1, with photography banned and ♿ access on ground floor only. The building, completed in 1908, was a memorial to Queen Victoria as well as a home for the several small collections scattered around the island — and the theme is archaeological.

From the cash desk, turn right and follow the floor plan anticlockwise if you want a chronological tour. The first large hall covers the **Neolithic and Chalcolithic** eras, from around 5,800 to 2,300BC, concentrating heavily on stone tools and simple pottery. The smaller room at the end covers the **Early Bronze Age,** and turns left into the hall devoted to **pottery** from the 19th cent BC to the end of the Hellenistic period, around 50BC.

The hall ends with an impressive **Late Bronze Age** display of terracotta votive offerings in human form from Ayia Irini (now Akdeniz in Northern Cyprus) ranging from 4in (10cm) to life size.

Left again into the long **Sculpture Gallery** with work from the 7th cent BC, including several life-size heads and a full-length carving of the child-god Eros (Cupid); all the exhibits from this hall come from temples and show the evolution of votive offerings as mortal man tried to ingratiate himself with the gods.

The next room holds the smaller display of **Roman sculpture,** dominated by the 6ft 10in (2.08m) statue of a nude Septimus Severus, Emperor of Rome from 193 to 211AD. The statue was found in pieces at Kythrea (now Değirmenlik) in 1928 and may have some association with the Roman aqueduct from the Kyrenia Mountains to Salamis.

Left again, and you find yourself in an exhibition of **bronzes,** showing the full range from swords and armour to a copper ingot weighing around 90lb (40kg). One side display concentrates on jewellery while a similar arrangement opposite has blown glass from

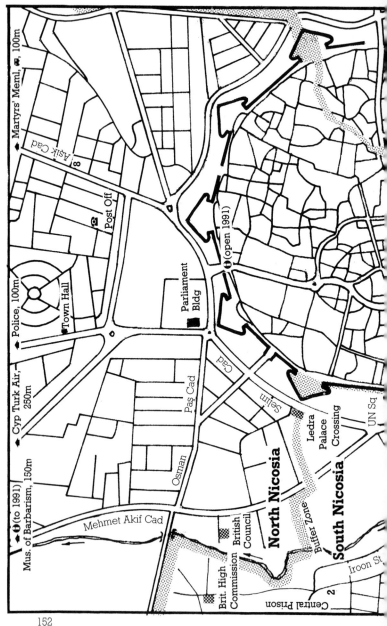

Martyrs' Meml, 🚉, 100m

Aşik Cad

Post Off

8

Town Hall

Police, 100m

Parliament Bldg

Cyp Turk Air, 250m

🛈 (open 1991)

Paş Cad

Cad

Selim

Osman

Ledra Palace Crossing

UN Sq

North Nicosia

🛈 (to 1991)

Mus. of Barbarism, 150m

Mehmet Akif Cad

British Council

Buffer Zone

South Nicosia

Brit. High Commission

Central Prison

2

Iroon St

NICOSIA

US Embassy

Cyprus Airways

A'bish Makarios Ave

A'bish Makarios Ave

Stasínou Ave

Santa Róza Ave

9

6

3

Post Off

(CTO head office)

Evagorou Ave

Ave

State Collection of Art

Dhigenis Ave

St Paul's Ch.

Cyp. Museum

Ho. of Representatives

J Nehru Ave

Givas

Geo

4

153

the 15th cent BC. For reference, the world's oldest known piece of glass, dated to the late 14th cent BC, was found on the seabed near Kaş in the world's oldest known shipwreck, and is now in the Glass Museum in Bodrum Castle, Turkey. The Shipwreck Museum in Kyrenia (Girne, in Northern Cyprus) has the remains of a vessel that sank in the 3rd cent BC.

From the Bronze Room a side passage leads to a museum extension built in 1935, and is as far as wheelchair visitors can go. Beyond a display of funeral ware, including urns and tombs, steps go down to a small room holding a reconstruction of a **Chalcolithic burial site,** including a human skeleton. Steps also go up to a similar room holding a reconstructed **Necropolis at Salamis.** The ivory bedframe from Salamis looks quite modern, but is from the 8th cent BC, as is a bronze urn about 4ft (1.2cm) in diameter.

The last room of all includes a reconstruction of an ancient copper or zinc mine, with the tools of the time.

No museum in Cyprus has yet incorporated animation, or offered the 'hands-on' experience which is so popular in the USA and is widely available in western Europe, but there are many dioramas, and captions are in English and Greek.

Other attractions. South of the museum along Leophoros Vyronos (Byron Ave), the first turning left takes you to **St Paul's Anglican Cathedral,** built in 1893 in the style and size of an English parish church. South again for 300m, where your road picks up Evagorou

Flat land is scarce in the Troodos, so houses may occasionally stride a river.

Ave, a sidestreet on the left leads to the **State Collection of Contemporary Art,** housing paintings and sculptures by Cypriots from 1930 to the present. Entry is free.

AROUND THE DISTRICT

ARCHANGELOS MICHAEL MONASTERY
One of the smaller monasteries, Michael the Archangel lies a little way from the Nicosia—Troodos road on its sweep south of the disused Nicosia Airport; it's difficult to find. The Byzantine church was rebuilt in 1713 when Kykko Monastery bought this monastery; the Archangel is seen in a fresco painted in 1785.

AYIOS HERAKLEIDIOS &
The old monastery of Ayios Herakleidios in Politiko village, two miles off the road from Nicosia to Makheras, was empty for years until the 1980s when around 27 nuns moved in and converted it into a pleasant convent, earning their living from the sale of honey, marzipan, and miniature icons. There's no overnight accommodation, and the convent closes its doors to visitors from 1200 to 1500 between mid May and mid September.

Herakleidos, whose name is alternatively spelt Irakleidos, was born near Kakopetria in the Troodos. He met the disciples Paul and Barnabas in Kition (Larnaca) and guided them to Tamassos; in return the holy men ordained Herakleidos as the Bishop of Tamassos. Herakleidos found a cave half a mile away and built his home there, and when he was murdered — according to legend at the age of 60 — he was buried in the cave; other versions of the story replace the cave with a Roman tomb but all agree that a monastery was founded on the spot around 400 and rebuilt at least twice, most of the present structure dating from 1773 and attributed to the restoration of Archbishop Chrysanthos.

Since World War Two, excavations around the convent's 15th-cent church have revealed a tomb in a crypt by the eastern wall though there is nothing to prove the bishop's body was buried in it; what is reputed to be his skull, and a bone from one of his hands, are kept in a gilded casket in the church.

The convent has a particularly pleasant courtyard garden with trailing vines casting shade on a modern mosaic floor.

AYIOS PANTELEIMON
The small convent of St Panteleimon lies at the end of a track north of Agrokipia village. Built in the 18th cent and restored in the 1960s, it is now a retreat for three nuns, who do not accept overnight guests.

DHALI
Idalion, called Idalium by the Romans, was one of the ten kingdoms of ancient Cyprus and has given its name to the modern village of

Dalı, or Dhali, perilously close to the Buffer Zone and the village of Louroujina, now Akıncılar in North Cyprus. Restoration work has not advanced far at Idalion, but I have not been able to see it as it is not signposted and I have yet to find anybody in Dalı village who has ever heard of it. I understand part of the city walls are visible on the site, said to be on high ground – but there's not much of that at Dalı.

Tradition claims that Idalion was founded by Kalkanor, one of the returning heroes from the Trojan War, and tradition (with a contribution from archaeology) places the end of *that* around 1200BC. Kalkanor and his companions had wandered from Salamis to Kythrea and had then turned south. Camping on this slight hill, one of the party drew attention to the rising sun: "Idou alion!" and so gave the new city its name.

Legend claims that Idalion spread across two hilltops and had 14 temples, of which the Temple of Aphrodite – known locally as Idalia – crowned one rise, Apollo's temple crowned the other, and the Temple of Athena sat in the Valley of Paradise between them. The Phoenicians were definitely here, and probably they had their own temple for Astarte.

Greek mythology tells the story of Aphrodite's passion for Adonis, the son of Zeus and Hera and brother of Ares (Mars to the Romans), the god of war. But Ares was also in love with Aphrodite, who was already married to Hephaestus (Vulcan). The plot thickens as Ares turns himself into a wild boar and kills Adonis – but Zeus is so shocked at this fratricide that he allows Adonis to spend half the year with the gods and the other half with the mortals. And Aphrodite was so grieved that her tears were transformed into anemone flowers.

Earlier this century the people of Dalı held a spring festival with anemones to mark the death of Adonis, the god who became associated with wheat as it spends half the year growing in the fields and is then absent for six months.

Tomb robbers. Idalion suffered greatly at the hands of tomb robbers in the mid-19th cent, ending only when Britain began administering Cyprus in 1878. There are reports of thousands of tombs being ransacked, particularly by diplomats normally based in Istanbul; the United States consul on Cyprus, Louis Palma di Cesnola, wrote in 1877 that in three years he had opened 'some 10,000 tombs, and had collected from them an immense number of vases,' most of which he shipped to the New York Metropolitan Museum of Art.

Cesnola was also responsible for the plundering of the Bronze Age site at Alambra (Alampra), 14 miles (22km) south of Nicosia. As if in compensation, American archaeologists came back to the site in 1974 and made further discoveries, now properly recorded and preserved. This site is not open to the public.

PANAYIA CHRYSOSPILIOTISSA

A natural cave in the village of Kato Dheftera formed the base for the ancient catacombs of Panayia Chrysospiliotissa, 7 miles (11km) south-west of Nicosia on a minor road. The early Christian burial chambers are the focus of a religious ceremony each August, dedicated to Our Lady of the Golden Cave.

TAMASSOS ⚹ (site only)

Tamassos, one of the ten city states in Cyprus's Geometric Period, is well-signposted and easily accessible from the Makheras–Nicosia road at Pera village. Open summer, Tues-Sun 0900-1200, 1600-1900; winter 0900-1300, 1400-1630. Admission 30c.

The setting is splendid, on a slight rise with the Troodos Mountains visible to the west and the Kyrenia Range to the north; approaching enemies would have found concealment difficult.

Tamassos probably owed its origins to the deposits of copper ores in the locality; the metal certainly made Tamassos wealthy, although it is recorded that its King Atmese had to pay tribute to the Assyrian King Esarhadon with the other nine city states of the island.

The main feature of interest in Tamassos is the two remaining royal tombs from 650 to 600BC, scientifically excavated in 1890 though left unguarded, allowing villagers to demolish the third tomb for its stone. The underground tombs are impressive for their size and architecture, with the funeral chambers having pitched roofs made of large slabs of sandstone.

The larger tomb has 22 steps – the top 11 rebuilt in 1972 – leading down to its two burial chambers, the first 10ft 5in by 9ft overall (3.17m by 2.79m), the second 10ft 6in by 9ft 1in (3.2m by 2.8m), with a maximum height of 8ft 5in (2.56m). The smaller tomb still has its sarcophagus in place, almost 8ft long by 4ft 1in wide (2.4m by 1.2m).

Recent digs have revealed part of the Temple of Aphrodite with copper slag on the floor, possible evidence that copper was seen as the gift of the gods and that it could be worked only by the gods' elect, the priests. In modern times those same copper veins have been worked by the Hellenic Mining Company.

During the 1830s, local farmers looking for water in the banks of the dry river, found a full-size bronze statue of Apollo weighing around 200lb (100kg). As they dragged it away, the head and all the limbs broke off the body; the farmers sold the head to an antique dealer but all the other pieces went to local smiths who turned the scrap into sheep bells, among other things. The sixth Duke of Devonshire bought Apollo's head in 1838 and kept it in the ancestral home of Chatsworth House, Derbyshire, from where it went to the British Museum in 1958 as part payment of death duties. A replica is now in the Cyprus Museum.

HOTELS

Five-star: Hilton, A'bish Mak Ave, 460⊨, ☎ ⌘ ✗ ⚹; **Four-star:** Churchill, 108⊨, ☎ ✗; New Ledra, Geo Grivas Dhigenis Ave (Leophoros Yeoryiou Griva Dhiyeni), 205⊨, ☎ ⌘ ✗ ⚹; Philoxenia, Eylenja Ave, 70⊨, ☎ ⌘ ✗; **Three-star:** Asty, 12 Prince Charles St,

105🛏, ☎ ✕; Cleopatra, 105🛏, ☎ ⇌ ✕; Europa, 16 Alceos St Engomi, 99🛏, ☎ ✕; Excelsior, 65🛏, ☎ ✕; Kennedy, 180🛏, ☎ ✕ ♿; **Two-star:** Averof, 50🛏, ☎ ✕; Lido, 72🛏, ☎ ✕; **One-star:** Alexandria, 72b; Capital, 96 Regaena St, 103b; Carlton, 41🛏, ☎; City, 65🛏, ☎; Crown, 13 Philellinon St, 58🛏, ☎; Denis, 51🛏, ☎; Nicosia Palace, 4 Pantelides Ave, 75🛏, ☎; Pisa Tower, 33 St Nikolaos St Engomi, 61🛏, ☎; Regina Palace, 74🛏, ☎; Sans Rival, 31🛏, ☎; Venetian Walls, ☎ ✕; **Unclassified:** Cottage, 13 Orpheos St Ay. Dhometios, 50🛏, Delphi, 24🛏 Royal, 15🛏.

GUEST HOUSES

Alasia, 23 Pigmalion St, 18🛏; Femina, 114 Ledra St, 24🛏; Gardenia, 23 Rigaena St, 22🛏; Kypros, 16 V. Voulgaroktonou St, 16🛏; Peter's, 5 Solonos St, 56🛏;

RESTAURANTS

There is a reasonable number of restaurants and tavernas in Nicosia, but scattered far and wide as they cater for the locals more than for tourists. For simplicity in finding them try the Archontico (1900-2400, ✆450080) or the Roylatico (✆455081), both in Laiki Yitonia, or the Athineon at 8 A'bish Makarios Ave (1200-2000, ✆444786).

NIGHTLIFE

The liveliest part of Nicosia by night radiates from Eleftheria Square. For Greek bouzouki music while you dine, try Kapello in Laiki Yitonia (✆450080, not Mon), or the Elysee Bouzoukia at 38 Evagoras Ave (✆473773). The Casanova Super Night Club is at 31 A'bish Makarios Ave (✆465082) and the Crazy Horse is at 185 J Nehru Ave, renamed from Homer Ave (✆473569). The British Council at 3 Museum St (✆445152) frequently has British-made films, though of necessity some are old.

The jetty at Gemikonağı in the north can no longer export the copper ores from the mines in the south.

16: PAPHOS

Aphrodite's birthplace

PAPHOS IS DIFFERENT. It is two towns in one — the newer Ktima at the top of the hill; and Kato Paphos, the old 'new' town on the coast. As a resort it is more down-market than either Limassol or Larnaca, its tourist hotels overflowing from the new town rather than forming a separate strip; it is arguably the most picturesque of the resorts south of the Green Line, and it certainly has more evidence of ancient history than anywhere else on the island.

Out of town. Paphos District has more isolated coves and beaches than any other part of Cyprus, each with its own hotel and bus service to Paphos town. South-east of the town, beyond Aphrodite's Temple at Kouklia, is the shingle beach and the rock of Petra tou Romiou where Ancient Greek mythology locates the birthplace of Aphrodite, the goddess of love, and north, beyond Polis, a year-round spring trickles into a little rocky pool that must be the playground of the gods — or the legendary Baths of Aphrodite.

PAPHOS IN HISTORY

APHRODITE'S TEMPLE &

Greek mythology claims that Pygmalion, an ancient King of Cyprus, carved an ivory statue of a maiden who was so beautiful that he fell in love with her. Seeing his quandary, Aphrodite brought the carving to life and named her Galatea, and when the ivory maiden gave Pygmalion a son, the child was named Paphos.

The original city of Paphos was 9 miles (15km) south-east of the present town on a site that had been occupied since the Late Bronze Age, and to avoid confusion with later communities we must think of it as Palaeopaphos, Old Paphos. It was here, around the 12th cent BC that, according to legend, King-and-High-Priest Cinyras built the Temple or Sanctuary of Aphrodite. This was the city which was to be one of the ten kingdoms of ancient Cyprus, and Homer, the Greek writer born somewhere between 1200 and 850BC, is among several authorities who tell of Old Paphos's great wealth. Homer specifically mentions in his *Iliad* that Cinyras had sent King Agamemnon of Mycenae a breastplate for the Trojan War.

But the town and the sanctuary stood for less than a century before being destroyed by an earth tremor.

Rebuilding. King Agapenor of Arcadia (now the Peloponnese) was returning home from the Trojan War when a storm blew him miles off course, to Cyprus, where he found the uninhabited ruins of Old Paphos. Proclaiming himself the King of Paphos he rebuilt the city and its Temple of Aphrodite.

Aphrodite was, understandably, among the most popular of the ancient gods and goddesses and she was revered in many temples around the eastern Mediterranean. Here in Old Paphos, the shrine closest to her birthplace in the sea foam, Agapenor had represented Aphrodite not as a beautiful female form but as a smooth column of stone, a phallic symbol, which was rubbed with oil at special ceremonies. And here in Old Paphos the springtime festival of the Goddess of Love soon took on a special meaning. In addition to the normal feasting, singing and dancing, the young maidens of the island, dressed in white robes and with wild flowers in their hair, joined the closing procession down to the coast where Aphrodite had emerged fully formed from the sea foam, and there they gave up their virginity in honour of their favourite goddess.

It is scarcely surprising that Old Paphos soon became Aphrodite's most popular and most important shrine, with pilgrims coming back year after year from as far afield as Athens and Phoenicia. Maybe there is a hint of the old pagan rites lingering in the modern ceremony of Kataklysmos when, after wining and dining, people take to the sea and soak each other.

It is difficult to imagine what the temple looked like in its prime. Homer had referred to the 'incense-burning altar' in the original, and Tacitus, the Roman historian born around 55AD and writing about Agapinor's rebuilt sanctuary with its stone column, speculated that the ancients didn't consider themselves worthy of capturing Aphrodite's beauty. Several Roman coins showed differing aspects of the temple from which we may suppose the column was in the centre of the floor while, outside, an altar at each side of the building had a perpetual flame on which, it was claimed, rain never fell: these altars could have been based on Homer's description of the original.

New Paphos. At the end of the 4th cent BC, Nicocles, the last ruler of Paphos, built a New Paphos on the coast to the north-west; it's now called Kato Paphos, 'Lower Paphos.'

New Paphos, of course, had its own Temple of Aphrodite still with a plain column of black stone in place of the goddess herself: this column has survived and is now in the Cyprus Museum, but the column from Old Paphos was lost in 1935.

Pilgrimages continued to come to both communities, with the new city gradually replacing the original town completely.

End of Aphrodite. And then, towards the close of the 4th cent AD, Emperor Theodosius banned all pagan cults and the temples of Aphrodite around the Roman Empire lost their appeal.

Kouklia. Meanwhile, Old Paphos had collapsed into decay, helped by the occasional earthquake. The Lusignans built a royal pavilion

The House of Dionysus has the island's most impressive in situ *mosaics.*

here, calling it La Covocle, probably from the Greek word *kouvouk-lia*, 'hemispherical,' describing the shape of the locality's tombs. The modern Cypriot village nearby corrupted the name to the present Kouklia.

Sugar. But that Lusignan Covocle was to become a large sugar refinery which in the 15th cent was built across the site of Aphrodite's Temple, destroying all but the foundations of Cinyras's orginal building.

Dig. A century later, Swiss and Venetian scholars recognised the significance of the area, and Louis Palma di Cesnola, the vandal of Tamassos, wrote of the 'fragments in marble and granite, bespeaking the wealth of a past age.' The first archaeological dig was in 1888 when a British team did little more than clear the site; the next major dig was from 1973 to '79 by a team financed by the University of Zurich.

Access and hours. There is now enough of Palaeopaphos exposed to justify a visit: turn north off the coast road by the sign to the temple; after 100ft (30m) turn right, and continue for 500m. The site is open in summer 0730-1930, closing in winter at sunset, and the fee is 50c.

Museum. An on-site museum is spread across two buildings, one covering an original mosaic floor, the other a reconstructed 13th-cent Lusignan fort. Among the many exhibits I found Bronze Age safety pins and fish-hooks particularly intriguing, but you can also see Mycenaean pottery, medieval potshards and Lusignan sugar-moulds.

NEW PAPHOS

New Paphos, better known as Kato Paphos, is the busy little town around the harbour, a mile from that *other* Paphos at the top of the hill, where you find the banks, the town hall, the bus stations and the telephone office.

New Paphos, which is a mere 2,400 years old, is now the centre of the district's tourist industry and is a charming example of the very old and the very new managing to live side by side — though some of the hotels by the Tombs of the Kings are too dazzling.

The walled city that King Nicocles founded, covered around 2,500 acres (1sq km) and had a harbour far larger than the present one; the breakwater stretched for almost a mile south-east from the present waterfront castle. When Alexander the Great died unexpectedly in 328BC without preparing an heir to his empire, his generals Ptolemy of Egypt and Antiochus of Antioch fought for the spoils, including Cyprus. Nicocles and his family were murdered to prevent them becoming hostage to either side, but eventually Cyprus fell to Ptolemy who made New Paphos his capital for the island in 294BC; the city remained the capital until 395AD when the Byzantines began their rule and transferred power to Salamis. These centuries of political prominence, followed by earthquakes, pirate raids, and 1,700 years of life as a small provincial town, have left New Paphos with a wealth of visible history comparable with some of the major sites in Asia Minor.

The small medieval castle guarding the harbour is open in summer Mon-Sat 0730-1330, and in winter Mon-Fri 0730-1400, Sat — 1300, for 50c.; &. Built by the Byzantines, rebuilt by the Lusignans in the 13th cent, demolished by the Venetians in 1570 for fear of its being seized by raiding pirates, it was rebuilt by the Ottomans soon after and, despite its chequered history, its tourist potential has yet to be realised. Behind it, within the confines of the original city walls, now scarcely visible, are the ruins of the **amphitheatre.**

Mosaics. A short walk north brings you to the most impressive display of in situ mosaics in Cyprus, protected by permanent modern buildings. The **House of Dionysus,** where the largest set of mosaics form the floor of a 3rd-cent AD villa, was discovered in 1962 by a peasant farmer whose plough went fractionally deeper than usual. The name Dionysus — Bacchus to the Romans — is arbitrary, chosen because the god is shown in several of the mosaics.

The 4th-cent AD **House of Aion,** discovered in 1983 by archaeologists from the University of Warsaw, is the most recently excavated and the smallest, with just two mosaics. Yet those two show the Queen of Sparta wooed by Zeus in the form of a swan; the young Dionysus being given by Hermes to his tutor; a beauty contest between Queen Cassiopeia and the Nereids (sea nymphs); an older Dionysus with the Satyrs; and Apollo declaring the punishment for Silenus Marsyas who challenged him to a flute-playing contest, and lost.

Warsaw University's archaeologists located the **House of Theseus** in 1965 and worked on it for several years. This house has mosaics of much larger stones, giving an appearance of coarseness, but the main floor undisputedly shows Theseus killing the Minotaur in the Labyrinth. Work is progressing on uncovering more mosaics here, notably a large circular one, and the protective building won't be put up until the extent of the house is known.

First Christian country? Nearby, the Polish diggers located the foundations and part of the floor of a once-imposing property which might have been the Roman governor's palace. If the assumption is correct, then this is probably the place where Governor Sergius Paulus met the apostles Paul and Barnabas in 45, and became converted to Christianity, thus making Cyprus the world's first country to have a Christian ruler. The site is not yet open to the public.

Hours and fee. A single ticket to all three houses costs C£1; open summer daily 0730-1930, in winter closing at sunset. Elevated walkways allow visitors to see all the mosaics without damaging them and, while there is sufficient light for photography, the colours lack brilliance, as a pebble from the sea does when it dries. &

The road leading back to the harbourside restaurants passes the ruins of the 5th-cent basilica-church of **Panayia Limaniotissa,** probably the burial place of King Eric 'Ever—good' Ejegod of Denmark, who died in Paphos in 1103 while on pilgrimage to the Holy Land. The basilica had been destroyed by 7th-cent Arab pirates and was destroyed again by a 'quake in 1153.

Castle of Forty Columns. The ruins of the Lusignan Castle of Saranta Kolones, the Castle of Forty Columns, feature on thousands of postcards. Begun at the end of the 12th cent, almost certainly on the ruins of a Byzantine castle which surrendered to Richard the Lionheart in 1191, the fortress was destroyed in the tremors of 1222 which flattened much of New Paphos.

Until modern times the overgrown site was dominated by a number of broken columns, which gave it its popular Greek name. Excavations began in 1957 and continued until the early 1980s, gradually revealing the nature of the jumbled masonry.

The ground plan is chaotic to the casual visitor, but the outer wall was square with a tower in each corner and another in the middle of each wall. Inside, the castle itself was also square and occupied the centre of the protected area, with quarters given to stables, a forge, a bathroom and two wells.

As the site is unfenced it is accessible at any time, without a fee.

Asklepion. As Asklepios was the Greek god of medicine and of healing, so a temple-cum-clinic raised to honour him was an asklepion. The only asklepion yet found in Cyprus was north-west of the Castle of Forty Columns, its few remaining pieces of masonry barely recognisable as a building before excavations began in the 1970s. The Polish archaeologists found several small figurines on site, including one of Asklepios himself, and near the House of Dionysus located several earthenware pots shaped like parts of the human

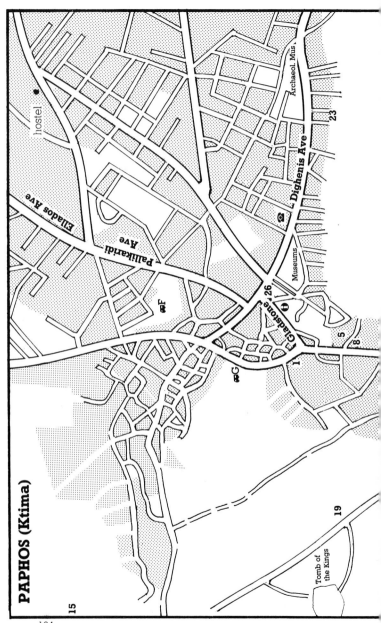

PAPHOS (Ktima)

hostel

Eliados Ave

Palikaridi Ave

Dighenis Ave

Archaeol. Mus.

Museums

Gladstone

Tomb of the Kings

15

23

26

5

8

19

164

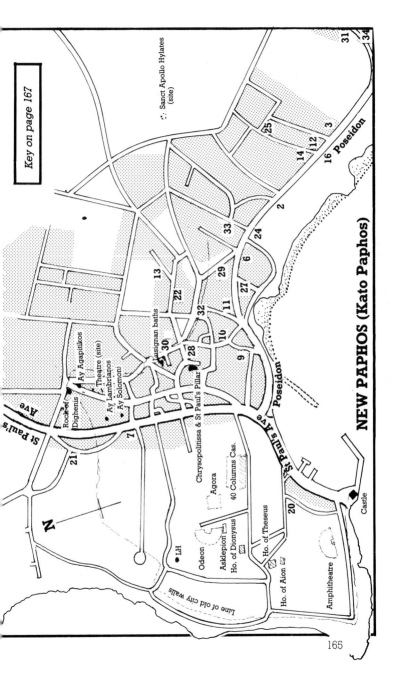

NEW PAPHOS (Kato Paphos)

Key on page 167

∴ Sanct Apollo Hylates (site)

N

St Paul's Ave

Rock of Dighenis
Ay Agapitkos
Theatre (site)
Ay Lambrianos
Ay Solomoni

Lusignan baths

Chrysopolitissa & St Paul's Pillar

Agora

40 Columns Cas.

Odeon

Asklepion
Ho. of Dionysus

Ho. of Theseus

Ho. of Aion

Amphitheatre

Ho. of Aion

Poseidon

St Paul's Ave

Castle

Line of old city walls

LH

31
34

25
3
12
14
16
2

33

24
6
29
27
13
22
32
11
30
16
28
9

21
7

20

Poseidon

body: an ear, a foot, a hand, but each capable of holding a balm used in treating ailments for that particular organ. The figurines, and the anatomical pots, are now in the District Museum in Paphos.

Asklepios has exerted a strange influence on medicine down to the present day. His mark of authority was a snake twisting around a staff, the symbol of modern medicine; and two of his daughters were named Hygea and Panakea, from which we have taken the words 'hygiene' and 'panacea,' the universal cure-all.

The asklepion, like the agora (ancient market place) and the totally-restored odeon (theatre) beside it, is unfenced. The tiny **odeon,** dated to the 2nd cent AD, was cleared of debris in 1973 and '74 and is now put to its original use several times a year.

Rock of Dighenis. Crossing St Paul's Avenue (Leoforos Apostolou Pavlou), the main road down to the harbour, you enter the shopping area of New Paphos where ancient ruins have been plundered for building stone, leaving little above ground level. The Rock of Dighenis is an exception, probably because of its size. Geologists explain that the rock occurred here naturally and is resistant to erosion, but the ancient folk claimed it had supernatural origins.

Dighenis fell in love with Regaena, the Queen of Cyprus, who promised to accept him if he first brought water to Paphos from the Kyrenia Range. Dighenis succeeded — the legend doesn't explain

The Monastery of Our Lady of the Golden Pomegranate is Chrysorroyiatissa's other name.

KEY TO HOTELS

1 Agapinor
2 Alexander The Great
3 Aloe
4 Aloma
5 Ambassador
6 Annabelle
7 Apollo
8 Axiothea
9 Daphne
10 Demetra
11 Dionysus
12 Evelyn
13 Fikardos
14 Georgiades-Marilena
15 Hilltop Gardens
16 Imperial Beach
17 Kings
18 Kissos
19 Land of the Kings
20 Limeniotissa
21 Melina
22 Mirofiori
23 New Olympus
24 Paphos Beach
25 Paphos Gardens
26 Paphos Palace
27 Porto Paphos
28 Pyramos
29 Rodothea
30 Sofiana
31 Theofane
32 Theoskepasti
33 Theseas
34 Veronica

Key to map on pages 164–165

how — but when Regaena broke her promise he hurled this boulder from the mountains at her palace . . . and missed.

Rock-chambers. The theatre is lost under the shops on the east side of Ayias Kyriakis St, and you will be lucky to find the rock-chambers of **Ayios Agapitikos** and his companion Ayios Missitikos, neither of whom is officially recognised by the Orthodox church. Agapitikos brought love, Missitikos brought hatred, and to activate these powers you must collect some dust from the relevant chamber and drop it in the drinking water of the person you want to love or hate.

The rock-chamber of Ayios Lambrianos and the catacomb of Ayia Solomoni are accessible from St Paul's Avenue, but neither is impressive. **St Solomoni's Catacomb** venerates the mother of seven children done to death in 158BC for their belief in Jehovah, and this catacomb was probably a pre-Christian Jewish synagogue. The tree inside the crumbling wall still has an occasional piece of rag tied to it, left in the hope that its owner will be blessed with good health.

Chrysopolitissa and St Paul's Pillar. The ruins of the 13th-cent Church of Chrysopolitissa mingle with the ruins of the largest early Byzantine castle on Cyprus, on a quarter-acre (1,000sq m) plot that is still being excavated. There are no signs to the site, and I had to go through a plain wooden gate to find the ruins, where archaeologists have now gone down many feet.

Before the dig began the only evidence above ground level was a white column, which is now the most obvious structure and appears to be part of the 14th-cent church more than a 3rd-cent basilica. That's a pity, for legend has long claimed this to be St Paul's Pillar, to which the apostle was tied and flogged in 45AD before he and Barnabas managed to convert the Roman Governor to Christianity. Paul wrote of his torments in II Corinthians XI, 23-25:

". . . In labours more abundant, in stripes above measure, in prisons more frequent, in deaths oft. Of the Jews five times received I forty stripes save one. Thrice I was beaten with rods, once I was stoned, thrice I suffered shipwreck. . ."

The 'forty less one' refers to the whip the Jews and Romans used, made of three thongs each of 13 'stripes' of leather. History records that Paul was flogged in Paphos — but it seems highly unlikely to have been at this column.

Theoskepasti. The parish church of Panayia Theoskepasti, near the long-vanished east gate to the old city, stands on the site of a 7th-cent church which, says tradition, was never raided by pirates because God always covered it with mist during an attack. Only one Saracen managed to find the church and when he entered to steal one of the icons painted by St Luke, a divine power sliced off his hands. You want proof? The incident is featured in another icon in this church.

Museums. Much of the treasure found in New Paphos's ancient ruins is on display in three museums, all of them in Ktima at the top of the hill.

The Archaeological Museum is open in summer Mon-Sat 0730-1330, 1600-1800, in winter Mon-Fri 0730-1400, 1500-1700, on Sat it closes for lunch an hour earlier; Sun 1000-1300 year round. Fee 50c. The Ethnographical and the Byzantine museums are both open in summer Mon-Sat 0900-1300, 1600-1900, but the Byzantine one doesn't reopen on Thurs or Sat afternoons. Winter hours are Mon-Sat 0900-1300, 1530-1730, again excluding those two afternoons. Fee, 50c.

NEW PAPHOS TODAY

New Paphos, Kato Paphos, is small enough to absorb in a day, but has plenty to keep you interested for a week even if you don't normally like wandering around ruins. The town is intimate and friendly, but parking is difficult at most times of the year and traffic jams are chaotic in high summer: avoid driving along the harbour even when vehicles are allowed down to the castle.

Despite the crowds, it is possible to find solitude down most backstreets where tourism has made less impact — though souvenir shops and bars are everywhere.

The harbour is wonderfully photogenic, and the end of the breakwater gives a good view of the municipal beach and the tourist hotels which stretch a little way south-east along the coast.

Beaches. The town beach is good, and there are several stretches of good sand by the main hotels, but elsewhere the sands are thin and you're more likely to be swimming off the rocks.

Boats. Ask at Steve's Pub on the waterfront and you'll be able to rent a self-drive motor boat for a leisurely cruise along the coast. The cost is C£25 per day for up to five people — or a party of 25 can charter a larger boat and crew for the day for C£75.

PAPHOS (KTIMA)

The new village at the top of the hill, a mile from New Paphos, is called Paphos without any 'new' or 'old.' Its optional name of Ktima — pronounced *k-teema* — means 'property,' and it was here that the Byzantine wealthy built their summer retreats. Ktima today is the administrative part of the Paphos twin-village complex, and is where to come for ordinary shopping — though the shopping centre is no rival to that of Limassol — for schools, buses, the post office and telephone exchange, hire cars, petrol, and the CTO office. West of the village, reached by taxi or on the Coral Bay bus, is Ktima's only ancient ruin, but it is the most impressive in the neighbourhood.

The Tombs of the Kings. A large outcrop of red sandstone gave the citizens of New Paphos ample scope for carving tombs and burial chambers from the living rock. All trace of human remains and of grave offerings vanished during Roman times but the tombs, chambers, caves and carved archways are still to be seen on this large site overlooking the sea.

Were kings buried here? The first burial chamber you see, cut into a large freestanding monolith, goes underground before leading you into a moderate-sized room, hacked from the heart of the rock and with separate alcoves for each corpse. We can guess that this chamber was for members of an influential family, but there is no evidence that the ruling classes were laid to rest on this hillside.

Elsewhere, tombs were carved almost at random and probably served as shelter for Christians during early persecutions and during later raids by pirates.

The site is open daily 0730-1930 in summer, to sunset in winter, for 50c.

AROUND THE DISTRICT

AIRPORT PICNIC SITE &

The spur road to Paphos Airport passes a grove of eucalyptus trees, with a picnic spot signposted; tap water is available. There is nothing of specific interest here, but I found the spot idyllic. A dirt track, passable to cars, leads down by a small conifer plantation to a lonely stretch of beach almost on the airport boundary fence.

AYII ANARGYRI

Just beyond the highest point along the road to Polis the village of Yiolou clings to a steep hillside. The next turning beyond the village leads to the mineral spring of Ayii Anargyri. The new Ayii Anargyri Hotel has piped the waters and now offers its guests the luxury of taking a mineral bath in their suite, but you can still do it the hard way by following the black plastic pipe southward into a small gorge and taking your bath *au naturel*.

The water has 1,860 parts per million of sulphates, with 590ppm

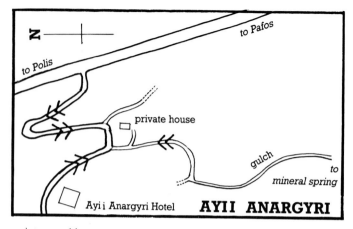

to Pafos

to Polis

N

private house

gulch

to
mineral spring

Ayi i Anargyri Hotel **AYII ANARGYRI**

calcium and lesser amounts of chlorine, sodium and magnesium, and is claimed to ease arthritis, spinal problems, gastritis and ulcers.

AYIOS NEOPHYTOS

Saint Neophytos, born around 1134 in Lefkara, was a hermit. He moved from the Monastery of Chrysostomos (now in North Cyprus) to the Paphos area in 1159, hacked several caves from the side of a ravine some six miles (9.5km) north of the town and so established a small monastic community. The cave church, now called the Ecleistra, has frescoes from the 12th to the 15th cents, including one of Neophytos himself done in 1183.

The present monastery, an austere building on the outside, stands around 100m from those original caves and surrounds an early church which has frescoes from the 15th cent, as well as the mortal remains of Saint Neophytos which were found in 1750.

Neophytos was a chronicler of considerable esteem, around 30 of his manuscripts surviving in the capials of Europe, although the University Library of Edinburgh has a copy of his greatest work, the Ritual Ordinance, made in 1214 by Basil, a priest of Paphos. The manuscript is open to view on special request.

BATHS OF APHRODITE

Seven miles (11km) north-west of Polis the tarmac road ends in a large car park with a CTO restaurant. From here a signed footpath leads 600ft (200m) into the scrubland on the lonely Akamas Peninsula to a small spring which flows all year round.

The water trickles from the limestone and falls around 15ft (5m) into a permanent pool about 12ft (4m) across: this is the Baths of Aphrodite, though there is only one.

It's a pleasant spot, though slightly overgrown, but it had no place in the original cult of Aphrodite as the region has always been uninhabited. Legend claims that young men whom Aphrodite spurned while she was bathing, went through the scrub to the Spring of Oblivion for a cold shower that would make them forget her.

The spring is unfenced and there's no admission fee.

Fontana Amorosa. A third spring, the Fontana Amorosa, is near the tip of the Akamas Peninsula at the end of a dirt road impassable to saloon cars. The spring here feeds several wells, one of which supposedly has the power to make anybody who drinks its water fall in love: this could be a good antidote to a shower from the Spring of Oblivion before a return visit to the Baths of Aphrodite! The walk to the Fontana Amorosa is pleasant, with good views of the Troodos Mountains, but the well is unrewarding.

Nature trail. From Aphrodite's Baths a simple nature trail leads through the woodland and back to the car park.

CORAL BAY

Coral Bay, one of several small coves on the west coast, takes its popular name from the traces of coral occasionally found on the beach, but it's also known as Maa. Maa Beach is small, with fine sand, and access through a large car park where there's a tiny bar. The village now being built here has up-market villas.

The road back to Paphos passes another stretch of sand by the Helios Bay Hotel; north, a minor road leads to **Ayios Yeoryios** whose church stands in isolation with not a single house left in the village. Cape Drepanon is a beautiful headland with a fishing harbour tucked into the base of the cliff; on the clifftop St George's restaurant grills its fish dishes to perfection.

A few ancient rock tombs cut into the top of the cliff are difficult to find, and probably not worth the effort. The beach begins north of the headland and parallels the track leading to **Lara Bay** and its turtle hatchery. You are now at the furthermost point of human habitation on the west coast of Akamas, and it's splendid country for walking provided you take everything you need and avoid the high temperatures of midsummer.

PETRA TOU ROMIOU

Petra Tou Romiou, the 'Rock of the Roman,' is the legendary birthplace of Aphrodite, goddess of love, who walked from the sea foam a fully-developed woman. Aphrodite, known to the Romans as Venus, was the wife of Hephaestus (Vulcan, the god who made volcanoes) and the mistress of Ares (Mars), Hermes (Mercury), Dionysus (Bacchus) and Poseidon (Neptune), as well as several mortal men.

But forget the mythology. Come to this rugged stretch of coastline, the most beautiful south of the Green Line and arguably the best on the island, and enjoy the scenery.

Access. Paths lead down to the beach which is too gritty for good sandcastles, but there's hours of fun to be had in wading around the rocks: don't swim if the wind is any stronger than a light breeze. A CTO pavilion is nearby (&), but access to the area is either in your hire car or by getting off a scheduled bus service along the coast road.

POLIS and Lachi.

Polis is a small resort at the end of the road north from Paphos. It has six tourist hotels, the smartest warranting two stars, but the scattering of notices offering rooms to rent for long or short periods labels it a downmarket resort.

Lachi, also spelled Latchi and Latsi, is a tiny fishing hamlet a mile west of Polis where a few new villas are creating a mid-market atmosphere.

The charm of Polis lies in its solitude, its casual attitude to life, and the splendid countryside all around; you make your own entertainment by day and by night, but for a touch of excitement you can hire a motorboat from Nicandro's Restaurant at Lachi.

The beach is a strange reversal of the normal, with large stones at the water's edge and the fine sand carried to the top of the beach by winds.

The first recorded settlement on this bay was known as Marion, but during the Ptolemaic dynasty in was renamed Arsinoe and was famed for its copper and gold.

Pomos. The coast road from Polis leads north-east towards Kokkina, the village which had a turbulent history between independence and the Turkish intervention of 1974. The road is good, serving the agricultural vilages on the slopes of the Troodos Mountains, and passes several stretches of totally undeveloped beach. By Kato Yialia a headland of flat rocks marks a change in the scenery, and the good road ends on the further side of Pomos.

For the next mile or two you travel on a narrow, winding lane that predates the events of 1974 until, suddenly, you see an oil drum standing in the middle of the road and you realise you are at journey's end. Kokkina is just ahead, but it's now renamed Erenköy and is in North Cyprus.

If you make a long detour into the foothills along unsignposted lanes, which also take you into Nicosia District, you may eventually find yourself on the coast again at Kato Pyrgos, which must be journey's end. The only other traffic you're likely to meet here is a Land Rover with UNFICYP registration plates. And, for interest, the single-track road meanders on for miles in North Cyprus, almost to the village of Karavostasi, now Gemikonağı.

YEROSKIPOU

Yeroskipou is an attractive village two miles (1.5km) east of Ktima, often confusingly spelled with a G- at the front and an -s at the back.

The name in Greek, Yeros Kipos, means 'sacred garden' and refers to the well-watered orchard and garden that stood here from recorded history until its spring dried up and it faded from memory.

The sacred garden was a popular stopover for pilgrims walking from New Paphos harbour to attend the orgies at the Temple of Aphrodite in Old Paphos, and a few of its mulberry trees are still standing, testimony to the silk industry that thrived here until the introduction of nylon.

Yeroskipou's attractions for the modern traveller are its growing Turkish delight industry — the delicacy is known locally as *loukoumia* — its church, and its museum.

The Church of Ayia Paraskevi is a 10th-cent Byzantine building with two aisles and five domes, the only one of its kind on the island; its frescoes have been dated to the 15th cent and earlier.

The Folk Art Museum, opened in 1976, is in the building which served as the British Consulate from 1799 to 1856. Admiral Nelson was looking for Napoleon's fleet in the eastern Mediterranean and called in at Paphos for news; his Commodore Sir William Smith found the time to appoint a British consul here at Yeroskipou before Nelson sailed on and eventually met Napoleon at the Battle of the Nile (see *Discover Malta*). The museum is open in summer, Mon-Sat 0730-1330; in winter Mon-Fri 0730-1400, Sat 0730-1300, for 50c.

HOTELS

Five-star: Imperial Beach, 484⋈, ☎ ⇆ ✕ ✿; **Four-star:** Alexander The Great, 344⋈, ☎ ⇆ ✕ ✿; Annabelle, 436⋈, ☎ ⇆ ✕ ₺; Cypria Maris, Poseidon, 474⋈, ☎ ⇆ ✕ ₺; Laoura Beach, Tomb of Kings Rd, 368⋈, ☎ ⇆ ✕ ₺; Ledra Beach, Poseidon, 520⋈, ☎ ⇆ ✕ ₺ ✿; Paphos Beach, 380⋈, ☎ ⇆ ✕ ₺ ✿; **Three-star:** Aloe, 213⋈, ☎ ⇆ ✕ ₺; Avlida, Tomb of Kings Rd, 190⋈, ☎ ⇆ ✕; Cynthiana Beach, Coral Bay Rd, 262⋈, ☎ ⇆ ✕ ✿; Dionysos, 179⋈, ☎ ⇆ ✕ ₺ T; Kissos, 137⋈, ☎ ⇆ ✕ ₺; Melina, 57⋈, ☎ ⇆ ✕ T; Nereus Sunotel, Constantia St, 144⋈, ☎ ⇆ ✕; Paphiana, Konia village, 162⋈, ☎ ⇆ ✕ ₺; Paphian Bay, Poseidon, 420⋈, ☎ ⇆ ✕; Paphiessa, Philonos St, 66⋈, ☎ ⇆ ✕ T; Porto Paphos, 97⋈, ☎ ⇆ ✕; Queen Bay, Coral Bay Rd, 353⋈, ☎ ⇆ ✕ ₺ ✿; Roman, Ay. Lambrianou St, 133⋈, ☎ ⇆ ✕ ₺ T; Theofano, 222⋈, ☎ ⇆ ✕; Veronica, 158⋈, ☎ ⇆ ✕; **Two-star:** Apollo, 61⋈, ☎ ⇆ ✕ ₺ T; Axiothea, 70⋈, ☎ ✕ T; King's, 51⋈, ☎ ⇆ ✕; Polis village, 108⋈, ☎ ⇆ ✕ ₺; Olympus, 43⋈, ☎ ✕ T; **One-star:** Agapinor, 50⋈, ☎ ✕ T; Ayii Anargyri, Yiolou village, 36⋈, ✕; G & P Latsi, Lachi village, 17⋈, ✿; Pyramos, 38⋈, T; Souli, Neokhorio village, 17⋈, ✕; Tylo Beach, Kato Pyrgos village, 60⋈, ✕; Yeronisos, Ayios Yeoryios village, 21⋈, ✕ ✿; **unclassified:** Akamas, Polis village, 34⋈, Paphos Palace, 27⋈, T.

GUEST HOUSES (CTO listed)

Pelican Inn, St Pauls Ave, 11⋈, T; Trianon, Makarios Ave, T.

APART-HOTELS

Aloma, 36🛏, T; Ambassador, 32🛏, T; Anemi, Kikerou St, 52🛏, ☎ ⌂ ♿ T; Bacchus, Coral Bay, 198🛏, ☎ ⌂ ❀; Daphne, 118🛏, ☎ ⌂ ♿ T; Demetra, 54🛏, ☎ T; Elia, Polis, 60🛏, ⌂; Euronest, Coral Bay, 40🛏, ☎ ⌂; Evelyn, 14🛏; Fikardos, 22🛏, T; Follow The Sun, Polis, 30🛏, ☎ ⌂; Georgiades-Marilena, 16🛏; Helios Bay, Coral Bay Rd, 64🛏, ☎ ⌂ ❀; Hilltop Gardens, 60🛏, ⌂; Kefalonitis, Pyramos St, 64🛏, ☎ ⌂ T; Land of the Kings, 208🛏, ⌂; Mariniki, Tomb of Kings Rd, 20🛏; Mirofiori, 107🛏, ☎ ⌂ T; Nicos & Olympia, Polis, 20🛏, ☎; Pandream, Poseidon, 48🛏, ☎ ⌂; Paphiessa, Philonos St, 52🛏, ☎ ⌂ T; Paphos Gardens Narkissus, 56🛏, ⌂; Rania, Poseidon, 112🛏, ☎ ⌂ ♿; Rodothea, 86🛏, ☎ ♿ T; Sofianna, 127🛏, ☎ ⌂ T; Stefanos, Polis, 64🛏, ☎ ⌂; Tasmaria, Tomb of Kings Rd, 60🛏, ☎ ⌂; Theseas, 40🛏, ☎ T; Vougenvilea, Polis, 20🛏, ☎.

YOUTH HOSTEL

The hostel (see map) has 20 beds in three rooms, with communal sleeping. The building is closed 0900-1600.

CAMPING

Polis Camping, 200 sites, C£1.50 per day per tent plus C£1 per day per person; Yeroskipou Zenon Gardens Camping, Yeroskipou, 95 sites, C£1 per tent, then as above.

RESTAURANTS

Pubs, cafes, bars and restaurants proliferate around the harbour in New Paphos. They are less obvious in Ktima but you'll find a few on Gladstone St. There are restaurants, too, at Coral Bay, Ayios Yeoryios, Polis and Lachi.

MINI-MOTOR BIKE HIRE

There are many places in Polis, including the campsite, where you can hire a Yamaha or similar 50cc mini-motor cycle. Rates are around C£3 per day for up to three days, C£2.50 per day for longer. The machines are not for long-distance use and helmets are seldom supplied. Polis campsite also has 350cc trials bikes at C£10 a day for up to three days.

17: TROODOS

Mountains and monasteries

THE TROODOS MOUNTAINS are the most magical part of the island. In a hire car, on your mountain cycle, or on foot, you can explore the heartland of Cyprus and feel yourself far from the bustle of towns, yet Limassol is only half an hour's drive from Troodos village and you can reach Nicosia comfortably in two hours even allowing for the hairpin bends.

The Troodos area is bisected north and south by the excellent new motor road, B8 to Limassol and B9 to Nicosia, though the numbers are seldom used. On the east-west axis, things are different. You may take all day to drive from Mt Olympus to Makheras Monastery along roads that vary startlingly from single-track lanes that contort themselves across the contours, to new roads wide enough to take three buses side by side, to unsurfaced tracks that crawl up and down the slopes and may have a loose boulder blocking the way around the next bend.

The climate varies considerably. In winter the mountaintops are snow-covered and many minor roads are impassable. In summer and autumn you can sunbathe in the thinner air, then take two paces into the shade of a tree and feel cool. And in spring you can crunch your way across snowfields that are frozen solid at daybreak but are mountain streams by mid afternoon.

For most of the time you are in valleys or on ridges, enveloped deep in the mountains, but occasionally as you reach a local summit the landscape of lower Cyprus unfolds itself before you, and when you stand near the top of Mt Olympus on a clear day you can see Paphos, Cape Gata, Nicosia, and the Kyrenia Mountains in North Cyprus. The big difference between these two ranges is that you go *into* the Troodos but you go *on* the Kyrenia Mountains. The Troodos are essentially introspective, a world within a world.

Forests. The Troodos Mountains are volcanic, but have been extinct for millennia, and the ample winter rains have rounded their contours and given a lush covering of mixed woodland. Throughout the ages, Cyprus's rulers have exploited this timber wherever the gradients allowed, never bothering to replant; the Troodos supplied most of the timber used in the Africa Campaign of World War Two, including almost every telephone pole from Cairo to Tunis. The British began a programme of conservation and reforestation which the

Asinou Church stands in isolation in the Troodos foothills.

independent government has intensified, involving the local people with an awareness of the need for a healthy forest. The result is that the Troodos Mountains now have what is claimed to be the best-managed woodlands in the eastern Mediterranean.

Main valleys. The massif is split by nature into several regions; from Mt Oylmpus at 6,401ft (1,951m) a spur runs north-west to Tryplos mountain at 4,620ft (1,408m) and on to the summit of Zakharou at 3,984ft (1,214m) with a splendid view of Polis and the Akamas Peninsula. The peak of Aphami at 3,784ft (1,153m) stands to the south-west, and another spur runs east to Kionia at 4,663ft (1,420m), near Makheras Monastery. Between these and lesser spurs are the valleys of Pitsilia to the south-east, noted for its vineyards and orchards; the Solea to the north, an area of dense conifer forest named from King Solon who ruled the ancient Kingdom of Soli, now in North Cyprus; and the Marathasa to the north-west, home of cherry orchards and the birthplace and tomb of Archbishop-President Makarios.

AROUND THE REGION

Most of the places in this chapter are without public transport or have at the most one ancient charabanc service a day. You need a car or a cycle — and a few locations are accessible only on foot.

AGROS

Agros, at 3,000ft on a south-facing slope, is the commercial centre of the Pitsilia valley, and with a good road down to Limassol. The 9th-cent monastery founded by monks from Constantinople was replaced in the 19th cent by a pseudo-Byzantine church. The village has three hotels.

ASINOU CHURCH &

The tiny 12th-cent church of Asinou is considered to be the most interesting Byzantine building on the island, though I feel this is an exaggeration. The church stands in near isolation except for the restaurant opposite and has an intriguing marble plaque by the gate which states that Asinou and eight other churches 'have been included in the World Heritage list.'

Inside, you find a barrel-vaulted roof and some excellent frescos, some dating back to the 12th cent.

Access. Access is difficult. Asinou is signposted from the main B9 road south of the E908 junction to Kalopanayiotis, but this takes you along 7 miles (11km) of dirt road from Ayios Theodhoros. The best approach is from the north, via Kato Koutraphas and Nikitari, especially as you need to stop at Nikitari to get the church key from a shop in the village centre with a tiny sign saying 'Asino Church Information.' The Nikitari priest, who doesn't speak a word of English, will probably come with you, and will expect a tip.

AYIA MONI MONASTERY &

Moni means 'monastery,' which gives Ayia Moni the Greek name of 'Holy Monastery.' Two miles (3km) south of Chrysorroyatissa, Ayia Moni stands on the site of a tiny 4th-cent BC Temple of Hera, the goddess who was both sister and wife to Zeus, and the mother of Ares. Hera, Juno to the Romans, was responsible for safe childbirth and was therefore associated with living creatures, particularly the pomegranate, the ancient symbol of fertility, and the cow; but here at this temple founded by King Nikoklis of Paphos the ancient Greeks sacrificed many animals in Hera's name.

Small galvanised iron screens hinged on the outer walls protect ancient Greek script, and at the back of the monastery you can see slots in the wall to allow people to consult the oracle (fortune-teller) hidden inside.

Ayia Moni, which comes under the control of Kykko Monastery, has been uninhabited since the Ottoman invasion of 1571 but is kept in good repair. It is among the smallest of monasteries on the island, its main hall measuring just 25ft by 22ft (7.5m by 6.5m) and now standing starkly bare. The nearby church is around 50ft (15m) long, a considerable improvement on the original church built in 310 by St Nikolas of Turkey — the original Father Christmas — which was four paces by three.

AYIOS NIKOLAOS TIS STEGIS

'St Nikolaos of the Roof' is an unusual church three miles (4km) south-west of Kakopetria along a poor track, with paper signs in plastic bags showing the way.

Steps lead down to the small plot where the church and its monastery were built in the 11th cent. The monastery was demolished some time in the 19th cent but the church remains, its original

Byzantine roof now protected by a much later one that stands several feet above it. Legends abound in Cyprus, but there is no explanation in fact or fiction why this church should have two roofs.

The interior walls of the church, open Mon-Sat 0900-1600, Sun 1100-1600 for a donation, are covered from floor to the original barrel-vaulted ceiling with frescos, except where the original plaster has crumbled. The painting is not of the best but the overall impression is of a gallery of Byzantine art from 11th to 15th cents.

Tomb of the Three Bishops. During the 19th cent Ottoman dominion, Turkish bandits roaming the island and looting wherever they could, struck Ayios Nikolaos tis Stegis while three bishops were staying at the monastery. The bishops fled into the mountains taking the order's treasures, which they managed to hide before the bandits caught them. No treasure: no bishops. The villagers of Kakopetria found the headless bodies in the forest and buried them on the spot. If you're prepared to search for a day or two you may find the three tombs somewhere on the mountainside; if you're lucky you might find the treasure of Ayios Nikolaos as well.

Aerial ropeway. Many maps show a chrome washer and an aerial ropeway up the valley from the church. The chrome mine on the north flank of Mt Olympus closed in 1974 and the ropeway and washer have gone.

CALEDONIAN FALLS

The Caledonian Falls is a beauty spot on the southern flank of Mt Olympus, accessible only on foot with an hour's easy hike in each direction. The southern access is hidden on the left of the trout farm (and that's worth looking at) on the main road north of Pano Platres; the northern access is around three miles north along the main road — keep a keen lookout for the sign, carved into a finger-post. Both tracks merge three-quarters of the way in, so hikers can use this route to bypass the tarmac road.

CEDAR VALLEY

Cedar Valley, on the southern slope of Mt Tryplos, is probably the most impressive beauty spot within the Troodos, as well as having a *cedrus brevifolia* tree estimated to have germinated around 1135, before Richard the Lionheart came here on the Third Crusade. Forestry workers estimate its height at almost 100ft (30m) and its total volume at 360 cubic feet (10.2cu m); for comparison, the world's largest tree in volume, General Sherman in California's Sequioa National Park, is well over 2,000 years old and is 275ft (83m) high, with a volume of 52,500 cu ft (1,500cu m).

Around 50,000 cedars grow in the valley, leaving a pleasant perfume on hot days.

Access. In Pano Panayia village take the side road by the Oak Tree Restaurant and after 1.5 miles (2.4km) follow signs to Ayios Yeoryios; at 5.2 miles (8.3km) the tarmac ends in a car park. Take the dirt road onward – at 0.6 mile (1km) a signpost can easily be missed – and go past the tiny isolated Ayios Yeoryios Church to the end of the track. A 1.5 mile (2km) hike is available through the most interesting part of Cedar Valley.

Ayios Yeoryios ton Emnon. The Church of St George, Ayios Yeoryios ton Emnon, was built at the request of President Makarios only a few days before he died, as the region held special memories for him. His father grazed sheep up here in the summer and the young Makarios had spent many nights on the mountain. The previous church on the site held an icon of St George, painted in 1772, which had long been moved to Panayia's Church of St George.

CHRYSORROYIATISSA &

The Monastery of Our Lady of the Golden Pomegranate, which is easier to say than Chrysorroyiatissa, stands around 3,750ft (1,125m) on Mount Royia, one of the most westerly spurs of the Troodos. Its setting is not only beautiful but spectacular, and the view from here extends to Paphos and the sea.

Legend, which has had so much to contribute to Cypriot history, claims that the monk Ignatius, investigating a fire on a beach near Paphos, found it to be coming from an icon of the Virgin Mary which was miraculously undamaged.

After Ignatius had salvaged the icon, he heard the Virgin Mary tell him to build a place of worship for it on the slopes of Mt Royia, Pomegranate Mountain. This was the beginning of the Monastery of Chrysorroyiatissa , back in the 12th cent, and Ignatius saw it expand to almost 70 brethren in his lifetime.

The present monastery was built around 1770 on the plan that has endured down the centuries and which almost all monasteries follow, with minor variations; a hollow square in two storeys, with offices, workshops, souvenir shops and small chapels on the ground floor and with dormitories above. And inside the protective courtyard stands the church, guarding all its treasures.

Chrysorroyiatissa has recently reintroduced its own special Monte Royia wine, rosé (blush), dry red or dry white, selling from the cellar shop from C£1.50 to C£5 per bottle.

The monastery also has a studio for the restoration of icons, established by a recent abbot who is famed as the greatest authority in Cyprus on the subject. As a result, the church is particularly well endowed with icons and has, among its other treasures, a holy shroud embroidered by Russian Orthodox priests in 1797. And cat-lovers should be pleased with the many feline inhabitants at the Golden Pomegranate.

On the edge of Chrysorroyiatissa's forecourt a *pinus brutia* tree leans precariously over the precipice, supporting a sign that states the tree 'is 110 years old' but forgets to add how old the sign is.

The monastery holds an important religious ceremony on 15 August, drawing large crowds, but on almost any other day the casual visitor might expect to find accommodation here and, as in all monasteries, there is no fee — you are expected to make a donation.

FIGARDOU

The village of Figardou, also written as Phikardou, is on a dirt road in the foothills of the Troodos, north of Makheras Monastery, and has therefore been bypassed by progress leaving its wooden houses virtually as they were when built in the 18th cent. The entire village is now under a preservation order.

GALATA

The new road across the Troodos Mountains bypasses every village, allowing Galata to preserve something of its older way of life yet benefiting from progress in the way that Figardou cannot.

Galata has several 'painted churches,' which refers to frescoes on the inner walls and not to painted plasterwork on the outside: Ayios Sozomenos, completed in 1513 and standing in the middle of the village; the small Ayia Paraskevi on the old road to Kakopetria, finished in 1514 and with frescoes from that date; Panayia Podithou, which was part of a monastery when built in 1502; and Panayia Theotokos, or the Archangel Michael, of 1514, a timber-roofed chapel north of the village.

KAKOPETRIA

Look for 'bad stones' — *kako petria* — when you come to this unique village on the north slope of the Troodos. The bad stones were boulders washed from the upper slopes and standing in the way of progress when settlers first moved into the valley.

Petra tou Androginou. (♿ with difficulty) Those that could be moved with levers were cleared; those that couldn't had houses built around and on them — except for Petra tou Androginou, the 'Stone of the Husband and Wife' the largest in the village and which was standing precariously on the spur of land where two streams meet. Over the centuries newly-weds in the village established the custom of walking around the stone, then standing on it to wish themselves lifelong love, as enduring as the boulder itself.

Legend claims that one couple were not so lucky. The stone shuddered, threw them off, then crushed them, which is why Petra tou Androginou is now firmly cemented in place. I find the legend impossible to believe for, if that giant boulder were rolling down the mountainside, I cannot see why it should have stopped where it is instead of crashing into the river. Look for yourself; the Husband and Wife Rock is up Paleas Kakopetrias St, beside the Village Pub and Restaurant which is on the upstream side of the bridge in the village centre.

Maryland at the Mill. Fifty yards away a dirt road leads upstream to an ancient watermill about the size of a small peasant cottage. Generations ago it was the most important mill for miles around, and farmers brought their grain here on muleback from as far afield as Paphos and Nicosia, sometimes having to wait several days for it to be milled. The fee was a quarter-oke of flour for every 22 okes of grain, and the mill continued grinding until 1950. Its horizontally-mounted paddle wheel is still visible beneath the floor of the stable, which is now a souvenir shop.

Hydro-electric. In order to drive the paddle wheel, the miller needed a vertical fall of water, brought along a small canal from further upstream. This prompted another villager to build a similar system with a 40ft (12m) drop of water onto a vertically-mounted wheel – which generated electricity. Kakopetria was therefore the second village in Cyprus to have a public electricity supply (the first was Morphou, now Güzelyurt), beginning in September 1927 and running until 1959 when the electricity board took over.

Hydro power was available from sunset until late in the evening, which meant that the villagers had to irrigate their fields by night, when the power station stopped work. The little canal and the tower which gave the 40-ft drop are still visible on the hillside, and there is a suggestion that the power station may be reopened as a museum piece.

Restaurant. (♿ using the lift) The most prominent building by the old water mill is a three-storey structure set into the hillside (the top floor has ground-level access at the rear) and looking like a medieval castle with modern Oriental balconies, though it was completed in 1987. This is Maryland at the Mill, one of the smartest

Ayios Sozomenos, one of Galata's 'painted churches.'

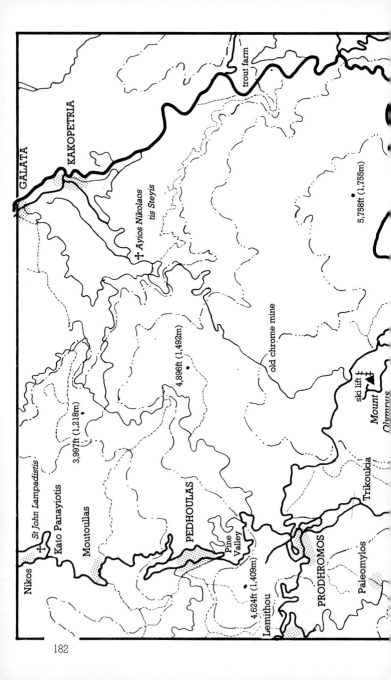

GALATA

KAKOPETRIA

trout farm

5,758ft (1,755m)

† *Ayios Nikolaos
tis Steyis*

old chrome mine

4,896ft (1,492m)

ski lift

*Mount
Olympus*

3,997ft (1,218m)

St John Lampadistis

Kato Panayiotis

Nikos

†

Moutoullas

PEDHOULAS

Pine
Valley

Trikoukia

PRODHROMOS

Paleomylos

4,624ft (1,409m)

Lemithou

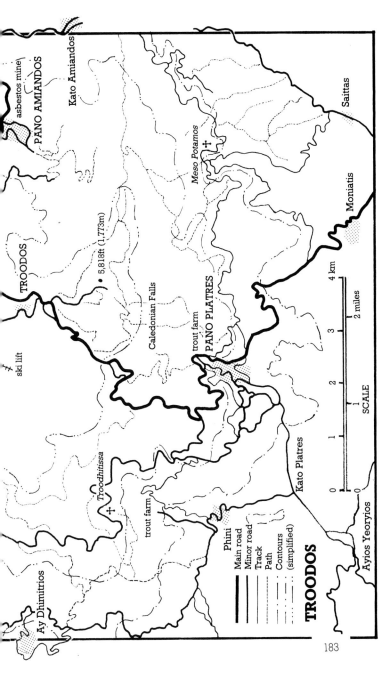

TROODOS

asbestos mine

PANO AMIANDOS

Kato Amiandos

Saittas

TROODOS

ski lift

• 5,818ft (1,773m)

Meso Potamos

Moniatis

Caledonian Falls

trout farm

PANO PLATRES

Troodhitissa

trout farm

Phini

Kato Platres

Ay Dhimitrios

Ayios Yeoryios

					SCALE		
0	1	2	3	4 km			
0		1		2 miles			

Main road

Minor road

Track

Path

Contours
(simplified)

183

restaurants on the island and certainly graced with the most distinctive location; its 400 seatings attract coachloads of tourists for lunch.

The restaurant's owner, John Aristides, nephew of the pioneering electrician, and his companion Dr Varos Karayioryis, campaigned for Kakopetria village to be placed under a preservation order and in 1976 they succeeded. From near dereliction at independence, the village is now a minor tourist attraction in its own right and most of the old houses are being restored.

Agilades. In 1938, amateur archaeologists found the remains of a 5th cent BC settlement with a Temple of Athena, the goddess of wisdom and of war, at the start of the track up to Ayios Nikolaos tis Stegis church. Athena was sometimes considered part human, hence her other name Parthenos, and the Parthenon in Athens (Athena's city) was built for her.

Old industries. Kakopetria has grown vines for centuries and until recent years the production of the local wine was a cottage industry, with each house having an earthenware wine jar around 6ft (2m) in diameter in a ground-floor room; the jars were so big that the house was built around them. A few families also distilled the grapeskins to make a potent spirit called *zivania*. These crafts have now gone and though a few houses still keep their wine jars your best chance of seeing one, even though it's smaller, is in Makarios's birthplace in Panayia.

Until the middle of this century Kakopetria's women were in the silk industry, from raising the silkworms to spinning and weaving the finished cloth; the British Government recruited them in World War Two to make the material for parachutes but later they were among the many economic victims of the invention of nylon. And several of the men were experienced saddlemakers who took their skills around the island each year from the first week in Lent (before Easter) to mid September. We all know what put an end to their trade.

Lampadou. Kakopetria is one of four communities that lay claim to being the site of Lampadou, birthplace of St John Lampadestis and the St Heraklidios who founded the monastery near Tamassos; the other claimants are Mitsero, Agros, and Kalopanayiotis.

KALOPANAYIOTIS

Kalopanayiotis probably has the strongest claim to being the site of old Lampadou as the deserted Monastery of St John Lampadistis ♿ is in the village, and the monastery's main church is dedicated to St Heraklidios. The fabric ranges from Byzantine to 18th cent and has many frescoes — and to see them you need to borrow the key from the local priest whose church is a short way uphill.

Kalopanayiotis also has three sulphur springs claimed to be beneficial for sufferers of digestive problems, anaemia, eczema, rheumatism, depression, and an accelerated heartbeat. The village's hotels have access to the waters.

KILANI

Kilani, the village where Emperor Comnenus took refuge from Richard the Lionheart, is in a wine-producing area. Its 12th-cent church of Ayia Mavri has 15th-cent frescoes.

KYKKO &

Kykko is the most popular, the wealthiest, the largest and certainly the best decorated monastery in Cyprus. Spotlessly clean and with the smell of polish lingering on the air, the first-floor balcony, overlooking the courtyard and its well, is lined with some of the best frescoes I have seen. Their style, colour, and the liberal use of gold leaf, make them look almost like mosaics.

The church, standing in the middle of the court, has more treasures than any other, the most important icon being of the Virgin Mary with the infant Jesus, allegedly one of the three painted by St Luke but now covered with silver to hide or protect the original work. Until more enlightened times, the peasants believed this icon to have the ability to bring rain when taken to the nearest mountaintop. And the church clock, of course, is never altered to summer time (daylight saving time).

The Byzantine Emperor Alexios Comnenus, an ancestor of Isaac who surrendered Cyprus to Richard Lionheart, founded the monastery in 1100 and presented St Luke's icon to it; despite several fires, the icon has presumably survived. The monastery's name comes from the species of oak, *quercus coccisera,* found in the locality.

Access. Kykko is signposted from Panayia and Pedhoulas. The road is twisty and narrow, but well-surfaced; if you're driving be prepared to meet several coachloads of tourists. As the monastery is one of those that accepts overnight guests, the independent traveller could plan his itinerary around a night here — but rooms are issued on a first-come basis.

Makarios. Michael Makarios, destined to be independent Cyprus's first president, came to Kykko in the late 1920s as a cadet soon after finishing his elementary schooling. The young Makarios studied his Gymnasium (high-school) lessons at Kykko and moved on to the Pancyprian Gymnasium from where he graduated in 1936 with fees paid by the monastery. Scholarships took him on to universities in Athens and Boston (Mass), and he was in the USA when he learned he'd been elected to the Bishopric of Kitium, in April 1948.

Soon politics became as important as religion in his life's work, and when Makarios joined General Grivas in the EOKA campaign, Kykko Monastery provided both men with a safe haven and used its contacts in the Orthodox church to raise funds and recruit helpers for EOKA.

Coup. Makarios soon saw that the drive for union with Greece was alienating the Turkish Cypriot minority and, as president, his policy was for continued independence. Greek army officers in Cyprus tried to assassinate him on 15 July 1974, but Makarios escaped to his haven at Kykko Monastery. It was from here that he broadcast his defiance and so proved he had survived the attempt. Now an ex-president, he was smuggled down to Paphos from where the British took him by helicopter to Akrotiri and on to London and exile. Five days after the coup the Turkish Army landed on the north coast by Kyrenia.

Throni. Makarios died in August 1977 and, at his wish, was buried at Throni, 1.5 miles from Kykko. His tomb now stands at the spot where those earlier peasants had come to pray for rain, bearing St Luke's icon in procession.

LAGOUDERA

For the best examples of frescoes in Cyprus, calculated in terms of quality as well as quantity, come to Lagoudera's 12th-cent church on the northern flanks of the Troodos. The paintings date back to 1192 and a team from Harvard University cleaned and restored them a few years ago. The nativity scene on the vaulted ceiling is among the largest.

Access. If you're in a hurry take the Troodos—Kyperounda—Khandria road, but be prepared for several miles of dirt road.

LOUVARAS

Louvaras sits on the north slope of one of the Troodos Mountains' southern spurs, accessible from the Limassol—Agros road south of Zoopiyi. The village's small church of Ayios Mamas, built in 1455, has a good display of frescoes.

MAKHERAS &

In 1125 the hermits Neophytos and Ignatius came from Palestine to Chrysostomas Monastery (now held by the Turkish Army in North Cyprus), but the Virgin Mother appeared to them with instructions to go to the eastern end of the Troodos Mountains, where they must follow a light. The light led them to a cave, and there they saw an icon of the Virgin Mother, but overgrown with brambles. A knife appeared, and the voice of God ordered them to use it to clear the undergrowth. They realised that they must then build a monastery by this holy spot, and so Makheras, 'the Knife,' was founded on a mountain that now bears the same name.

There is some confusion with the story of the founding of Ayios Neophytos near Paphos in 1159, also by a hermit named Neophytos, and some records claim Makheras was established in 1148, not 1125.

Makheras is a beautiful monastery, but not as immaculate as Kykko, and its few icons are confined to the church. The most treasured of the icons shows the Virgin Mary, and is attributed to St Luke which, if true, means that two of Luke's three paintings of the Virgin are here in Cyprus.

Outside, a perilously thin flying buttress carries an open-air stairway to the church's belfry. Swallows nest under the eaves, and tangerines grow in the courtyard.

Walk around the inside of the buildings which form the monastery's exterior walls, and you can trace Makheras's history in Greek and English captions to a series of plaques, beginning with a memorial to the monastery's four spiritual children: two monks martyred in 1232; Archbishop Kyprianos, hanged in 1821; and the unidentified Kalogheros Ioannikios, martyred in 1833.

Other plaques continue the story. The Apostle Luke paints the icon of the Holy Virgin of Makheras, one of 70 icons credited to him; an unnamed hermit leaves Asia Minor in 750 to rescue the icon; the icon is hidden in a cave by a holy spring; Neophytos and Ignatios arrive in 1125 and find it; in 1165 they go to Constantinople to ask Emperor Comnenus for help and receive the monastery's independence plus a large estate.

In 1172 Nilos leaves Palestine, becomes the abbot at Makheras, and enlarges the monastery; in 1175 it becomes stavropegaic (independent of the local bishop and answerable only to the archbishop of Cyprus, as are Ayios Neophytos and Kykko); then in 1232 Nilos and two companions refuse to accept new rules, are dragged by horses over the rocks until they die, and their bodies are burned.

The story continues: in 1340 a burning carob tree has a crucifix hidden among its branches, but the crucifix isn't damaged. Later, the Bishop of Famagusta tests the cross by plunging it in fire, with the same result. And Queen Alice of Cyprus, struck dumb three years earlier for venturing into Makheras when women were banned, regains her voice.

In 1393 the unnamed Lusignan king and queen of Cyprus leave Macheras barefoot for Nicosia to pray for an end to the plague. The story jumps to 9 July 1821 when Archbishop Kyprianos blesses the gallows and forgives the hangman — but history records that Kyprianos was hanged from the branch of a mulberry tree. Finally, on 5 September 1892, Makheras is destroyed by fire in three hours, but the monks save Luke's icon. The icon returns to the rebuilt monastery in 1900.

Access. The drive from Troodos takes hours. The best access is from Nicosia and Tamassos, with a good road all the way.

Modern martyr. In March 1957, British troops burned Grigori Afxentiou to death in his hideout near the monastery after a 10-hour fight. Afxentiou was deputy leader of EOKA and the cave is now a place of pilgrimage for many Cypriots.

MESA POTAMOS

Mesa Potamos, 'between the rivers,' is a deserted monastery on the lower slopes of Troodos, south of Pano Amiandos.

MOUTOULLAS

Moutoullas's tiny 13th-cent chapel of Panayia tou Moutoulla has some of the oldest frescoes on the island, going back to 1280. The chapel's key is available from the neighbour's house.

OMODHOS

The small village of Omodhos is part of the Krassochoria, the 'wine villages,' on Troodos's southern shoulder. Originally the property of the English Crusader Sir John de Brie, the Prince of Galilee, the village has the tiny Monastery of Stavros, noted for its woodcarving and its small museum to the struggle for independence.

PALEKHORI

Palekhori, west of Makheras, has the Church of the Transfiguration of Christ, a 16th-cent chapel on the hillside beyond the village whose wall paintings come a close second to those of Kalopanayiotis. Access along the mountain ridge is difficult and you'll need to ask for directions in the village.

PANO AMIANDOS

Pano Amiandos has the world's largest open-cast asbestos mine, scarring acres of the mountainside south of the main road, though with some reforestation now in progress. This mine, which is forced to close when snow covers the slopes, yields short-fibre mineral used in asbestos-cement for roofing and fireproofing panels, and samples of rock lying by the roadside reveal the blues and greys typical of asbestos. These short fibres are not visible until the rock is crushed, but long-fibre asbestos — the more dangerous type — is apparent in the raw rock. See Chapter 3, Economy and Industry.

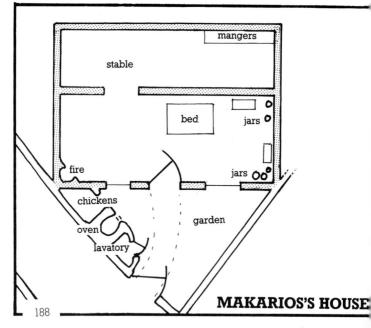

MAKARIOS'S HOUSE

PANO PANAYIA

Pano Panayia is the village where President Makarios was born, but you could easily pass through without realising it.

Yet if you looked the other way, you could not fail to see the large statue of the archbishop-president gazing towards the Makarios III Centre, a tiny museum open Tues-Sun 1000-1300, 1400-1600 for a small donation (&). Elsewhere in the village, the one-room elementary (primary) school which Makarios attended has given way to the Makarios III Gymnasium.

The Makarios home. & A discreet sign in the village centre points to the simple peasant cottage 100m away, where on 13 August 1913 Michael was born to Christodoulos and Heleni Makarios. The house is open daily 1000-1300, 1400-1800, with a donation expected. If the sturdy gate is closed during these hours, ask Maria for the key; go 50ft (15m) back to the tarmac street, turn right, and try the second house on the left.

The house is basic and simple, the kind of home all mountain shepherds have lived in for generations. Behind that sturdy gate is the garden, with the earth-closet lavatory, the simple oven for baking bread, and the henhouse.

Inside, there are just two rooms, the first for the family and the second for the donkeys. The family room has a simple window each side of the door, and an open fireplace in one corner. The brass bedstead, the proudest possession of the household, stands facing the door and is for as many of the family as can sleep in it. Some wooden chests, a big earthenware pot for wine, smaller ones for yoghourt and cheese, and the smallest of all for water, complete the main furnishings. Luxuries are a small mirror, a glass vial for rosewater, and a shelf of assorted plates. A *tapadyia,* a rope basket hanging from the ceiling, keeps the bread out of reach of the mice.

An open doorway leads to the windowless stable where two or three donkeys are quartered, their body heat helping to warm the house on winter nights.

PELENDRIA

South-east of Kato Amiandos, Pelendria once belonged to Jean de Lusignan, son of King Hugh IV of Cyprus. Its 14th-cent Church of Timiou Stavrou and the 16th-cent Panayia Katholiki both have frescoes.

PRODHROMOS

The village of Prodhromos suffered an economic decline when its major hotel, the Berengaria, closed in 1980. Six of the seven taxis moved out and the sole survivor had little work, but now, with the promise of a remodelled five-star Berengaria reopening, the village is coming back to life. During the bad times the Bank of Cyprus, in the Post Office, opened only on Wednesday, and the telephone office opened only Mon-Fri 0900-1300, 1600-1800.

Pinewood Valley. North of the village and its Forestry College (not open to visitors), the Pinewood Valley Hotel on the edge of Pedhoulas is at the start of a long downhill hike to Kakopetria.

Pedhoulas. Pedhoulas village missed the worst of the depression but it has too many rusting corrugated iron roofs to be prosperous. Both villages are a little too far from the main road to have a big share in the tourist boom, and neither can live well enough off the land despite Pedhoulas's cherry orchards.

You can visit the parish church of the Archangel Michael, completed in 1474, if you get the key from the house next door.

STAVROS TIS PSOKAS

The monastery at Stavros tis Psokas, a corruption of the Greek for Cross of Measels, has long disappeared, but the forest lookout station which replaced it in the late 19th cent has now become a rest house. From this vantage point between the peaks of Zakharou and Tryplos, there are splendid views over the forest to the coastal plains, and if you are extremely lucky you may see moufflon − wild sheep − in the timberland.

For an overnight stay in the rest house, contact the Department of Forests in Nicosia or the Divisional Forest Officer of Troodos, ✆ 020.922454. There is water, electricity, but no means of cooking, and there's a small fee. Getting there involves travelling several miles of unmade road.

TROODHITISSA ♿

Two monks who shared a cave high in the Troodos also shared a dream in which the Virgin Mary told them to build a church. Soon the church became a monastery, and the result was Troodhitissa, founded in 1250 although the present and third building was completed in 1731

Ayios Nikolaos tis Stegis, the church with two roofs.

after two disastrous forest fires.

The church's most important relic is an gilded icon brought from Asia Minor, but its best known treasure is a sacred girdle. Legend claims that any woman wanting a son must wear this belt as she prays, but if her prayers are answered she must either put her son into the ministry or buy his redemption.

TROODOS & Mt Olympus

Troodos is not a village. At the highest point of the main road which crosses the mountains from north to south, Troodos is a BP petrol station, an old-style GPO telephone box painted green, a large public toilet (restroom) which suffers from being frozen every night for eight months of the year, a police station, tiny post office, and several restaurants including two in corrugated iron shacks. The two two-star hotels are nearby.

From Troodos, a good road climbs the last few hundred feet to the RAF radar station on the summit of Mt Olympus, with a spur to the radio and television transmitters of the Cyprus Broadcasting Corporation. The views are good but, as the peak is flattish, not as spectacular as you might imagine — and don't point your camera at the radar station.

WALKS in the mountains

The CTO produces an eight-page booklet called *Nature Trails on Troodos* in several languages, listing four trails purely for hikers. Prepared in co-operation with the Forestry Department and the Cyprus Ornithological Society, the booklet, and the trails, name the trees and birds you may see.

Birds in the Troodos. The list of birds has only 48 species, but they include as residents the imperial eagle, *aquila heliaca*; griffon vulture, *gyps fulvus*; scops owl, *otus scops cyprius*; crag martin, *hirundo rupestris*; common wren, *troglodytes troglodytes*; coal and great tits, *parus ater cypriotis, parus major aphrodite*; short-toed tree-creeper (abundant), *certhis brachydactyla dorotheae*; chaffinch, *fringilla coelebs cypriotis*; serin, *serinus serinus*; greenfinch, *carduelis chloris*; goldfinch, *carduelis carduelis*; linnet, *acanthis canabina*; crossbil, *loxia curvirostra*; house sparrow, *passer domesticus*; jay *garrulus glandarius* and raven, *corvus corax*.

Other common species include a diversity such as the woodcock, nightjar, hoopoe, masked shrike and blackbird, with the list of exotics having the crane and the pied flycatcher.

Trees in the Troodos. The main conifers present are the Aleppo and corsican pine, *pinus brutia, p. nigra calabrica*; juniper, *juniperus foetidissima*; cedar, *cedrus brevifolia*; and golden oak, *quercus alnifolia*.

The nature trails identify and label many tree species as well as pointing out other vegetation such as the dog rose *rosa canina* and, at the other end of the scale, an exotic *sequoia gigantica* from California.

The Cyprus Ornithological Society is at 4 Kanaris St, Strovolos 154, Nicosia, ✆(02)420703; the Forestry Department at Loukis Akritas Ave, Nicosia, ✆(02).450168.

The trails. Trail One starts at Troodos Post Office and runs 5.5 miles (9km) along the same contour, ending on the Prodhromos road near the base of the ski lift; recommended time 5 hours. A spring of fresh water is near the midway point.

Trail Two starts from the south end of Troodos and runs 2 miles (3km) south-east, downhill, with the return along the same route.

Trail Three starts at the Presidential Cottage 0.6 mile (1km) south of Troodos and goes 1.2 miles (2km) south and downhill to the Caledonian Falls, with the return along the same route − or you can come back on either of the dirt roads.

Trail Four starts and ends near the start of the spur road to Mt Troodos and circles the summit at the same contour.

HOTELS

Four-star: Forest Park, Platres, 182🛏, ☎ ⌫ ✕ ♿. **Three-star:** Churchill Pinewood Valley, Pedhoulas, 63🛏, ☎ ⌫ ✕ ♿; Hellas, Kakopetria, 55b, ∅ ✕; Makris Sunotel, Kakopetria, 57🛏, ✕; Rodon, Agros, 128🛏, ☎ ⌫ ✕. **Two-star:** Edelweiss, Platres, 42🛏, ✕; Hekali, Kakopetria, 52🛏, ☎ ✕; Jubilee, Troodos, 70🛏, ☎ ✕; Marangos, Pedhoulas, 92🛏, ✕; New Helvetia, Platres, 32🛏, ☎ ✕; Pendeli, Platres, 63🛏, ☎ ✕; Troodos, Troodos, 27🛏, ✕. **One-star:** Central, Pedhoulas, 34🛏, ✕; Jacks, Pedhoulas, 20🛏, ✕; Kifissia, Kakopetria, 70🛏, ✕; Krystal, Kakopetria, 59🛏, ☎ ✕; Lanterns, Platres, 28🛏, ✕; Minerva, Platres, 26🛏, ☎ ✕; Rialto, Galata, 52🛏, ☎ ✕; Splendid, Platres, 85🛏, ☎; Vlachos, Agros, 42🛏, ✕. **Unclassified:** Alps, Prodhromos, 32🛏, Christy's Palace, Pedhoulas, 33🛏, ✕; Drakos, Kalopanayiotis, 12🛏, ✕; Elyssia, Pedhoulas, 49🛏, ✕; Helioupolis, Kalopanayiotis, 26🛏, ✕; Kallithea, Pedhoulas, 12🛏, Kallithea, Platres, 28🛏, ✕; Kambos, Kambos, 10🛏, ✕; Kastalia, Kalopanayiotis, 17🛏, ✕; Koundouris, Pedhoulas, 20🛏, ✕; Loukoudi, Kakopetria, 30🛏, ✕; Loutraki, Kalopanayiotis, 26🛏, ✕; Mount Royal, Platres, 46🛏, ✕; Overhill, Prodhromos, 40🛏, ✕; Pafsilypon, Platres, 62🛏, ✕; Paradisos, Perapedhi, 22🛏, Perapedhi, Perapedhi, 24🛏, ✕; Petit Palais, Platres, 28🛏, Semiramis, Platres, 29🛏, ✕; Spring, Platres, 29🛏, ✕; Synnos, Kalopanayiotis, 15🛏, Vienna, Platres, 18🛏, ✕.

GUEST HOUSES

Livadhia, Kyperounda, 25🛏, ✕; Meteora, Agros, 18🛏, ✕.

HOTEL APARTMENT

Paul's, Platres, 31🛏.♿

❶ In the centre of Pano Platres, open May-Aug, Mon-Sat 0900-1300, and Mon,Wed,Thur,Fri 1530-1815; open Sep and April Mon-Sat 0900-1500. Closed rest of year.

18: THE BRITISH SOVEREIGN BASES

Episkopi, Akrotiri, Dhekelia

THE TWO MAIN SOVEREIGN BASES are British Dependent Territories, which makes them as British as those remote Atlantic islands of South Georgia, Ascension, and St Helena. They were not included in the territory of the Republic of Cyprus that was granted independence on 16 August 1960, and it was disagreement between Britain and the emerging republic over the bases' area that delayed independence from the planned date of 19 February.

The sovereign base areas, known to the military as SBAs, are in two main chunks, the Episkopi Army base and the adjoining RAF Akrotiri near Limassol forming the Western SBA, and the Dhekelia Army base between Larnaca and Ayia Napa forming the Eastern SBA. Their total area is between 98 and 99 square miles (around 256sq km).

No borders. The SBAs are unique in that there are no borders, not even a simple fence. British people on the bases travel freely in Cyprus, and Cypriots drive freely across the bases. Military personnel and their families can, with the right documents, drive from the Dhekelia base into Famagusta through the Four-Mile Crossing, and North Cypriots come the other way, to work on the base.

Dual nationality. Almost all Cypriot private property was excluded from the bases by clever manipulation of the borders on maps, resulting in the villages of Xylotimbou and Ormidhia being enclaves in the Dhekelia base, but Akrotiri village is unique by being on SBA territory – so its citizens automatically got joint British and Cypriot nationality, and any baby born there now can still claim a British passport. The ancient city of Curium, the Temple of Apollo, and the Monastery of St Nikolaos of the Cats, are all on SBA territory, and Kolossi Castle is only just over the border.

Retained sites. Strangely, the SBAs have their own dependent territories elsewhere in Cyprus, the 15 or so 'retained sites.' One on the Akamas Peninsula is used as a light weapons firing range, the Berengaria site is for housing and the NAAFI, and the British East Mediterranean Relay Station at Zygi broadcasts BBC World Service programmes, but the most obvious is the radar installation of RAF Mt Olympus, on the island's topmost peak.

Mt Olympus. The large white spheres of the radar base dominate the Troodos skyline and on a clear day can be seen from Limassol, Paphos, and the Kyrenia Range in North Cyprus. They provide radar information for the Akrotiri air traffic controllers and, at around 6,500ft altitude (including their own height above the summit), are strategically sited near a sensitive part of the world; it's an open secret that Britain uses its bases to keep in touch with what's happening in the Near East, picking up information that's not available in any other way. The bases are not part of NATO.

The official explanation for the SBAs' existence is that Britain needs to maintain a permanent military presence at a strategically situated point in the eastern Mediterranean, providing a staging post for military aircraft, as well as communications, and administrative support for the British contingent in the UN troops in Cyprus — though the two forces are entirely separate except that the British boys in blue berets draw their supplies from Episkopi. The SBAs are needed for a quick reaction if trouble brews in the Near East or the Gulf of Iran, as when Iraq seized Kuwaitand they also provide somewhere to train the troops in the cold northern winter.

Red Arrows. If you come to Cyprus in late winter or early spring you may see the Red Arrows RAF display team rehearsing over the Akrotiri airfield.

Who rules? The SBAs operate under their own civil law which is as near as possible the law of Cyprus, which in turn is based on British law from colonial times. The SBAs have their own Sovereign Base Police which is separate from the Cypriot force, their own civil court and judge, and their own prison at Dhekelia. The head of state in this mini-dependency alternates between a major general and an air marshall, responsible to the Secretary of State for Defence in Whitehall and not to the Foreign and Commonwealth Office.

Population. On average there are 2,700 Army and 1,500 RAF personnel, 230 British civilians, and their dependents on the bases, making around 9,000; most troops are on two-year or six-month tours. There's also work for 2,600 Cypriot civilian employees, and around 3,500 soldiers come to Cyprus each year for training — which may include hiking in the Troodos and scuba diving near the Temple of Apollo.

The SBAs are a popular posting for British troops — but a six-month tour with UNFICYP is not so welcome, due to the strict conditions imposed on the soldiers.

THE TURKISH REPUBLIC OF NORTH CYPRUS

19: GAZİMAĞUSA

Famagusta and the Panhandle

GAZİMAĞUSA IS BY FAR THE LARGEST DISTRICT in North Cyprus, reaching from the boundary with the Dhekelia Sovereign Base in the south, to within sight of Ercan Airport in the west, and to the tip of the Panhandle in the north-east.

Gazimağusa city has the finest beaches on the entire island but, sadly, most of them have been behind barbed wire since August 1974. Indeed, the Greek name for the city, Ammochostos, means 'covered by sand.' The Turks, who for generations have occupied the area within the walls, corrupted that to Mağosa and then added *gazi*, which means a fighter for the cause of Islam.

Old Famagusta is a strange place. Its Great Mosque, the Lala Mustafa Paşa, is still the Gothic cathedral of St Nicholas with its pews removed and a tiny minaret added. Within the Kaleiçi, the old city, there are many buildings which trace the island's history — yet there are vast open spaces which could never be tolerated in the bustle and pressure of an old medina in the Arab world. Famagusta is unlike anything else in Islam in so many ways that you need constant reminders you are not in some Christian backwater.

Yet when you come to know the old city you appreciate its unique character. Turkey it is not. It is certainly not Arabia. Nor is it Italy despite its Venetian connections. It is not Spain, nor France, nor even Britain. It is not even Mediterranean. It is unique.

Other attractions. A few miles up the coast stands the ruined city of Salamis and the scarcely-visible remains of the Bronze Age city of Engomi. Nearby stands the once-great Monastery of St Barnabas (Apostolos Varnavas), empty since 1976 but in good repair.

Famagusta Bay sweeps round to meet Kirpaşa, the long peninsula of the Panhandle guarded at its blunt end by the Byzantine fortress of Kantara Castle and at its pointed end by the isolated monastery of Apostolos Andreas, still occupied by a few miserable Greek nuns.

The Panhandle is a remote area, seldom visited by tourists, yet it has some splendid viewsfrom its backbone of hills, its beaches have

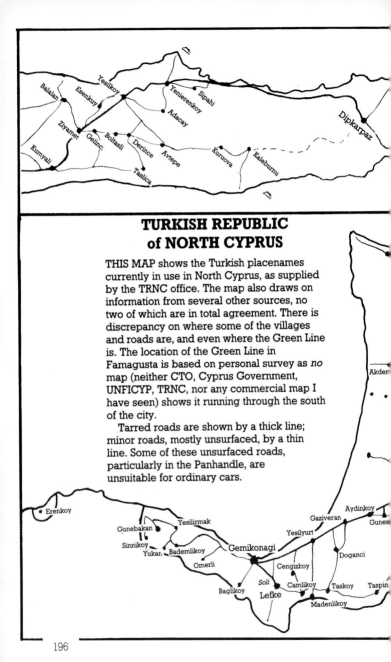

TURKISH REPUBLIC of NORTH CYPRUS

THIS MAP shows the Turkish placenames currently in use in North Cyprus, as supplied by the TRNC office. The map also draws on information from several other sources, no two of which are in total agreement. There is discrepancy on where some of the villages and roads are, and even where the Green Line is. The location of the Green Line in Famagusta is based on personal survey as *no* map (neither CTO, Cyprus Government, UNFICYP, TRNC, nor any commercial map I have seen) shows it running through the south of the city.

Tarred roads are shown by a thick line; minor roads, mostly unsurfaced, by a thin line. Some of these unsurfaced roads, particularly in the Panhandle, are unsuitable for ordinary cars.

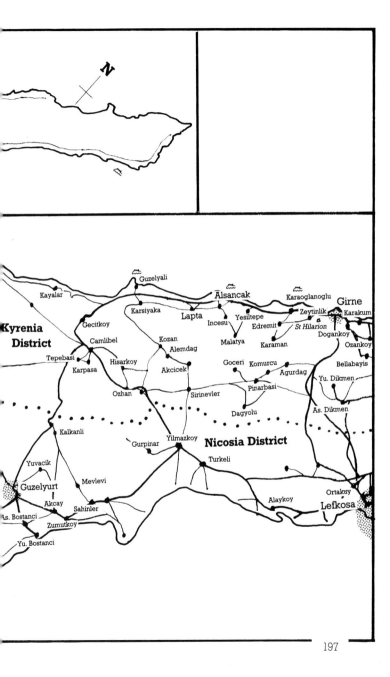

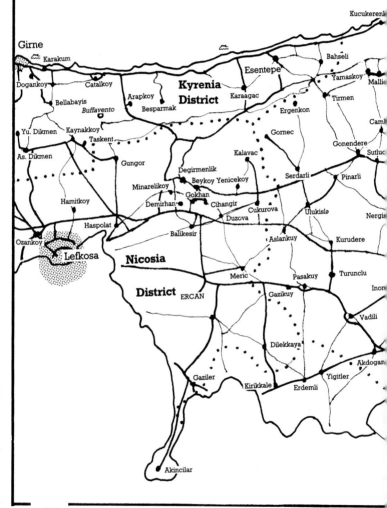

TURKISH REPUBLIC
of NORTH CYPRUS

Girne

Karakum

Kucukerenl

Bahseli

Dogankoy

Catalkoy

Kyrenia
District

Esentepe

Yamaskoy

Malli

Arapkoy

Besparmak

Karaagac

Tirmen

Bellabayis

Buffavento

Ergenkon

Yu. Dikmen

Kaynakkoy

Gornec

Caml

Taskent

As. Dikmen

Gungor

Kalavac

Gonendere

Sutlu

Degirmenlik

Serdarli

Pinarli

Minarelikoy

Beykoy Yenicekoy

Hamitkoy

Demirhan

Gokhan

Cihangir

Cukurova

Ulukisla

Nergis

Haspolat

Duzova

Balikesir

Ozankoy

Aslankuy

Kurudere

Lefkosa

Nicosia

Meric

Pasakuy

Turunclu

District ERCAN

Gazikuy

Inon

Vadili

Dilekkaya

Akdogan

Gaziler

Yigitler

Kirikkale

Erdemli

Akincilar

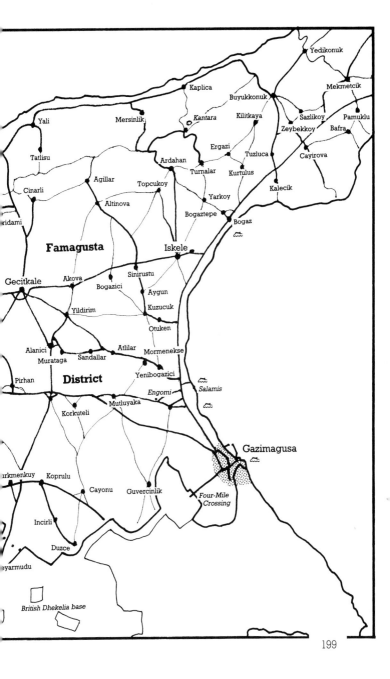

few human footprints in them, and its wildlife is less disturbed by mankind than anywhere else on the island. Come in early summer and you will see hen quail leading their chicks across the road. Come at any time and you may see the non-venomous six-foot black snakes that live in the area.

By contrast, the central plain, the island's breadbasket that the Greeks call Mesaoria, has little of tourist interest.

GAZIMAĞUSA

Gazimağusa is two cities. The old city, still surrounded by its Venetian walls, is the Kaleiçi, literally 'castle inside' and pronounced *kah-lay ee-chee*. It has been Moslem since the Ottoman Empire took it by siege in 1571. The new city, mainly to the south, is Maraş (Varosha) and its satellites Namik Kemal, Canbulat, and Kamilpaşa, named from characters in the city's history.

KALEIÇI

The first known settlement on this spot was established by Ptolemy Philadelphus, who lived from 285 to 247BC during Cyprus's Hellenistic era. The city grew steadily but unspectacularly for a millennium, finding a small role in the Crusades as the last haven for Christians before they met the perils of the Seljuk Sultanate, which had closed off the Holy Land to Christian pilgrims.

The Crusades. The First Crusade went overland in 1096 and was a fiasco, but it regrouped in Constantinople in 1097 and seized Jerusalem in 1099. The Second Crusade of 1147, with Louis VII of France at its head, was a disaster and in 1187 the Sultan Saladdin recaptured Jerusalem. The Third Crusade, which had England's Richard the Lionheart among its leaders, captured Acre in 1191.

Exactly a century later, the Mameluk Sultanate seized Acre and sent its Christian residents into exile. Many of them came to Famagusta and quickly made this the busiest and wealthiest port in the eastern Mediterranean, with one of its merchants soon to be considered the richest man in the world as his daughter had more jewels than there were in the French crown.

Change of rule. In 1184 the self-styled Emperor of Cyprus, Isaac Comnenus, took the island out of Byzantine control, only to lose it to Richard of England in 1191. But Richard couldn't keep it and sold it to the Knights Templar who in turn sold it to the Lusignans, the French Crusaders, in 1192.

St Nicholas's Cathedral. The Lusignans increased Famagusta's prosperity, building St Nicholas's Cathedral between 1298 and 1312 (now the Sinan Paşa Mosque), adding the Church of Sts Peter and Paul in 1358-60, and their Royal Palace (now the Venetian Palace). The Lusignan kings were crowned in the cathedral and lived in the palace, which made Famagusta the most important city on the island — yet Nicosia was still its capital.

Catherine Cornaro. The Venetians had been on the island since the Crusades, but not with sufficient strength to overthrow the Lusignans — until 1489 when they stage-managed the abdication of Queen Catherine Cornaro. She made her first announcement on 26 February in the main square in her beloved Famagusta, which thus became the first Cypriot city to fall under Venetian rule. (See chapters 9 and 13 for the Cornaro story.)

Venetian Walls. The Venetians were never a powerful force, and the growing threat from the Ottoman Empire urged them to increase the island's defences. They replaced the weak Lusignan city walls with the massive structure you see today, up to 30ft (9m) thick and 60ft (18m) high, and stretching 2.2 miles (3.5km).

The Martinengo Bastion (now the Tophane) at the north-west corner was almost a castle in its own right; the Land Gate in the south-west was a well-defended tunnel, though the modern road goes in through a new gate beside it; and in the south-east corner the arsenal (now the Canbulat, pronounced the Turkish way) guarded the approach to the Sea Gate, the only other access.

Othello's Tower. The *Castella* was in the middle of the wall facing the sea, with an extending wall down to the water's edge. Shakespeare set Act II Scene I of his *Othello* in 'a seaport in Cyprus' and gave Cassio the lines:

> "Great Jove, Othello guard
> And swell his sail with thine own powerful breath,
> That he may bless this bay with his tall ship,
> Make love's quick pants in Desdemona's arms,
> Give renew'd fire to our extincted spirits,
> And bring all Cyprus comfort!"

Shakespeare never specified Famagusta, but the city was the island's chief port. And so for the sake of four words the castle came to be known as Othello's Tower. It's open daily 0730-1530, but stays open longer if there are enough visitors. Admission is 25p (40¢). Today's visitors can explore the sturdy fortress and from its flat top look down at the commercial port 100m away; the main court leads to a sunken nave with a hint of Byzantinian influence in its architecture. You may be lucky enough to find some signature marks made by the Venetian masons, but much of the exposed structure is weathering into those contorted shapes which are typical of globigerina limestone.

Venetian lion. The *Porta del Mare* had the statue of a lion, the symbol of Venice, guarding it on the inside: it's still there today. Folklore claims that the lion has swallowed a treasure which some lucky person will recover by thrusting his hand down the animal's mouth on the one occasion in the year when this miracle happens. But nobody knows the time or date of the miracle.

Siege of Famagusta. The walls took a severe battering when the Ottoman general Lala Mustafa laid siege to Famagusta for four months in 1571, sending — according to legend — 100,000 cannonballs into

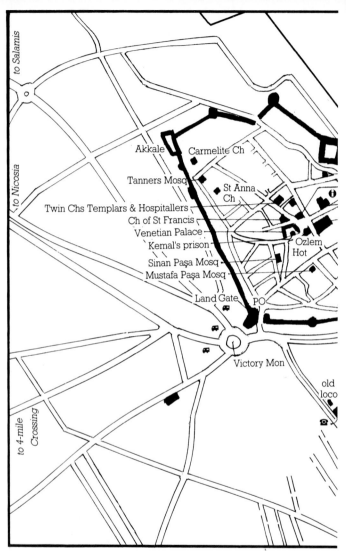

to Salamis

to Nicosia

Akkale

Carmelite Ch

Tanners Mosq

St Anna Ch

Twin Chs Templars & Hospitallers

Ch of St Francis

Venetian Palace

Kemal's prison

Sinan Paşa Mosq

Mustafa Paşa Mosq

Ozlem Hot

Land Gate

PO

to 4-mile Crossing

Victory Mon

old loco

the city and destroying almost everything but the buildings in the centre.

Canbulat's tomb. ⅂ The Bey (ruler) of the Turkish town of Kilis was confronted with the horrifying wheel of knives which the Venetians had put in a tiny opening into their arsenal. Bey Çanbulat's solution to the problem was to charge the revolving knives on horseback at the

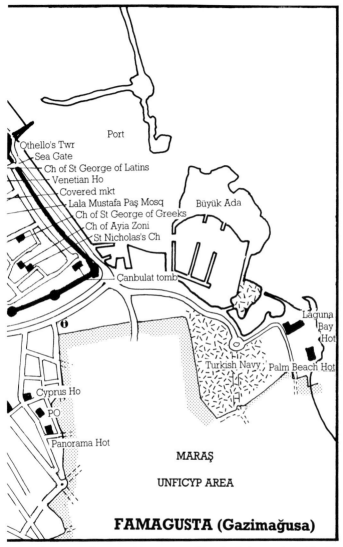

Othello's Twr
Sea Gate
Ch of St George of Latins
Venetian Ho
Covered mkt
Lala Mustafa Paş Mosq
Ch of St George of Greeks
Ch of Ayia Zoni
St Nicholas's Ch
Çanbulat tomb

Port

Büyük Ada

Laguna Bay Hot

Turkish Navy
Palm Beach Hot

Cyprus Ho
PO

Panorama Hot

MARAŞ

UNFICYP AREA

FAMAGUSTA (Gazimağusa)

cost of his own life – and the horse's. The Canbulat tomb inside the
arsenal holds his remains, and for years was considered a holy place
as women prayed there for sons as brave as Canbulat. The irony was
that his sacrifice never led to the Venetians' surrender: that was due
to starvation.

Akkale. The Land Gate was the first part of the defences to fall, and the white flag of surrender which the Venetians waved over the parapet gave the Turks their name for the bastion: *Ak kale*, 'white tower.'

Surrender. When Marc Antonio Bragadino conceded defeat it was with the guarantee of safe passage for all his people from Famagusta to Crete, but Mustafa, who had lost 80,000 men in the siege, changed his mind when he saw how few men had been resisting him. He slaughtered every one of the defenders then had Bragadino tortured, flayed alive, and finally he paraded the skin from Syria to Constantinople. It was the worst incident in the Turkish rule of Cyprus, and the Greeks still don't forget it.

The Turks like to point out in mitigation that, apart from this incident, their rule was much more benign than the Venetian. They abolished serfdom, and granted the Greek Orthodox Church the right to practise its religion, relieving it from 310 years of oppression from the Catholic Church.

They also repaired Famagusta's walls but did little other restoration in the old city, and when the British arrived in 1878 they found much of the Kaleiçi was an open prison for criminals from Turkey.

Suez Canal. The British are mainly responsible for the destruction of old Famagusta; they shipped the loose masonry to Egypt to build Port Said and its quays, following the opening of the Suez Canal in 1869.

Lala Mustafa Paşa Mosque. ♿ St Nicholas's Cathedral became the Santa Sophia Mosque of Famagusta, named from the Byzantine church in İstanbul which had been rededicated after the Turkish conquest of that city. Externally, it is only the small and slender minaret on the left tower which shows this is no longer a Christian church. Its splendid Gothic facade is as impressive as many others in Europe, and it is indeed the biggest Gothic church in the eastern Mediterranean.

Inside, the main difference is the absence of pews. The floor is carpeted in green right to the door, which means you must take off your shoes before you enter. An attendant sprinkles rosewater on your hands and isn't concerned whether you are Moslem, Christian or Jew. Leave a donation in the offertory box and walk down the nave. Look at the 12 massive columns supporting the roof, whitewashed like every square inch of stonework from floor to ceiling. Then look at the windows, whose plate tracery design is exactly as you would find in Early English architecture. Yet this *is* a mosque!

In 1954 St Sophia was renamed the Lala Mustafa Paşa Mosque in honour of the commander of the Ottoman invading troops in 1571.

Access. The mosque is open at all times and there is no restriction on access during prayers or other services. Wear what you would when going to your own parish church, and behave in the same manner.

Venetian Palace. The Lusignan kings of Cyprus had their Royal Palace conveniently near their cathedral, using it until 1369 when

Peter II moved to Nicosia. The Venetians took it over with the abdication of Queen Catherine Cornaro and the place became known as the Palazzo del Proveditore or the Venetian Palace, but it was no longer used by the monarchy.

Above the central arch facing the square is the coat of arms of the Captain of Cyprus in 1552, the palace's last days of glory, for the Turks used it as the Ottomans state prison.

Prison of Namil Kemal. Only the cell of Namil Kemal now remains of the many built in the palace. Kemal was a Turkish writer, poet and dissident and, after he staged a controversial play in İstanbul in 1873 he was imprisoned here for 38 months. The cell is small and utterly bare and is supposed to be open to the public, but you can see its gaunt interior through the barred window.

Kemal's bust stands on a marble plinth beside the paved front court of the Lala Mustafa Mosque, with an inscription in Turkish telling his story.

An earthquake destroyed most of the Venetian Palace, leaving only two of the walls, Kemal's cell, and the arched facade. Where the Lusignan royalty once held court, the citizens of Famagusta now park their cars.

Sinan Paşa Mosque. The merchant Simon Nostrano allegedly financed the building of the Church of Sts Peter and Paul, between 1358 and '60, with the proceeds of one business deal in Syria. The newly-arrived Turks restored it in 1571 and converted it into the Sinan

St Nicholas's Cathedral is now the Lala Mustafa Paşa Mosque in Famagusta.

Paşa Mosque, but the British tastelessly used it as a warehouse for cereals and potatoes, giving rise to the name of the Wheat Mosque.

After another restoration in 1964 it became the town hall, and it now sees duty as a public library.

28 Çelebi. Among the few graves beside the Wheat Mosque is that of the former Turkish ambassador to Paris with the unusual name of Mehmet Faizi 28 Çelebi, who died here in 1732 in exile. *Mehmet* is Turkish for 'Mahomet,' and *Çelebi,* which means 'gentleman,' was his given surname when he joined the Janissaries; he was presumably the 28th gentleman. The Janissaries, the *yeni çeri* or 'new soldiers,' were boys stolen from Christian lands as infants and brought up as fanatical Moslem troops almost with a kamikaze urge; they were disbanded in 1826 after they rebelled against the sultan.

Other points of interest. There is little else of interest within the old city. A World War One cemetery near the Land Gate, Akkale, holds the remains of many Turkish soldiers who died in a British prisoner of war camp in the city after being captured in the Suez Canal and the Dardanelles.

Elsewhere, you have a tour of the ruins of a very few of the 365 churches which the Lusignans are claimed to have built in the city. **St Nicholas's Church** and the nearby church of **Ayia Zoni,** the 'Blessed Girdle' of the Virgin Mary, were 15th-cent Byzantine; the **Church of the Holy Cross,** later the Mustafa Paşa Mosque, was 16th-cent.

The Church of **St George of the Greeks** was the old Orthodox cathedral, but nothing is known of **St George of the Latins** except that it was 13th-cent. Nothing is known about the two 15th-cent churches inside the Land Gate; all that's known of the **Church of St Anna** is its name; it is known that the **Carmelite Church** was one of the most important, but it's a ruin like all the others. The Tanners' Mosque had begun life in the 16th cent as a church, but its history is unknown; and the **Church of St Francis** had an underground passage linking it with the Venetian church.

Only the small, 14th-cent Twin Churches of the **Knights Templars and Hospitallers** have been restored.

Polly Peck International. After seeing such desolation in the old city, it's rewarding to hear of a success story unequalled in Cyprus's history. Asil Nadir was born in 1953 in Lefke (Lefka), now in the far west of North Cyprus, son of a prominent Turkish Cypriot business-man. He read economics at İstanbul University then joined his parents in Britain in 1963 as racial tension increased.

Three years later he was running a textile company in London, selling to the Near East as well as to the British market. In 1980 he bought a controlling stake in a small company called Polly Peck and within ten years his Midas touch had turned it into a leading multinational company worth billions of pounds sterling. Polly Peck International is the biggest company in North Cyprus and is responsible for the country's exceptional trade with Britain.

PPI's orange-hulled ships bring manufactured goods into Famagusta and take out citrus fruit, grapes and other products; the company's growing interest in fruit led to its purchase in 1989 of the Del Monte giant in the USA for $875,000,000 (£557,000,000). In addition to food and textiles it now has interests in the electronics firm Sanusi in Japan and Turkey, and is expanding rapidly into the leisure industry with the building of the luxury Sheraton Voyager Hotel in Antalya, Turkey; it already owns the Palm Beach Hotel in Famagusta and has built the Girne View, the Jasmin Court and the Crystal Cove in Kyrenia.

Noble Air. Mr Nadir's sister, Mrs Bilge Nevzat, runs Noble Raredons, the company which includes Noble Air and Mosaic Holidays, firms which specialise in taking Britons on holiday to North Cyprus.

THE NEW TOWN

Maraş. Maraş, the heart of new Famagusta, is where the 30 or so tourist hotels of pre-intervention days stand behind oil drums and barbed wire, silent museum pieces to the stupidity of mankind. Eleven of them were four-star, including the 448-room Golden Sands, and together they had 3,143 beds.

The only operating hotels in Maraş are the Laguna Beach apart-hotel, the five-star Palm Beach, and the Panorama near the Police Station, and they all suffer the mild indignity of not having any water supply on Sundays as the Greek Cypriots south of the Green Line pump it for only six days a week.

The Palm Beach's neighbour to the south is a private house, with a narrow path beside it giving public access to the sands. This path was as far as the Turkish Army could advance before the cease-fire in August 1974, and its southern fence is the boundary of North Cyprus; 200m away, the next hotel has not seen a guest since the intervention and its north wall is badly holed, exposing some of the rooms and the lift shaft to the weather.

Cyprus Railway. The British built a railway from Morphou (now Güzelyurt) to Nicosia and on to Famagusta. One of the original 0−6−0 locomotives, number 846 built by the Hunslet Engine Co in Leeds in 1904, stands on a short section of track beside the Post Office on Polatpaşa Blv, with another which I couldn't find said to be in Güzelyurt.

The narrow-gauge Government Railway closed in 1951. The track has been gone for years, and the last railway building was demolished in Dörtyol − 'four roads,' but Prastio to the Greeks − in 1990 to make way for road widening.

AROUND THE DISTRICT

Somewhere south of Famagusta is the site of **Leucolla,** a small city off which was fought one of the biggest naval battles in ancient history.

Antigonus, one of Alexander the Great's generals, sent his son Demetrius Poliorkitis to take Cyprus in 305BC. Demetrius raided the tip of the Panhandle and fought his way down the coast to Salamis from the safety of his 108 ships. King Ptolemeos of Egypt came to the rescue of King Menelaos of Salamis, bringing 140 galleys and a small fleet of merchant vessels. Demetrios hid in Leucolla harbour until the Egyptians were passing, then sailed out to the attack, sinking all but eight of the Egyptian ships.

Louis Palma de Cesnola, the United States consul in Cyprus who plundered several ancient sites, wrote in 1877: '. . . after digging a few days at random I came upon the foundations of a building . . . From the situation of the ruins they can be no other than those of Leucolla.' Maybe Cesnola found it; maybe not. But now it is lost again.

SALAMIS &

Teucer (or Tefkros), son of the ruler of the isle of Salamis, near Athens, was exiled by his father after the Trojan War — around 1180BC — so he came to Cyprus and founded a Salamis of his own.

In 707BC it had to join the other nine city states of the island in paying tribute to Assyria though it was to become the greatest of them. King Eulethon claimed on his coinage, minted from around 560BC, that he was ruler of the entire island.

Persian satrap. This first period of supremacy was brief, as the Persians seized Cyprus in 540, making it the fifth of its 20 satraps (provinces).

When the mainland Greeks revolted against Persian rule, Eulethon's great-grandson Gorgos of Salamis refused to join in, so his brother Onesilo seized the throne and led the anti-Persian revolt of 499-8. The Persians crushed the opposition in the following winter and so Salamis remained in the Persian fold.

Evagoras. Evagoras seized the dynastic throne in 410BC, won the Persians' respect in battle though failed to defeat them, and so gained the right to rule Cyprus as a vassal to Persia's King Artaxerxes. Evagoras restored Cypriot fortunes, making his reign the golden era in the island's affairs, and soon Salamis was once more the chief city with a thriving trade in copper, corn, salt, and olive oil.

Persian domination continued until the Greeks' Alexander the Great defeated the Persians' Darius the Great in 333 near İskenderun, Turkey. Then, surprisingly, Alexander died of a fever in 323 at the age of 32, and the civilized world was again in turmoil.

Evagoras's successor Pnytagoras had helped Alexander at the siege of Tyre and was rewarded with Tamassos; now Nicroceon gambled and chose the winning successor to Alexander's empire, and was rewarded with the remainder of Cyprus.

Leucolla again. But Antigonus, who was the less fortunate successor to Alexander, sent his general Demetrios Poliorkitis to seize Cyprus, and King Menelaos, successor to Nicocreon, saw the tide of battle go against him at Leucolla (see above). Demtrios took Salamis and Cyprus.

The Ptolemys eventually controlled the island, which resulted in

Salamis losing the status of chief city in 294BC to Paphos.

Brutal interest. The city continued to thrive under the Romans though in 56BC it needed a loan. Marcus Brutus, who helped kill Caesar in 44, arranged the finance — at 48% interest — and when the repayments stopped, he locked up Salamis's senators until five had starved to death.

St Barnabas. Barnabas was born in Salamis into a Jewish family at some unrecorded date. He went to school in Jerusalem, heard the teaching of Jesus, and was converted to Christianity. Although Barnabas was not one of the Twelve Apostles, he was regarded as an apostle when he came back to Cyprus with Paul in 45. There is no evidence that Barnabas and Paul made Salamis the first Christian city outside of Palestine, but this was indeed the city where Christianity began its long journey around the world. Barnabas and Paul travelled on to Paphos, the capital, where they convinced the Roman Governor Sergius Paulus of their beliefs, so making Cyprus the world's first Christian country.

Eventually Barnabas was murdered in an attempt to stop the spread of this new theology, and that led ultimately to the founding of St Barnabas's Monastery (see below).

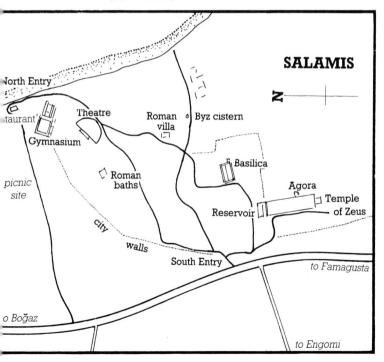

SALAMIS

North Entry

staurant

Theatre

Roman villa

Byz cistern

Gymnasium

picnic site

Roman baths

Basilica

Agora

Temple of Zeus

Reservoir

city

walls

South Entry

to Famagusta

o Boğaz

to Engomi

Slow demise. Salamis was badly hit by the earthquake of 76 or 77AD, and again in the Jewish uprising of 116, but it recovered. The city was one of three in Cyprus to send a bishop to the Council of Nicaea (now İznik in Turkey) which decided, among other issues, how to calculate the date for Easter. The tremor of 332 shook the city badly, and the 'quake and tsunami of 342 dealt it a near mortal blow.

Emperor Constantius rebuilt it on a smaller scale at the century's end, renaming it Constantia, and it briefly became the island's chief city again. It took the full force of the first of many Arab raids in 647 when it was besieged, sacked, and its entire population slaughtered. Once again it was rebuilt, but more earthquakes, more raids, and the silting of the harbour forced its people to abandon it to the drifting sands. The nearby city of Ammochostis — Famagusta — began its rise to prominence.

SALAMIS TODAY &

The Salamis ruins have two entrances; the south gate, by the custodian's office, is near the side-road to Tuzla, Engomi and St Barnabas's Abbey; for the north gate, turn right onto a dirt track 0.4 mile (700m) up the road and continue for 0.6 mile (1km) to a car park and restaurant, with the ticket office on the coast. Admission is 25p (40¢); times vary slightly but you can reckon on 0800-1700, with the south gate closing an hour earlier.

Students of archaeology can spend a week in Salamis and find it not long enough but, even if you are bored by ruined cities, the gymnasium and the theatre are worth an hour of your time. As the booklet occasionally available at the ticket office is scant on information, I offer a more detailed tour of the city.

Little remains of what was Evagoras's Salamis, but these are the most impressive ruins on the island. The **theatre** is the largest in Cyprus and among the largest in Byzantium; its proscenium (stage) is almost 90ft (27m) in diameter, and the 50 rows of seats could hold around 20,000 people. Probably the most amazing fact is that the theatre is intact, having survived earthquakes, Arabs, and medieval builders, and it was rediscovered in 1959 under its covering of sand and shrubbery.

The **gymnasium** suffered far worse, but many of its marble columns have been re-erected, though some are suffering from the corrosion of iron staples holding them together. The largest complex at Salamis, it was discovered in 1882, with serious excavation beginning as late as 1952, although this was the public building and bath-house of the Byzantine Constantia, standing on the site of the Roman baths but with little evidence of that older structure surviving. The gymnasium and its baths are 420ft long by 250ft wide (125m x 75m), the south portico with its restored columns and Corinthian capping stones being photogenic as well as impressive.

Doorways lead north from this portico into the palaestra (wrestling-school), but the triple door has in its step a rare relic of the Hellenistic gymnasium, a dedication to Ptolemy V Epiphanes of 205-180BC. The west and north porticos had all their doorways sealed, but at the corner where they meet is the only columnar base stone that was found in place.

The east portico's taller columns are out of place, prompting the suggestion that they were brought in by builders – probably in the time of Constantius – from pagan temples of the 2nd cent BC. In the middle of this portico stood the marble altar of Hermes, now languishing in the Famagusta District Museum amid the derelict hotels.

East of the east portico lies the main building. Look for a pit dug in front of one of the connecting doorways in 1890 and you may see some of the oldest masonry on the site, believed to be 4th-cent BC.

The main building is primarily a large central hall sandwiched between two narrower halls; of these, the north hall gives access to the praefurnium, the stoker's room, where a fire created the hot air that went through the hypocaust, an early form of central heating. The Byzantines evidently didn't like cold baths even in this climate, but they may have had to tolerate smoke as well.

The outer wall of the main building shows some good examples of flying buttresses and, where it faces the sea, exaggerated erosion of the globigerina limestone. The inside of a split-open dome reveals a mosaic of an orange growing on the tree.

The **Basilica of St Epiphanius** at 190ft by 138ft (58m x 42m) is Cyprus's largest, and was presumably the church of Constantia as St Epiphanius is known to have been the bishop from 368 to 403. The original church had six naves, each separated from its neighbour by 14 columns, but during rebuilding, probably when the domes were added, the two inner naves became one.

The second nave from the south has a marble-lined tomb at its eastern end, probably for Epiphanius's remains, but it has been empty for almost 1,100 years as the Byzantine emperor Leo the Wise is reported to have taken the relics to Constantinople.

The church survived 'quake and raids and may be the building which a Christian pilgrim noted in 1344, but its ruins were covered by sand and undergrowth when discovered in 1924.

Between the basilica and the theatre, Salamis's builders had provided a water **cistern,** probably the world's biggest when it was created. Remains of columns in the tank hint of the presence of a roof, and historical records infer that the water came along a 35-mile (56km) aqueduct from Değirmenlik (Kythrea).

The **agora** or market place may have had a monumental five-arch gateway at the north; the open space, 750ft long by 180ft wide (225m x 54m) would warrant such an approach.

The **Temple of Zeus** was at the south end of the agora and again built on the massive scale. At the height of its influence this temple was one of the top three of Cyprus, and from 22AD the right of asylum was granted to any fugitive who managed to reach it.

OUTSIDE OF SALAMIS

If you leave Salamis by the southern gate and head towards Tuzla, you'll see **St Catherine's Prison** on your left. It's a sad-looking cell of darkened ashlar limestone, fenced off from public inspection, but it was here — according to legend — that St Catherine was imprisoned, though legend is reluctant to name her crime. She later went to Egypt and tried to convert the Roman Emperor Maximinus Thrax to Christianity around 236, and for her reward was condemned to die strapped to a turning wheel. A miracle destroyed the wheel, but there was no miracle to prevent Catherine being beheaded, although angels took her body to Mt Sinai: Jebel Katerina at 8,550ft (2,605m) is the highest peak of Sinai Mountain.

Catherine wheel. Her holy day is 25 November, close enough to Guy Fawkes Day (5 November) for British children to remember the saint in their spinning fireworks known as Catherine wheels.

Around the prison, but inaccessible to the public, are several royal tombs from the 8th and 7th cents BC.

Monastery of St Barnabas. ♿ Half a mile (0.8km) takes you to the

Amathus: Richard the Lionheart was here.

Monastery of St Barnabas — Apostolos Varnavas to the Greeks — built in 1756 in the style of a Byzantine church on the site of the first monastery of 477; it's one of the few on the island not to stand protectively around a central courtyard.

Hidden among trees on the north of the road, the monastery has been empty since 1976 when the three monks who stayed on after the Turkish intervention of 1974, moved south. The buildings are locked, but the key to the church is at the ticket office: admission 25p, 40¢, hours unpredictable. The church is dismal in comparison with those south of the Green Line but if this is the only monastery you are likely to visit, then come. You might see the four life-size murals in the church which tell the story of the founding of this monastery.

Resentment had built up in Salamis to Bishop Barnabas's preachings, prompting a group of Syrian Jews to stone him to death and throw the body on a fire. The fire refused to burn and during the night Barnabas's nephew (or cousin) John removed the body. . . . But wait. Another version of the story says the body was dumped in a swamp, with some of Barnabas's pupils as unintended witnesses to the deed.

Both stories agree that the corpse was smuggled away and hidden in a cave . . . or buried in a tomb under a carob tree . . . with a copy of St Matthew's Gospel lying on Barnabas's chest.

St Mark's Gospel. Meanwhile, John had other things to do. He changed his name to Mark, wrote his version of events in the Gospel according to St Mark, and subsequently took Christianity to Alexandria.

Move forward to 476 and the first of those four murals. Bishop Anticitus has a dream which shows him where Barnabas's body was buried. In the second mural Anticitus exhumes the remains, finds the copy of St Matthew's Gospel still on the apostle's chest, and so proclaims that this is, indeed, Barnabas.

Red ink. The third mural shows Byzantine Emperor Zeno, in Constantinople, agreeing that the gospel proves the remains are those of Barnabas, and in the final mural Zeno funds the building of the first monastery near the site of the grave . . . or the cave. He also settles a longstanding dispute between the churches of Antioch and Cyprus, declaring that as the Cypriot Church was founded by St Barnabas it owes no allegiance to Antioch. Religious independence brings the right of Cypriot archbishops to wear cloaks of imperial purple and to sign in red ink — and when Archbishop Makarios signed the deed of political independence in 1960 in red ink, he wore a purple cloak.

Mausoleum. A woman in Nicosia financed the building in 1953 of a mausoleum over the spot where Barnabas's body was found. It's 100m east of the monastery, but locked.

ENGOMI.

The ancient city of Engomi, also known as Alasia, Asy, Isi or Enkomi, is poorly signposted. From the centre of Tuzla (the Greeks still know the modern village as Engomi) ask for the road to Lefkoşa. About a mile out, you'll find the ruins on your left opposite a water tower. The site is unfenced and there's no guardian, no visiting hours, no fee — just walk in. But if you're not interested in archaeology, don't bother.

This Late Bronze Age community thrived between 1600 and 1050BC but was destroyed by earthquake, fire and repeated flooding so that today nothing survives above ground level. There are, nonetheless, plenty of foundations to see, covering about a square mile (250ha).

A British Museum expedition discovered the site in 1896 and found a wealth of Mycenaean pottery and jewellery, much of which is in London, although grave robbers had already been at work. Later expeditions proved this to be the richest Mycenaen city in Cyprus, with the treasures now going to the Cyprus Museum in Nicosia, and out of reach of visitors to North Cyprus. Among the most important discoveries are a clay tablet bearing Minoan writing yet to be decoded, and a 12th-cent BC bronze figure 21in (55cm) tall, probably of a horned god.

Further digs after World War Two revealed that most of the tombs had been placed under the houses, and that the population could have reached 15,000. And some of the stones in the city walls were 12ft (4m) long and weighed 60 tons.

Birdwatchers' delight. South of Salamis but north of the military zone lies a haven for birdwatchers. An unmarked dirt road leads directly to the beach — a splendid stretch of sand with very few human visitors — and to some salt pans where you can see black-winged stilts, herons, and even spoonbills.

KANTARA CASTLE

The Byzantines built the original castles of St Hilarion, Buffavento and Kantara, guarding the Girne Dağlar (the Kyrenia Mountains) and so protecting Cyprus's north coast. The siting of this trio was critical: each could control its own section of shoreline and communicate instantly by mirrors with the lowlands to the south, and so with Nicosia. And the castles on the flanks, St Hilarion and Kantara, could also communicate with Buffavento in the middle. Without them, invading Saracens could seize Kyrenia before anybody in the capital had a word of warning.

Strangely, the castle's name is the Arabic for 'bridge, arch,' but there is neither up here on this crest, nor any apparent Arabic link in the neighbourhood. The Lusignans, who called the place 'Candare,' reinforced all three castles and added royal apartments, but as the methods of waging war and carrying news were changing, the Venetians decided there was no longer any need for the formidable trio and abandoned them in 1525.

St Hilarion and Buffavento are in Girne District, but Kantara is at the eastern end of the range, where the mountains lose height and become the hills of the Kırpaş Peninsula.

Access. Kantara is well signposted from İskele (Trikomo) on Famagusta Bay, but you still have an hour's drive ahead as the road climbs, twists, and becomes single track. The final stretch is along the crest of the mountains ending in a small car park at the base of the castle. The view from here is splendid; climb the last 200ft (60m) of track to Kantara — no gate, no fence, no opening hours, no fee — and the view is exhilarating, taking in both coastlines and, on a clear day, stretching back to Famagusta.

Kantara is in a surprisingly good state of repair, so that most of its features can be recognised. You enter, for example, near the south-east tower, where the main room, which was formerly a prison, now has an unguarded hole in the centre of the floor giving direct access to the cistern — drop a stone and you'll hear there's plenty of water.

The path leads on to three vaulted chambers with good views to the south, but look by the last room for a chamber of another sort — the medieval lavatory, a slit in the wall.

More vaulted rooms are in the north wall, and on top of them is the ruined tower from where the garrison sent messages to Buffavento. The top of this tower is — or was — 2,068ft (993m) high.

THE KIRPAŞA PENINSULA

It's anybody's guess where the Kirpaşa Peninsula begins, but **İskele** is a convenient starting-place. The village, called Trikomo by the Greeks, is small despite its prominence on the map, and its chief claim to recognition is as the birthplace of George Grivas, co-founder of EOKA and the main campaigner for *enosis,* union with Greece. At independence the village had 2,088 Greek Cypriots and seven Turkish — but every inhabitant today is Turkish.

Ardahan, the village between İskele and Kantara castle, was Ardhana before the events of 1974, and every one of its 450 Greek inhabitants has fled. Today most of the houses are empty and crumbling back into mother earth, and the few that are inhabited by Turks are not allowed to be repaired. The church here is ruined, derelict, empty and desecrated, one little proof of the accusation on the notice by the Ledra Palace crossing in Nicosia.

Boğaz (Boghaz) has always been Turkish, and as the name means 'narrow entrance'among other things, this coastal village could be considered an optional entry to the Panhandle. You'll find a small and narrow beach here, with the Boğaz Hotel facing it across the road.

A few miles further you see North Cyprus's petrol tanker terminal on your right, and from here on, the Panhandle becomes a region of small hill farms mixed with patches of woodland, and with only one decent tarmac road running its length. Villages are tiny, primitive, and few people know more than a smattering of English — then you meet an old man who has spent half a lifetime in England and wants to take you home and spend the day reminiscing. Every village has a narrow tarmac lane linking it with this main road, but the village-to-village network is of unmade tracks some of which have boulders so big they would shatter your car's sump.

The Greek village of Ayios Theodoros with 800 people at independence, is now the Turkish **Çayırova** while the neighbouring village of Ayios Evstathios, which was always Turkish, has become **Zeybekköy. Pamuklu,** once the Greek Tavros, has kept its ornately decorated church but converted it to a mosque, though only the muezzin's loudspeaker shows the change. Houses stand in ruins, women wear the *Şalvar*, the unisex baggy trousers, and a bust of Kemal Atatürk stands in the village square.

Turn off the main road at Ziyamet (Leonarisso) and take the tarred side road to **Boltaşlı** (Lythrangomi) for the Church of the Blessed Virgin Mary, also known as **Panayia Kanakaria,** an early Byzantine church and adjoining cemetery which are all that remain of a monastery. Before the events of 1974 a farmer lived in one part of the church and used the other as his barn; now only doves and lizards live here, but the church is still the most impressive on the Karpaş.

The church had a mosaic of the Virgin and Child but due to the old belief that a segment of the stone had the ability to cure skin disease, much of the Virgin and most of the archangels had gone before modern medicine came on the scene.

The Kanakaria mosaics. And then came the Turks on 18 August 1974. Soon the remaining mosaics were packed in plaster and cut from the floor. An art dealer got permission from the North Cypriot authorities to export them and they went via Geneva to Indianapolis where they were sold for $1,800,000. They were offered to the Getty Museum for $20,000,000 but before the sale went through a local court ruled the mosaics were the property of the Orthodox Church in Cyprus, arguing that as the North Cypriot government was illegal, so was its export licence. As I write the mosaics are still in Indianapolis, pending an appeal.

The tarmac ends at **Kaleburnu,** a quaint village with twisting streets not designed for the automobile. Just before the village the road bends left by a football field, a track goes straight ahead, and another turns right. Take this right route for Üsküdar Plaj, a good-sized beach of reddish sand served by a ruined restaurant.

This small beach near Yenierenköy on the Panhandle has its own fish restaurant.

The road ahead to Dipkarpaz is passable only to trucks and tractors, so you must turn back for **Yenierenköy,** 'New Erenköy,' the biggest community on the peninsula and home to the refugees of the original Erenköy that was the scene of bitter fighting in 1964 when it was called Kokkina. Yenierenköy, Yialousa to the Greeks, has a petrol station which closes for lunch, a simple hotel, and a large derelict warehouse for fumigated tobacco leaves.

Beyond the village the road passes Karpaz Plaj and its beachfront restaurant, with a tiny fishing harbour nearby. This beach, on the north of the Panhandle, has too much plastic rubbish lapping at the shoreline.

The road is narrower by the time you reach **Dipkarpaz,** (Rizokarpaso) probably the most astounding village in North Cyprus as several hundred of its 3,000 Greeks stayed on despite the Turkish intervention. You will be lucky to identify any of them, and shopkeepers who speak English go deaf when you raise the subject. The Turkish Army didn't come this far and after both sides had sorted out their refugees, the people of Dipkarpaz realised they could stay. But there are difficulties. They rely on a weekly UNFICYP convoy of supplies sent up from the south, and their children may be taught in the village school only up to the age of 11: after that, if they want more learning, they must go to the south and *never* come back. I heard the sad joke that most of the villagers would like to take that one-way journey south but the Cypriot Government had told them to stay; it would soon be coming to collect them.

A twisty road leads to the north shore and the ruins of **Ayios Philon,** a ruined church and restaurant set in a little bay that would be beautiful if it were not for the lorryload of plastic rubbish swirling around. Some of it comes from the Lebanon and Syria, judging by the labels, but I hear that the Famagusta−Mersin ferry contributes its share. The road ends at Aphendrika, which is yet another ruin.

The other road from Dipkarpaz follows the south coast to the tip of the Panhandle − and here you find the most beautiful and most isolated beaches on the entire island, totally free of rubbish. The Blue Sea hotel and restaurant serves good meals and you can have bed and breakfast for two for less than £10 (for $15).

Monastery of Apostolos Andreas. The tarmac road ends at the Monastery of Apostolos Andreas, &, St Andrew's Monastery, the only Orthodox one functioning in North Cyprus although under considerable duress. When you drive into the open-sided court, big enough for a parade ground, a policeman beckons you over, checks your passport − the only such check in North Cyprus outside the ports of entry − and enters details in his log book, with the exact time. He calls over one of the seven remaining Greeks, who shows you around the basement church with its splendid icons and candelabra, now showing distinct signs of neglect. The police forbid photography but the Greeks urge you to take a surreptitious picture.

When I wandered around the parade ground examining the grim, barrack-like monastery buildings, I noticed another example of the battle of nerves between Greek and Turk, Orthodoxy and Islam. The biggest sow I have seen on the island was wandering around — Moslems consider the pig to be unclean — but nearby, an overlarge sign in several languages pointed to a building converted to the 'Municipal toilet of Dipkarpaz.'

There are no set opening hours and there is no fee, but most visitors slip a few thousand lire to the Greeks when the police aren't watching, as the monastery and its nuns are obviously poor.

Apostle Andrew. Andrew was, like his brother Peter, a fisherman on Lake Kinneret (the Sea of Galilee) when he heard Jesus's preachings. Andrew was the first of the apostles, hence his Greek name *O Protoklitos,* 'the first-called.' Some years later Andrew was a passenger on a ship sailing past the Cyprus Panhandle when he realised water supplies were dangerously low. He told the captain to put ashore as there were several wells; when his prophesy was proved correct other travellers called here, more as a pilgrimage than for the water itself.

Isaac Comnenus. The well brought increasing numbers of pilgrims over the passing centuries, and history records that when Richard the Lionheart took Cyprus in 1191 there was a 'fortified abbey' on this spot. One story adds that Isaac Comnenus, the self-styled Emperor of Cyprus, surrendered to Richard at this abbey, but another version places the surrender at Kyrenia Castle.

The pilgrimage survived into modern times, with thousands visting the sacred well each year, many of them seeking a cure for their ailments; those that couldn't make the journey would throw a bottle of olive oil into the sea, hoping St Andrew, controller of the winds, would

Kantara Castle commands the approaches to the Panhandle.

direct it to Cape Andreas. The monastery prospered and was rebuilt in 1867, the sad structure you see today, and a century later had an income estimated at £150,000,000 a year, sterling.

Sacred head. St Andrew was crucified on an olive tree at Patras, Greece, at the age of 80, and then beheaded. His skull stayed in Patras until 1460 when the threat of Turkish invasion prompted its removal to Ancona, Italy, and eventually to St Peter's Basilica in Rome. Pope Paul VI sent it back to Patras in 1964 and a Greek destroyer brought it to Famagusta for the centenary celebrations at Apostolos Andreas Monastery.

HOTELS

Five-star: Palm Beach, 108r, ☎ ⇌ ✕ ✿ ✆036.62000; **Four-star:** Park, Salamis, 93r, ☎ ⇌ ✕ ✿ ✆036.65511; Salamis Bay, Salamis, 369r, ☎ ⇌ ✕ ✿ ✆036.67200; **Three-star:** Boğaz, Boğaz, 40r, ✕ ☎ ✿ ✆037.12559; Giranel, 20r, on main road north of Famagusta, ⇌ ✆037.12455; Mimoza, beside Salamis Hotel, 51r, ☎ ✕ ✆036.65460; Sea View, Boğaz, 30r, ☎ ✕ ✆037.12459; **One-star and unclassified:** Altun Tabya, 14r, ☎ ✕ T; Blue Sea, Dipkarpaz (Rizokarpaso), 5b, ✕; Ozlem Pansiyon, T; Panorama. 15b, ☎ ✕ T; Side Pansiyon, T; Sönmez, T, ✆036.65601; Yengin, Yenierenköy.

HOTEL APARTMENTS

Cyprus Gardens, 18 bungalows, ☎, ✆020.74662; Khan Hotel, 10 apartments, ✆036. 66999; Kutup Hotel, 20 apartments, ☎, ✆036.65431; Laguna Beach, 39 apartments, ☎, ✆036.66660; Onur, Yeni Iskele, 18 bungalows, ⇌ ✿ ✆037.65314; Salamis Bay Bugalows, 8 bungalows, ☎ ⇌ ✆036.67200;

MOTEL

Kocareis, by Salamis Bay Hotel. Basic but clean; restaurant.

CAMPING

Halk Plaj, Yenierenköy; Onur Camping, Yeni Iskele, ✆037.65314.

RESTAURANTS

Basic restaurants and lokantas are in Liman Yolu (Port St) beside the Lala Mustafa Mosque, while Cyprus Gardens opposite the post office in the Maraş district is the only smart one in town. The Kocareis (pronounced 'koja') Motel by the Salamis Bay Hotel serves good fish dishes and is probably the cheapest out-of-town place to eat; the restaurant at the Salamis site is popular for lunch but often empty in the evening. The Blue Sea hotel-restaurant at Dipkarpaz is an ideal spot for meals near the tip of the Panhandle.

❶The tourist office is on Fevzi Cakmak Cad. You can find other information, notably about excursions around North Cyprus, at the Champion Guiding Office at 27 Liman Yolu, beside the main mosque.

KYRENIA (GIRNE)

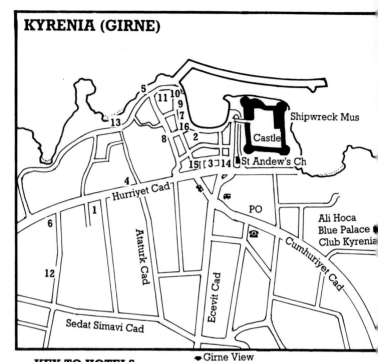

KEY TO HOTELS and PENSIONS

1 Aradol
2 Atlantis
3 Bingöl
4 Bristol
5 Dome
6 Dorana
7 Ergenekon

8 Kanguru
9 King's House
10 Kordon
11 Liman
12 P.88
13 Roks
14 Set
15 Sidelya
16 Swan

20: GIRNE

Kyrenia and the north coast

KYRENIA HAS ONE OF THE MOST BEAUTIFUL HARBOURS in the Mediterranean, rivalling Marmaris, Bizerte and even Santorini. The semicircular port, protected by a breakwater to the north and the imposing castle to the east, has picturesque shops and restaurants along its southern side, many set in medieval stone buildings.

The town behind it is small, having around 3,400 people at independence and around double that figure today. Hürriyet Caddesi, Freedom St, has the majority of the shops and the traffic, while its neighbour Cumhuriyet Cadessi, Independence St (note the subtle difference in spelling), has the post and telephone offices. The two palm trees outside the post office are the town's public notice board, carrying everything from adverts for rooms to rent on short or long lets, to the phone number of the British Residents' Society, which meets behind the office every Saturday morning.

At the moment there is no bus station, so buses and dolmuşes leave from an open site on Ecevit Cad near the post office, and on the street 50m west. The market which shares the bus site is also the best place in town to buy fresh fruit.

1974. Kyrenia suffered from the aftermath of the Turkish intervention of 1974, but it had been suffering long before that. Between the seizure of the town on 20 July and the armistice on 16 August, the economy was shattered. One shop remained open, and for several weeks it was possible to walk through the town without seeing anybody. There had been almost 2,400 Greeks at independence, all of whom had fled south, leaving only a few hundred Turks. The Royal Navy had evacuated the tourists, and the many British expatriates who favoured the area – and who still do. Recovery was painfully slow; it could be argued that Kyrenia can never recover fully, but the little town is now the centre of the reviving tourist trade of North Cyprus with a steady trickle of Europeans buying old property – Turkish-owned, *never* Greek-owned – and converting it into luxury holiday homes. A British Member of Parliament is among them.

What to see. You can get the feel of Kyrenia in half a day, on foot, but you will find yourself coming back to that harbour for yet another look from yet another viewpoint. You will eventually find the **Folk Art Museum** in a three-storey building that was originally a granary with living accommodation above but which now offers a display of household tools of the past 300 years.

The small **St Andrew's Church,** &, backing onto the castle, treasures a union flag which covered the bodies of General Orde Wingate and other British troops killed in Burma during World War Two. The church sorely needs treasure of another kind: a larger congregation, to fill its 67 seats and meet its running costs.

The seafront promenade, Kordonboyu, has a casino, several hotels including the impressive Dome and, in the west, a small beach. As Kyrenia, like most towns on the island, lacks a good beach, you need to travel a few miles west to Altınkaya or Çikama Plaj, or east to Club Acapulco.

But the biggest attraction in Kyrenia is its castle, from where you have an even better view of that beautiful harbour and its backdrop of blue mountains.

KYRENIA CASTLE and SHIPWRECK MUSEUM

Kyrenia's castle was built by the Byzantinians, probably on the ruins of a Roman fort, but its first mention in recorded history is in the account of Richard the Lionheart's seizure of Cyprus in 1191. After taking Limassol and Larnaca, Richard added Nicosia and the three castle of the Kyrenia Range, St Hilarion, Buffavento and Kantara, to his prizes, leaving his companion Guy de Lusignan, founder of the Lusignan dynasty, to capture Kyrenia.

Guy found the wife and daughter of the deposed Isaac Comnenus hiding in the castle, then he dashed to Kantara and found Comnenus himself seeking refuge. This account contrasts with the story that Richard took Comnenus prisoner at Apostolos Andreas Monastery, and both look equally believable.

How much and when? The castle changed hands only once as a result of direct attack, when the Venetians snatched it from the Lusignans in 1491, though the Venetians bombarded it in 1373. But once in control they repaired the damage and extended the west and south defences, which means we have a castle in remarkably good repair. It's open daily 0800-1300, 1400-1700 for 25p (40¢), with access over a bridge which crossed a moat in the 14th cent.

&. Disabled visitors can approach along a flat path from the police station or St Andrew's Church and can see the castle's courtyard and enter the Shipwreck Museum, but the upper court of the castle, and the shipwreck itself, are accessible only by stairs. You can also reach the castle by a flight of steps from the east end of the harbour.

Mixed styles. The bridge leads through the Venetian walls, past the Lusignan guardroom, to the Byzantine Chapel of St George whose Corinthian capitals have been added in restoration since 1974 — such is the mixture of architectural styles.

In more detail, the early Byzantine structure is the north wall; the north-east tower and parts of the north-west; the chapel, undercroft and the south-west tower; and the royal guard rooms, now holding the Shipwreck Museum. The Lusignans added the guardroom and most of the inner offices north of the courtyard; the Venetians added the rest, including the north-west, south-west and south-east towers which swallowed much of the Byzantine original.

Shipwreck Museum. The Shipwreck Museum, set in the western side of the courtyard, has a separate entrance fee of 25p (40¢) which lets you explore four rooms devoted to the actual timbers and cargo of what is claimed to be oldest trading ship known. This vessel was about 47ft long by 14ft 6in wide (14.3m x 4.4m), built of Aleppo pine which has been carbon-dated to 389±44BC. Among its cargo were some 9,000 almonds, whose kernels have been dated to 288±62 BC Assuming the almonds were fresh, the ship could have been up to 100 years old when she sank around − give or take − 389BC. Most of her bottom timbers − a section 39ft 10in (12.15m) long − have been raised from the sea bed and are now on display in the museum.

By contrast, the world's oldest known shipwreck happened 3,200 years ago off Kaş, Turkey, but only its cargo survived.

Examination of more than 400 amphorae (wine jars) in the cargo show that the ship called at Samos and Rhodes, and masons' marks on the millstones aboard can add Kos to the itinerary. Personal gear for four people hints at the size of the crew, and other evidence shows they fished during the voyage but put ashore to cook their meals.

Pennsylvania University. Michael Katsev and a team from Pennsylvania University surveyed the coast in 1967 after a sponge diver showed them the wreck, and in '68 and '69 archaeologists in

Pin your notices to these trees in front of Kyrenia post office.

diving gear photographed and raised the wreck and its cargo. Preservation of the timbers took four years, and the museum opened in 1976.

The ground floor has a modern mock-up of the ship's mid-section with some of the actual wine jars aboard, showing how their tapered shape makes for ideal stowage aboard ship. The vessel's remains are in the next room, but viewing is only from the gallery.

THE KYRENIA RANGE and THE NORTH COAST

The Kyrenia Mountains are spectacular, running in a gentle curve with their jagged crest between two and four miles from the coast. The average gradient of the upper slopes is around 60°, making them a formidable barrier to invasion. Several natural passes allow relatively easy crossing points, but St Hilarion Castle commands the road from Kyrenia to Nicosia and Buffavento commands two passes to the east, with Kantara controlling the eastern end of the range.

You cannot go *into* these mountains; you go *on* them. They lack depth, which means your eye is always directed to the view, either north to the narrow coastal strip and, in winter, a tempting glimpse of the snows of the Taurus Mountains in Turkey, or south to the plains, Nicosia, Famagusta, the Troodos and the isolated peak of Stavrovouni near Larnaca. It is only from up here that you can appreciate the strategy behind the Turkish intervention, for no army, ancient or modern, can draw its front line across the middle of the Mesaoria. Cyprus is not big, but from up here it looks positively small.

I have driven through all the passes and around both ends, and I recommend the journey south from Esentepe (Ayios Amvrosios) for a sudden and enchanting view of the plains. By the way, there are no signs to the isolated **Church of Antifanitis** marked on Greek Cypriot maps in this area, and I doubt it has survived.

Crusader tombs. A narrow road climbing from **Karşıyaka** (Vasilia) over the western end of the range, takes you into an area where several Crusader tombs are hidden among the rocks and undergrowth. This is scenic country, popular with British residents despite the number of Greek peasant homes in ruins. **Güzelyalı,** 'beautiful shore' but Vavilas to the Greeks, has the small German-run Hotel Sunkiss (15DM or £5 bed and breakfast) near the tiny beach, and the smarter Club Güzelyalı is to the west, on a miserable bit of beach. The village, like most along this coast, is unspoiled, but 'beautiful' is a stretch of the imagination.

Turin Shroud. Lapta (Lapithos) and its neighbour Alsancak (Karavas) are popular with German visitors and residents, but there's little to see of the twin villages' former glory. Here stood the old **Monastery of Akhiropitios,** 'built without hands' because the Virgin Mary brought the entire edifice over from Asia Minor during one night. Before 1974 it was an army barrack and it now stands empty and derelict like the nearby 16th-cent Church of Evlalios. Legend claims that Christ's shroud was in the monastery for generations until a Princess of Savoy took it to Italy, where it gained fame as the Turin

Shroud.

In medieval times the villagers harnessed the mountain streams for irrigation and, later, to turn a flour mill, which was an early rival to the mill at Kakopetria in the northern Troodos. Most of the aqueducts are still in use for irrigation.

The ancient city state of Lapithos, known to the Greeks as Lambousa, 'shining,' was on the coast near Alsancak but it was captured and destroyed several times, the final blow being repeated 7th-cent attacks by Arab raiders. Some splendid silver plate and gold ornaments, found here in 1902 and named the Lambousa Treasure, are in the Cyprus Museum, with other trophies in the New York Metropolitan and the British Museum. You will need to search hard for what little there is left of the city.

Hotel luxury. Lapta is the beginning of the tourist strip, with the five-star Celebrity Hotel and the Marmaris. Alsancak has the five-star de luxe Crystal Cove, opened in 1990 with a specification that omits nothing, and the three-star Mare Monte.

Beaches. Sand is still a rare commodity on the shoreline, but Alsancak Plaj is good, though small, helped by a stone breakwater.

Karaoğlanoğlu. Before 1974 less than 2,000 Turkish Cypriots lived on the north coast, from the Panhandle's tip to Korucam Point (Cape Kormakiti). Ayios Yeoryios was all Greek, and every one of them fled south on or after 20 July 1974 when the Turkish Army landed on the village beach at 4am. The village's new name, Karaoğlanoğlu − think of it as 'kara−lana−loo' for simplicity − comes from the military commander who lost his life in the landing. An artless concrete monument on the roadside marks the spot, with a nearby car park at the top of a path down to the renamed Çikarma Plaj, the best stretch of beach west of Kyrenia and perfect for sandcastles, sunbathing, swimming, or the occasional invasion. The Altınkaya and the Bambi fish restaurants are down at the water's edge.

Back at road level, the Karaoğlanoğlu Şehitligi is the Martyr's Memorial, holding the graves of 71 Turkish soldiers killed in the operation, with a display of knocked-out military vehicles.

St HILARION CASTLE

The Byzantine Castle of St Hilarion is well signposted from Kyrenia town centre. Take the road through the mountains towards Nicosia and turn off right onto a smaller tarmac track that climbs steeply through open woodland. Signs warn 'no photography, no stopping,' as there is an army camp laid out beneath you, but there is no restriction on walking up to the castle, which encircles the 2,402ft (732m) peak of its own little mountain and has a panorama on the majestic scale.

Hours. The castle is open daily 0830-1700 for the equivalent of 25p (40¢). Wheelchair access is impossible but photography is allowed.

History and mystery. St Hilarion the Great established the first monasteries in Palestine and died near Paphos around 371. Another St Hilarion, often confused with him, was a 6th-cent hermit in Syria who fled to Cyprus ahead of the wave of Islam. But which Hilarion came to this mountaintop to live out his life as a hermit?

The Byzantines built a church here in the 10th cent, followed by a small monastery which was soon converted into or absorbed by, a castle, as the first written record of St Hilarion Castle is in the accounts of Richard the Lionheart's seizure of Cyprus in 1191. The castle's own guidebook says that Richard captured Isaac Comnenus, the Emperor of Cyprus, at Tremethousa (now Erdemli), but that was the scene of the battle from which Comnenus escaped. Other authorities place Comnenus's capture at Kantara or Apostolos Andreas.

Richard the Lionheart. Richard *did* put Comnenus's daughter, captured at the fall of Kyrenia Castle, here in St Hilarion as a hostage against reprisal attacks while Comnenus himself was still at liberty. Later, Richard brought his new queen, Berengaria, for a brief honeymoon look at the castle. And 800 years later Walt Disney used St Hilarion as the basis for his fairytale castle in *Snow White* — or is that just another legend?

God of love. Around the 12th cent St Hilarion was known as Didymos, 'twins,' from its double peak, and when the Lusignans took over Cyprus from England's Richard I, they corrupted the name to Dieu d'Amour. They also fortified the castle, knowing that love was not strong enough to deter invasion.

Refuge. Holy Roman Emperor and King of Germany, Frederick II, put in at Limassol in 1228 to demand the regency of Cyprus, but John

Open-cast asbestos mines at Pano Amiandos.

d'Ibelin, who held the regency while King Henry I was a minor, refused – and incarcerated himself at St Hilarion. After a truce d'Ibelin agreed to go on the crusade with Frederick but, when he came home the next year, he found the emperor's supporters had seized the island. He defeated them at Nicosia and they fled north – and shut themselves in St Hilarion. Two years later, d'Ibelin and Frederick were in Syria when other invaders hit Cyprus. This time Frederick's family sought refuge in St Hilarion and were saved when Henry I, now of age to take the throne, came back and saved the day. He also saved Cyprus from any further threat from Germany.

Prince John's Tower. Late in the 14th cent, Prince John of Antioch took refuge here with his Bulgarian bodyguards. But Queen Eleanor of Cyprus wanted revenge, knowing that John had murdered her husband, King Peter I, who was also John's brother. She persuaded John that the Bulgarians were plotting to kill him, so he sent them one by one to the top of a tower from where they were thrown to their death. John, without his bodyguard, didn't last much longer.

The castle today. The castle is in a 60% state of repair and stands at three levels. The first level is the Lower Ward where the guards, the men-at-arms, and the draught animals were quartered, all enclosed within a wall which strides down a 50° slope before making a sharp turn to follow the contour. A path leads through rough land to the Middle Ward, accessible through a massive Byzantine gatehouse with Lusignan additions.

The cluster of buildings in the Middle Ward is the most impressive part of the fortress, its Byzantine church having parts of the roof domes still surviving – though the arches on the east facade were rebuilt in 1959 to prevent collapse. North-east of the church is the belvedere, the lookout post, backing onto the remains of a great hall.

Here, too, are the kitchens, a water tank now restored, and other rooms which may have been part of the monastery. The north face of this cluster of buildings was beyond the crest of the ridge and so could be built up, and down, to take four storeys, all with a splendid view out to sea.

A path climbs steeply to the Upper Ward, where the little remaining Byzantine masonry is overlaid by the Lusignan royal apartments. And from this topmost part of the castle complex another path goes downhill to Prince John's Tower, from where King John's bodyguards were hurled onto the jagged rocks.

The main road east from Kyrenia passes the large and modern terminal for the passenger ferry to Taşucu, Turkey, and the three-star Club Acapulco Hotel beside a good beach. But if you want to go to Bellapais Abbey look for signs to *Bellabayıs*.

BELLAPAIS ABBEY

The North Cyprus tourist map infers that you can reach Bellapais from the Nicosia road. You can not. Access is only from the coast road

The Selimiye Mosque in North Nicosia began life as a Gothic cathedral.

east of town, Cumhuriyet Cad, and right again into Kurtuluş Cad; follow the signs and go right through the village of Bellabayıs.

Hours. The abbey is open 0830-1700 for 25p (40¢); &, with minor problems.

The 14th cent abbey is the most outstanding example of Gothic architecture in Cyprus, excelling the former St Nicholas's Cathedral in Famagusta for splendour if not in its state of preservation. Around 200ft (65m) square with its outbuildings, it surrounds a central cloister 110ft (37m) long, with the church to the south, facing the road and the village, the chapter house and undercroft to the east, facing the car park, and the refectory to the north, overlooking a cliff and with an excellent view across the lowlands to the sea.

The refectory, 90ft by 32ft (27.5m x 9.7m) is the most impressive and best preserved part of the abbey, with the Lusignan coat of arms carved in the lintel of its mock-13th-cent doorway, as this section was the work of King Hugh IV who ruled for five years from 1324. A staircase set into the wall leads to the pulpit where a monk read the scriptures during meals. The kitchen, west of the refectory, has a staircase leading down to the crypt where the monks stored the abbey's farm produce, particularly its olive oil.

The church is the oldest part of the abbey and also in near-perfect order, but there are no plaques or other memorials to the Cypriot monarchy who lie under its floor. The undercroft, the abbey's workroom, has the monks' dormitories above, each with a good early-morning view across the countryside.

Abbey of Peace. Bellapais's origins are unknown, but the first recorded monks were Augustinians who were persuaded in the early 13th cent to change allegiance to the Order of the Premontre, established in Laon (France) in 1120 and also known as the Premonstratensians or the Norbertines; St Norbert, the founder, had been Archbishop of Magdeburg before making the long trek to France.

The Norbertines called this the *Abbaie de la Pais* in the Old French spelling, which the Venetians corrupted to the present name, Bellapais, and which the Turks modified to Beylarbayi before settling on Bellabayıs. But as the peace-loving, austere-living, hard-praying, devoutly Catholic monks wore white robes, this was also the *Abbaye Blanche,* the White Abbey.

True Cross. Roger the Norman, descendant of the man who snatched Malta from the Arabs in 1090, presented Bellapais with a fragment of the True Cross and a small fortune in cash in 1246, on the understanding that prayers should be said for him and his wife in perpetuity. While not questioning the validity of this piece of the Cross, it is a fact that if all such fragments around the world were brought together they would probably make several crosses.

But the abbey's main benefactor was Hugh III (1267-84) who financed most of the surviving structure, granted the abbott the right to wear a bishop's mitre and golden spurs, and carry a gilded sword. Hugh died at Tyre and is buried under the church floor in a grave now unmarked.

Debauchery. When the Venetians took over from the Lusignans, standards tumbled in the abbey and the once-celibate order now had monks with wives — occasionally with two wives. The Ottomans sacked the abbey in 1570 shortly before they seized the island, and handed the wreckage to the Greek Orthodox Church.

BUFFAVENTO CASTLE

The central castle in the trio striding the ridge of the Kyrenia Mountains is Buffavento, often spelled with just one 'f' as it may have come from the Italian *bufèra di vènto,* 'storm of wind.' Other authorities claim the name is a corruption of the Greek *koutsaventys,* the 'lame master' who established the tiny village of Koutsovendis in the foothills to the south — it's now called **Güngör** and is the most derelict community I have seen in North Cyprus.

Access. The North Cyprus tourist map infers the best approach is from the south, via Kaynakköy (Sykhari) and Taşkent (Vouno) to Güngür (Koutsovendis). Combine this information with maps specialising in Greek Cyprus and you'll realise the route also takes in the Monastery of Chrysostomos.

Don't try it. The road is bad and the countryside so derelict you'll have difficulty in finding anybody to tell you the way — in Turkish, not English. And while you may see Buffavento from Güngür, the track is not only impassable to cars but as it goes through a Turkish military camp it is closed to tourists.

The only access is from the east, from the highest point of the main Kyrenia—Ercan road. Look for the layby at the summit; from here a track leads 3.8 miles (6.1km) along the countour to a small parking area at the base of Buffavento. Don't be deterred by the bad appearance of this track as the boulders are only on the first 200m, and if you're alone in a left-hand-drive car you'll probably not see the castle, so check your distance carefully.

A fainter track leads from this car park towards the mountains; drive along it to another parking area under a tree, from where you have a stiff walk on a cliff-face path, which takes at least 45 minutes up and 30 down. The ruined castle is unfenced and there's nobody to collect an entry fee.

Panorama. I found the view from Buffavento to be the best on the island, taking in Nicosia, Mt Olympus and its radar domes, Mt Stavrovouni, Famagusta, Ercan Airport, and miles of the north coast.

Taşkent. Taşkent, of course, is the village that has cause to remember the events of 1974 with particular bitterness, and it is here that the flag of the Turkish Republic of North Cyprus is painted on the hillside in a defiant gesture to southern Nicosia.

Monastery of Chrysostomos. The legendary origins of the Monastery of Chrysostomos have much in common with Ayia Napa Monastery, but here the heroine was a queen who lived in Buffavento Castle. Both she and her pet dog suffered from a skin disease, but the dog eventually went down the mountain each day and found relief in a spring. When the queen realised her pet was being cured she followed him, found the holy spring, and shared in its healing powers. She built the monastery in gratitude in 1090, 100m from the spring.

St John Chrysostomos follows the design of the times, with a fortress-like outer frame protecting the church in the central court — but here there are two churches, the Holy Trinity and St John Chrysostomos, the latter named from a saint born in Antioch in 354 who became patriarch of Constantinople; Chrysostomos refers to his great eloquence.

When St John's church was restored in 1891 its new door was hailed as a work of art — and of craftsmanship as it didn't have a single nail. You won't see the door as the entire monastery is now occupied by the Turkish Army and is out of bounds.

Beşparmak. Back at the layby from where the track leads to Buffavento, there is a good view of the most distinctive peak in the Kyrenia Range, Beşparmak, known to the Greeks as Pentadactylos. Both words translate into English as 'five fingers' and allude to the mountain's five individual summits, the highest of which rises to 2,282ft (749m).

Turtle Beach. East of the turning for Beşparmak village, the road runs beside the shoreline for a few hundred metres at the place unofficially known as Turtle Beach. The beach is good but totally ignored by humans — and maybe we should leave it that way.

KORUÇAM BURNU (CAPE KORMAKITI)

The main road west from Kyrenia swings south around the end of the mountains just past the new Club Güzelyalı Hotel. If you turn right to Kayalar you enter a part of the country where time has stood still since 1974. The only Turkish Cypriots were in the villages of Camlıbel (Kambyli, near the Greek Myrtou) and Akdeniz (Ayia Irini). Özhan (Asomatos), Karpaşa (Karpasha) and Koruçam (Kormakiti) were near-total Maronite, members of a Christian sect that accepted the teachings of a monk named Maro in the 8th cent; others of their number are still in the Lebanon. Greek Cypriots prevailed in the six other villages, their numbers around 2,500 at independence.

Desolation. All the Greeks fled in 1974, and few Turks have moved into the area to borrow the empty homes: an agreement drawn up between the governments north and south of the Green Line allows each people to live rent-free in homes abandoned by the other, but they may not repair or maintain the property. The result of this policy is starkly evident in what was Orga — 139 Greeks at independence — and is now Kayalar, home to maybe five Turks. Not a pane of glass survives. Some doors that were locked and bolted when their owners fled are still fastened, but elsewhere doorways stand gaunt and chickens walk through to roost on bales of straw in what were front

The iconostasis in the Apostolos Andreas Monastery has most of North Cyprus's remaining icons. Many were stolen in 1974.

parlours. Roofs are collapsing, weeds are growing in walls, and grass is pushing up through the tarmac in the main street.

The road into Kayalar is untouched since the early days of the motor car, but west of the village a wide new road stretches along the lonely coast to Sadrazamköy (Liveras) and on to Koruçam Burnu, the headland the Greeks call Cape Kormakiti. I suspect that as you read this the road will have bypassed Kayalar and linked up with the main coast road to Kyrenia.

From Sadrazamköy back to Koruçam (Kormakiti) village the old road is narrow but adequate, cutting through poor farmland where the peasant way of life barely survives.

Koruçam. The Maronites of Koruçam had no quarrel with the Turkish Cypriots. They had not joined EOKA nor campaigned for *enosis,* so when the Turkish Army took the headland between 8th and 16th August it went around the Maronite villages.

Churches in neighbouring Greek villages were hit by gunfire, and some were destroyed, but the large pseudo-Byzantine church in Koruçam is untouched and its Maronite sisters live on undisturbed, running the infirmary for the local people and maintaining the church. You would like to see inside it? With the church behind you, turn left and you are facing the infirmary, with the village tap at the base of its wall. Ask at the infirmary and a sister will show you inside the church, including the icons now stored in the vestry for safety, as the Turkish children can be troublesome.

The Maronites continue to worship in their giant church in Koruçam, formerly Kormakiti.

Akdeniz. West of Tepebaşı (Dhiorios) a road leads through open woodland and sandhills to Akdeniz (Ayia Iniri). The country to the north is a military area with photography prohibited, and the military has also taken over the beach though there are no signs and your first warning will probably be from a soldier speaking only Turkish. The village church of St Iniri is smart and well tended, its pews replaced by prayer mats and it roof bearing a small minaret. Akdeniz means 'white sea,' but the two words Ak Deniz specifically mean the Mediterranean.

HOTELS

Five-star: Celebrity, Lapta, 43r, ☎ ✕ private ✿, casino, ∅082.18751; Crystal Cove, Alsancak, 213r, ☎ ✕ ≈ private ✿, casino, ∅081.54989; **Four-star:** Dome, 161r, ☎ ✕ ≈ private ✿, T ∅081.52453; **Three-star:** Club Acapulco, 68r, ☎ ✕ private ✿ ∅081.53510; Club Kyrenia, 64r, ☎ ✕ ≈ ✿ ∅081.54801; Deniz Kizi, Alsancak, 55r, ☎ ✕ ✿ ∅082.18710; Dorana, 33r, ☎ ✕ T ∅081.53521; Grand Rock, 46r, ☎ ✕ ≈ ✿ ∅081.52238; Liman, 16r, ☎ ✕ T ∅081.52001; Mare Monte, Alsancak, 78r, ☎ ✕ ✿ ∅082.18310; **Two-star:** Anadol, 22r, ☎ ✕ T ∅081.52319; Atlantis, 14r, ☎ ✕ T ∅081.52242; Ergenekon, 16r, ☎ ✕ T ∅081.52240; Golden Bay, Alsancak, 25r, ☎ ✕ ✿ ∅082.18540; Socrates, 16r, ☎ ✕ T ∅081.52157; **One-star:** Bristol, ☎ ✕ T ∅081.52298; **Unclassified:** Sunkiss, Güzelyalı, 13r, ✕ ✿ ∅082.18588; **New:** Blue Palace, Dr Fazil Küçük (by ferry terminal); Club Güzelyalı, west of Güzelyalı, opened June 1990; Jasmine Court, Kyrenia, opened June 1990.

PENSIONS

Ali Hoca Pansiyon, Paküllü Cad; Bingül Pansiyon, Efeler Cad; Kanguru Pansiyon, Canbulat Cad; King's House, Efal Akca Cad; Kordon Pansiyon, Kordon Boyu; Riviera Mocamp, Karaoğlanoğlu; Set Pansiyon, Efeler Cad; Sidelya Pansiyon, Efeled Cad; Swan Pansiyon, Efel Akca Cad; P 88, Fehmi Ercan;

HOTEL APARTMENTS

Ambelia, Bellapais, 18 studios, 32 villas, ☎ ≈ ∅081.52175; Celebrity, Lapta, 33 bungalows, 3 villas, ☎ ≈ private ✿ ∅082.18751; Girne View, 39 apartments, ☎ ∅081.54989; Kanarya, ☎ ∅081.53878; Kings, Alsancak, ☎ ∅082.18745; Philecia Court, ☎ ∅081.52165; Riviera, ☎ ∅081.53369; Şerif Apartments, Karaoğlanoğlu. ∅81.54782; Silver Waves, Karaoğlanoğlu, ☎ ∅081.53480; Villa Club, Yeşiltepe (Motidhes, near Alsancak), ☎ ∅082.18400.

TOUR OPERATORS

At least 15 independent tour operators in Kyrenia arrange conducted excursions to other parts of the country. There is no point in supplying full addresses and phone numbers as you can find these at the telephone office or the town hall (belediye) and make your arrangements face to face. These are the main operators and their street:

Adatur, Ergene; Ali Aksu, Beycam Cad; Ankara Seyahat, Kordon Boyu; Bofor Turizm, Ersin Aydın Cad; Celebrity Turizm, Cumhuriet Cad; Golden Turizm, Atatürk Cad; K.T.H. Yolları, Kordon Boyu; Mehmet Doğansoy, Hurriyet Cad; Naz Arda, Ertaçlar Pasaji; Nil Turizm, Kordon Boyu; Ozari Turizm, Kurtuluş; Roots Turizm, Ertaçlar Pasaji; Side Turizm, Canbulat Cad; Uskşdar Turizm, Hurriyet Cad.

RESTAURANTS

There are more eating-places in the Kyrenia area than in the rest of North Cyprus. If you don't want to search, just go down to the harbour at midday or in the evening and take your pick – or read on. Ignoring the hotel restaurants and the small beach-side bars, here are some worth trying for their special character: *Abbey House Restaurant,* Bellapais; *Dragon House,* patronised by Laurence Durrell, Spike Milligan and Peter Sellers; *Harbour Club,* established 1950 and patronised by many, including Tommy Handley of *ITMA* radio fame, British comediennes Elsie and Doris Waters, politician Duncan Sandys, and many news correspondents; *Rita on the Rocks,* on a tiny rock bay near Karaoğlanoğlu; *Sunderland Bar,* Özanköy (near Bellapais), named from a British football team and patronised by President Denktaş.

NIGHTLIFE

The hotels and restaurants provide most of the nightlife, but for the 'best music and light show in town' try the Girne Tunnel Disco from 2230 every night. It's near the Girne View Hotel on Ecevit Cad, ✆081.54430.

LAVATORY

The most convenient 'conveniences' in Kyrenia are at the start of the harbour breakwater, but they emit a smell – and so does the harbour at times. People who know their way around town usually call in at the Dome Hotel, inside the front door and on the left.

❶ The tourist information office is on the harbourfront, ✆081.52145.

21: LEFKOŞA

Northern Nicosia

THERE IS A DISTINCT DIFFERENCE between the Turkish and Greek sectors of Nicosia. A building boom is in progress in the suburbs but there is still a small-town atmosphere about the place. It is only when you reach the Turkish part of the old walled city that you can appreciate the presence of permanence, of history, and of substance.

THE OLD CITY
The story of Nicosia's Venetian walls, and the origin of its name, are told in Chapter 15 — except for that of the Kyrenia Gate.

KYRENIA GATE
The Kyrenia Gate was the only entry to the walled city from the north and is still the main entrance to north Nicosia. Today's traffic swirls past on each side, leaving the original gateway, built in 1567, as an island in the middle of the road. Look at the inner side of the gate, above the portcullis, and you may see the inscription GR 1931, marking the year the motor age breached the ancient walls. The two upended cannon are a relic of Ottoman times.

The Venetians called this the *Porta del Proveditore,* the 'military governor's gate,' and as the bastion to the east is named from one Signor Barbaro we can assume that he was the governor.

Tourist Office. The Turks added a guard room on top of the gate in 1821, as a protection against a Greek rebellion, and from 1991 the tourist office has its home here.

BEDESTAN
Between the Selimiye Mosque and the covered bazaar stands a 6th-cent Byzantine church that was partly demolished in the 14th cent to make way for a larger church in Gothic style, resulting in the glorious architectural mix seen today. The Gothic extension, when new, briefly served as the Orthodox Cathedral and the Archbishopric. The picture is complex already, but some authorities make it even more complicated by arguing that the Gothic addition was the Church of St Nicolai Anglicorum, 'St Nicholas of the English,' belonging to the Order of St Thomas the Martyr of Canterbury — Thomas à Beckett — who fled from the island in 1373 during an attack by Genoa. If that

The Greeks called it Orga, the Turks renamed it Kayalar, but it's now a ghost village.

The Kyrenia Gate guards the entrance to North Nicosia.

were so, why was it not St Thomas's Church?

The Ottomans used both buildings as a covered market, a *bedestan,* which is the name it still has today, although the true covered market is much larger and just across the street. Later the Turks had their cloth market in the twin churches and, later still, they stored grain here.

Back under Turkish rule again, the Bedestan is empty, unused, and normally kept locked.

BÜYÜK HAN

The 'Great Inn,' Büyük Han, standing almost in the city centre, was the work of Muzaffer Paşa, the first Governor of Cyprus under the Ottoman rule and one of the generals leading the invasion of 1571. A *han* is a caravanserai, a hostel for travellers, stabling for their animals, and a warehouse for their merchandise, all under the same roof. Many hans survive in Turkey today, but this is the only one in Cyprus.

Muzaffer financed this han by levying a local tax but, as he did it without approval from İstanbul, he was recalled in disgrace.

The Great Han is built to the same basic plan as the early Orthodox monasteries; four sturdy walls, mainly blank to the outside but supporting on the inside two storeys totalling 67 rooms, the upper storey having a verandah all around. On the ground floor are the stables and warehouses, with the travellers' rooms above, accessible by staircases. Whereas a monastery would have a church in the centre of the court, the Great Han has an octagonal mosque standing on pillars, with the ablutions fountains beneath.

The British used the Grean Han as a prison from soon after their arrival in 1878 until 1893, when it became a hostel again, this time for destitute Turkish families. In 1963 the Cypriot Government closed the han for renovation and conversion to a museum of Turkish art, but the civil unrest in the city delayed the work and the building now stands empty.

COVERED BAZAAR

South of the Bedestan, which is no longer the covered market that its name implies, there is the new Covered Bazaar — which is never called a bedestan although it is one. This is a true market in the Turkish sense and is worth a visit for the atmosphere even if you have no intention of buying. Language is no problem even though a few traders speak only Turkish, for there are many others ready to reminisce about their years in England, running a stall on the Portobello Road or a small shop in north London and now back in North Cyprus because it's their home country and they want to give it a chance.

The covered market sells a wide range of low-price goods, starting with fruit and veg, through frozen meat, Turkish delight, audio casettes, alcohol and souvenirs, to the top of the range household items. It is the main fruit market in north Nicosia yet trade is surprisingly light — but 100m to the south, beyond the barbed wire, a smaller fruit market does much more business.

SELIMIYE MOSQUE

The Selimiye Mosque is the most impressive building in north Nicosia, but it still looks more like the Gothic Cathedral of St Sophia which it originally was. Founded in 1209 by the Lusignan dynasty, it was consecrated on 5 November 1326 while still not complete. The Archbishop dedicated the cathedral to Ayia Sophia, 'holy wisdom,' and later a number of Lusignan monarchs were crowned here.

The Ottomans seized the city on 9 September 1570 and converted it to a mosque, stripping out all the pews, the pulpit, and anything else that reminded them of Catholicism, yet they never changed its name until 13 August 1954 when the Mufti (Turkish equivalent of an archbishop) reconsecrated the building in honour of Sultan Selim II, ruler of the Ottoman Empire back in 1570.

The mosque today. The upper parts of the twin towers spanning the main door were victims of the Ottoman invasion and they're now capped, and the twin minarets, rising to 160ft (49m), are much more distinctive than the single minaret at the Lala Mustafa Paşa Mosque in Famagusta.

Inside, most of the detailed stone carvings of angels have been plastered over as Islam does not like anything which can be considered the likeness of a living creature. The walls, ceiling, and

Arguably the best beach in North Cyprus, near the tip of the Panhandle.

the main columns along the nave, are all whitewashed, giving a clean but empty appearance. The nave is carpeted, and visitors of either sex and any religion may enter — ♿ included — wearing shoes, provided they do not step on the carpets. There are no set hours, and no fee, but a donation is welcome.

SULTAN MAHMUT'S LIBRARY

Ali Ruhi, Governor of Cyprus, established the Library of Sultan Mahmut II in 1829, in what is now Selimiye Meydanı (Square) at the rear of the Selimiye Mosque. Its architecture hints of the grand establishment this was, holding not just a wide selection of manuscripts in Turkish, Arabic and Persian, plus a gift of books from the sultan's own library in İstanbul, but also the *Büyük Medresse*, the Great Koranic School.

The main part of the building is octagonal, with flying buttresses in western European style, and it is only the small domes over the front door, topped with the crescent of Islam, that proves this is no Christian building.

Sadly, the building is now permanently closed.

TURKISH MUSEUM ♿

A long, low building, looking like a row of oversized beehives and quite out of place in a city centre, is the Turkish Museum, just inside the Kyrenia Gate.

It began life in the early 17th cent as the Tekke of the Mevlevi Dervishes, which needs to be explained. A *tekke* is a convent, used here by members of the Mevlevi Order, established by the *mevlana,* 'guide, leader,' Celaleddin Rumi in the 13th cent in Konya, Turkey. *Derviş* is Turkish for 'beggar.' The order's philosophy was admirable for the times, concentrating on equality of the sexes, the pursuit of righteousness, and communion with God.

And the way they did it was to dance, spinning on the spot with arms outstretched, the right palm facing heaven to receive a blessing and the left palm facing the earth to pass on that blessing.

The Whirling Dervishes earned their notoriety in western Europe for their fanaticism and their ruthless support for Islam in the field of battle, yet at other times they were tolerant to other religions.

Celaleddin was born in Balkh, then in Persia but now a district in north Afghanistan, but he is known in the west more as a poet than the founder of the dervishes. His *Mesnevi,* a six-volume tome on Sufism, with a mixture of anecdotes, was published in English in the 1930s.

Arab Ahmet. The pasha Arab Ahmet, who helped in the Ottoman conquest of Cyprus, was a fervent dervish. He built the Tekke on land given by a devout woman, Emine Hatun, and took an active role in the services for years. The male dervishes were the dancers, wearing calf-length white dresses whose skirts flared out as they whirled to the music of a reed pipe and a drum.

The Tekke today. The Dervish Order was suppressed in Turkey in

1925 but allowed to re-emerge in 1947, and the dervishes draw vast crowds to their early December festival in Konya, Turkey. In contrast, the Nicosia Tekke is now a humble museum to the Dervish Order, with a mixture of other exhibits. Here are the dervish costumes, photographs of dervishes, and some of their reed pipes. Here, too, are Korans of the 16th, 17th and 18th cents, an assortment of nine tombs including that of Arab Ahmet Paşa — and Mrs Denktaş's HMV gramophone.

Hours. The museum is open daily 0800-1400, 1500-1800 for 25p (40¢).

VENETIAN COLUMN

The 20-ft (6m) tall marble column in the centre of Atatürk Square commemorates the Venetian conquest of the island in 1489, and was probably stolen from the ruins of Salamis. The Venetians capped it with a stone lion and carved the coats of arms of their leading families in the base.

The Ottomans didn't want reminders of other conquerors, so they took it down, but by 1915 the British rulers were developing a sense of history and put it back again, minus the lion.

It was the focal point of the Turkish community in north Nicosia long before independence, and it is now the symbol of Turkish rule. The square has been named from Kemal Atatürk for many years.

Nicosian miscellany. The old city of north Nicosia is much quieter than the city south of the barbed wire, its main **shopping district** being Girne Cad from Kyrenia Gate to the Venetian Column, and then through a maze of streets down to the Selimiye Mosque, but you can find some interesting shops and small restaurants along Ermu Cad, parallel with the Green Line. Along here, too, you touch the northern tip of south Nicosia's Ledra Street, where you can see the North Cypriot, Turkish, Cypriot and Greek flags flying within a few feet of each other.

Move to the south-west part of the city, by the Roccas Bastion, and you see a different face of Nicosia where the houses are standing derelict and the streets are almost empty.

There are several mosques in the city, such as the Arabahmet, built in 1845 but named from the founder of the Tekke, and the Yeni Cami or 'New Mosque.' East of the Selimiye Mosque is the **Lapidary Museum** occupying the 15th-cent Venetian House which is probably more interesting than the collection of lapidary it contains.

NICOSIA OUTSIDE THE WALLS

There is absolutely nothing of historic interest outside the walls of the northern part of old Nicosia: the Venetians levelled it. The North Cyprus **Parliament** building, near Kyrenia Gate, is new and unimpressive, but if you go around the Martyrs' Memorial into Selim Cad, you find yourself in the smartest district in the suburbs, far smarter than the Greek sector beyond the barbed wire.

Selim Cad, of course, leads to the **Ledra Palace Crossing,** the only place on the island where tourists may cross between north and south. Here are car rental agencies and insurance offices, all specialising in one-day hire, money changers who accept Cyprus pounds, and the small customs office. North Cyprus, understandably, welcoms visitors from the south, if only for the day; Cyprus, equally understandably, doesn't welcome them from the north.

Mehmet Akif Cad leads to what the North Cyprus map marks as the **British High Commissioner's Residence.** It isn't, of course, but the elegant building now serves as the British High Commission Consular Section, open Mon-Fri 0730-1300, and the British Council, open during consular hours plus Mon, Tues, Thurs, Fri 1530-1800. Its public reference library has a large range of books in English and the latest British newspapers, and the council also arranges exhibitions and film shows.

Museum of Barbarism. Continue north along Mehmet Akif Cad to the house where EOKA terorists killed Mrs Ilhan and her family in 1963; Major Ilhan was a doctor in a Turkish army regiment. The house is now the Museum of Barbarism with absolutely nothing outside to draw your attention to it, which is why I can't report on what's inside. Dead opposite is the **tourist office,** open in summer Mon-Fri 0730-1400 and Tues-Fri 1530-1800; in winter Mon-Fri 0800-1300, 1400-1700, but closing permanently when the replacement office opens at Kyrenia Gate.

Kemal Atatürk and the Venetian Column dominate Atatürk Square in North Nicosia.

AROUND THE DISTRICT

You may feel tempted to drive your hire car down to **Akıncılar**
(Louroujina), at the tip of that long spur of territory of North Cyprus
which pierces deep into the heart of Cyprus. The village had 1,547
Turks and three lonely Greeks at independence, making it the
second largest Turkish village in the island — Lefke topped the list
with 3,585 Turk to 224 Greek. The Turkish Army swept down over the
lowlands to seize (or liberate, according to your point of view) the
village in the last few hours before the 27 August cease-fire.

Later, the Turks had to cut a road to the village as the Greeks
controlled all the existing accesses, and the area has been politically
sensitive since 1974, with the Buffer Zone at its widest point to the east
of this corridor.

So you would like to visit Akıncılar? You can't. You'll be stopped at
a military barrier a little south of Ercan Airport, which is as far as you
go without a permit. And you won't get a permit without a good
reason.

West of Nicosia, the Maronites are still in their village of Ayia
Marina, now Gürpınar, and your next place of interest is Güzelyurt.

Güzelyurt. The village of Morphou, with 6,500 Greeks at independence to 125 Turks, is now Güzelyurt, 'beautiful place,' pronounced
goo—*zell*—yert. The beauty lies in the surrounding country which
produces most of Cyprus's citrus crop, and the loss of this in 1974 was
a major blow to the republic's economy.

The town cannot really be called beautiful. Functional, bustling, full
of character — yes. And it has escaped those two great despoilers,
war and tourism. Although most of the property is still owned by
Greeks who fled to the south as refugees, there is no sign of
dereliction as the Turkish rent-free tenants are obviously making
repair when necessary despite the agreed ban on doing anything to
property abandoned by a Cypriot who has fled to the other side of the
Green Line. There is nothing here for the tourist so the only hotel is a
simple one-star affair. All the buses and dolmuşes operate from a
terminal sensibly located on the edge of town, leaving the centre to
the small shopkeepers who sell anything and everything the average
villager could need. Here is where I bought a cylinder of butane gas
in a video shop.

Cyprus Mines. The road meets the sea at Yeşilyurt 'green place,'
but the beach is shingle. Soon you are in the industrial area around
Gemikonağı (Karavostasi) where the crumbling remains of a jetty, a
small cargo ship rusting on the beach, and the empty storage tanks of
the Cyprus Mines company are another reminder of the events of
1974, for the mines are in Cyprus, only a few miles to the south but
totally out of reach. To be fair, the little port handles other seaborne
cargoes.

Beyond Gemikonağı you are right out of tourist country. The road
narrows, UNFICYP Land Rovers form much of the scant traffic, and
United Nations troops have sole use of a beachfront hotel at Halke

Tourists are dwarfed by Keo's vast vats.

Plaj.

Soli and Vouni. North Cyprus is now reduced to a strip of land 11 miles long by three miles wide (17km x 5km), served by a narrow lane that twists its way around the contours of the Troodos foothills, past villages where time seems to have stopped in the 1950s. Yet here are the remains of one of the ten city states of ancient Cyprus, Soli, and its associated palace of Vouni.

Soli took its name from an Athenian statesman who retired here around 510BC and introduced a new code of laws to the city and the island, then Soli gave its name to the valley of Solea on the northern slopes of the Troodos. The two are interlocked, for the copper mines of the Solea gave Soli its wealth and prominence, and seams in that same area were worked until 1974.

A team from Sweden excavated the city's late 2nd-cent AD Roman theatre in 1929, with the Cyprus Government restoring it in 1963 — arguably too well, as it now looks too new. Researchers from Quebec discovered the basilica and the ruins of a palace in the acropolis (hill-top fortifications) between 1964 and 1974.

The same Swedish team located the royal palace at Vouni, four miles (6km) north-west and standing on a headland overlooking the sea some 800ft (250m) beneath. The palace was built around 480BC and destroyed by natural causes in 400BC. During its brief existence the sumptuous building of 137 rooms was home to one of the kings of Soli.

. . . *concluded on page 250*

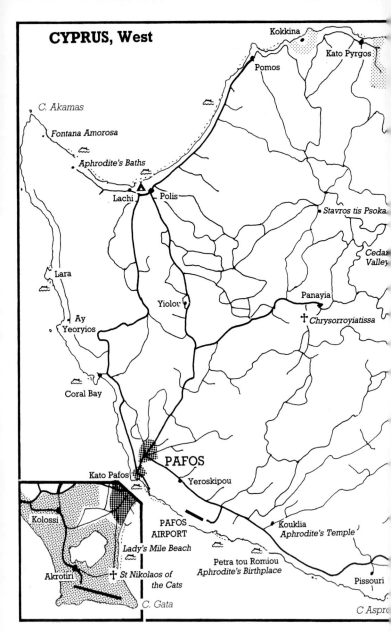

CYPRUS, West

Kokkina

Kato Pyrgos

Pomos

C. Akamas

Fontana Amorosa

Aphrodite's Baths

Lachi · Polis

Stavros tis Psoka

Ceda Valley

Lara

Yiolov

Panayia

† *Chrysorroyiatissa*

Ay Yeoryios

Coral Bay

PAFOS

Kato Pafos

Yeroskipou

Kolossi

PAFOS AIRPORT

Lady's Mile Beach

Kouklia

Aphrodite's Temple

Akrotiri

† St Nikolaos of the Cats

C. Gata

Petra tou Romiou

Aphrodite's Birthplace

Pissouri

C Aspro

244

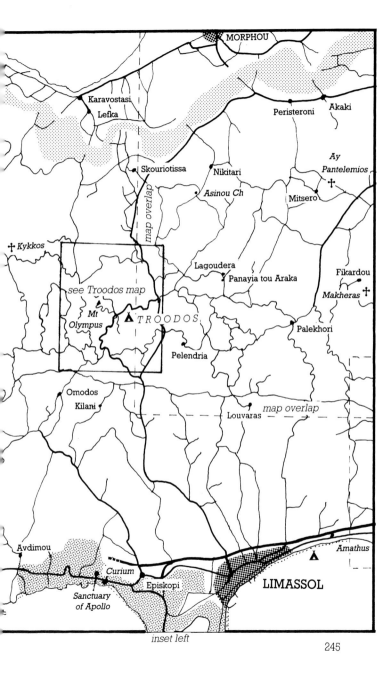

MORPHOU

Karavostasi
Lefka

Peristeroni   Akaki

Skouriotissa   Nikitari

Ay
Pantelemios †

Asinou Ch

Mitsero

† *Kykkos*

map overlap

Lagoudera
Panayia tou Araka

Fikardou

Makheras †

see Troodos map

Mt
Olympus   ⛰ *TROODOS*

Palekhori

Pelendria

Omodos
Kilani

Louvaras   *map overlap*

Avdimou

Curium

Amathus

Episkopi   ⛰

Sanctuary
of Apollo

LIMASSOL

inset left

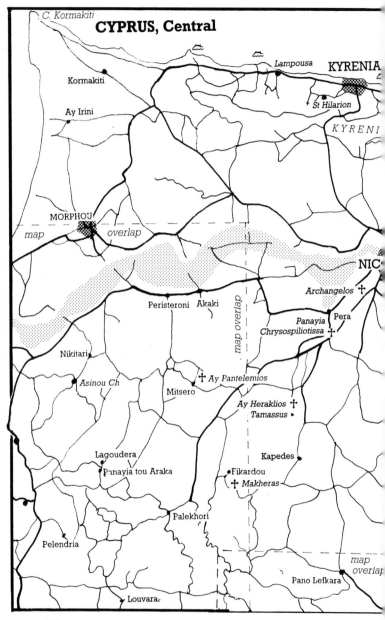

CYPRUS, Central

C. Kormakiti

Lampousa

KYRENIA

Kormakiti

St Hilarion

Ay Irini

KYRENI

MORPHOU

map *overlap*

NIC

Archangelos †

Peristeroni Akaki

map overlap

Panayia Pera
Chrysospiliotissa †

Nikitari

† Ay Pantelemios

Asinou Ch

Mitsero

Ay Heraklios †
Tamassus •

Lagoudera

Kapedes •

Panayia tou Araka

Fikardou •
† *Makheras*

Palekhori

Pelendria

map overlap

Pano Lefkara

Louvara

246

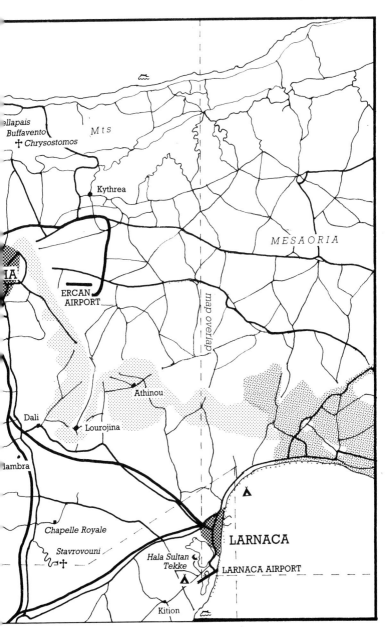

Bellapais
Buffavento
✝ Chrysostomos

Mts

Kythrea

MESAORIA

IA

ERCAN
AIRPORT

map overlap

Athinou

Dali

Lourojina

lambra

Chapelle Royale

Stavrovouni
☩✝

Hala Sultan
Tekke

LARNACA

LARNACA AIRPORT

Kition

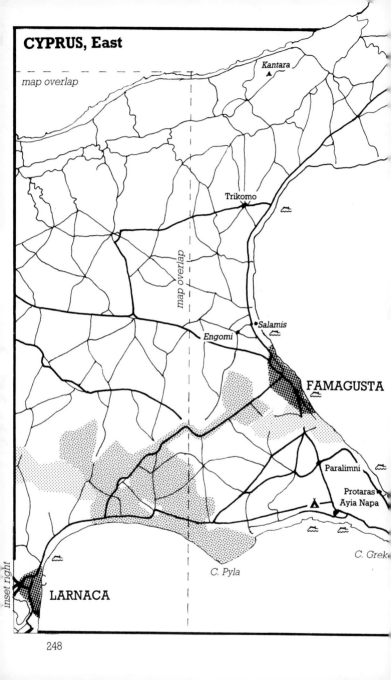

CYPRUS, East

map overlap

map overlap

Kantara

Trikomo

Engomi •Salamis

FAMAGUSTA

Paralimni

Protaras
Ayia Napa

inset right

C. Pyla

C. Grek

LARNACA

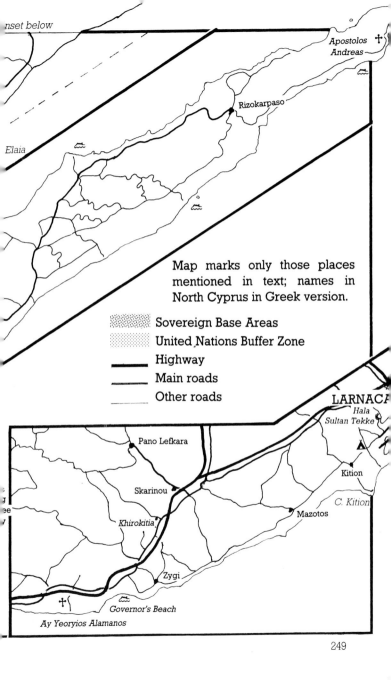

nset below

Apostolos
Andreas ✝

Rizokarpaso ◆

Elaia

Map marks only those places
mentioned in text; names in
North Cyprus in Greek version.

▒ Sovereign Base Areas
░ United Nations Buffer Zone
━ Highway
━ Main roads
━ Other roads

LARNACA
*Hala
Sultan Tekke*

Pano Lefkara ◆

Kition ◆

Skarinou ◆

C. Kition

Khirokitia ◆

Mazotos ◆

Zygi ◆

✝

Governor's Beach

Ay Yeoryios Alamanos

continued from page 243 . . .

Soli is signposted from Gemikonağı and there is unrestricted access to the site, but there is nothing to point the way to Vouni although a tarmac road was laid to it in 1959.

The road swings through Bademliköy (Loutros) to Yeşilırmak (Limnitis) near the tiny isle of Petra tou Limniti, the 'rock of Limnitis,' but before it reaches Günebaken (Amadhies) there is a notice warning visitors to go no further. Here, in the foothills of the Troodos Mountains, is the effective end of the Turkish Republic of North Cyprus.

HOTELS

Three-star: Saray, 74⇄, ☎ ✕ T ✆020.71115; **One-star:** Picnic, ☎ ✕ T ✆020.72122; Sabris Orient, ☎ ✕ T ✆020.72162.

PENSIONS

Aile, 20⇄; Altın, 36⇄; Anadolu, 16⇄; Antalya, 15⇄; Bursa Uludağ, 14⇄; Efes, 16⇄; Gözde 2, 11⇄; Güzel; Konak, 24⇄; Kurtulus, 30⇄; Side (Sarı Gül), 20⇄; Sönmez.

All hotels and pensions except the Gözde are in the old city. Pensions are continually coming onto the market in Nicosia but not all are granted licenses, nor do all licensed premises stay in business. This list is therefore subject to change; for the latest information ask at the Town Hall (Belediye).

HOTEL in Güzelyurt.

Güzelyurt, one-star, 14r, ☎ ✆071.43412.

OTHER SERVICES

There is no restaurant of distinction in Nicosia District, but there are enough simple lokantas and other eating houses to supply the needs of the relatively few tourists. Nightlife is non-existent.

Petra tou Roumio, where Aphrodite emerged from the sea foam.

INDEX

The Green Line in Nicosia at the only street barricade you may photograph.